CLAUDIO MONTEVERDI

Monteverdi in old age

Frontispiece]

HANS FERDINAND REDLICH

CLAUDIO MONTEVERDI

LIFE AND WORKS

Translated by Kathleen Dale

". . . e credete che il moderno
compositore fabrica sopra
li fondamenti della
verità."
(From the preface to Madrigal Book V, 1605)

GREENWOOD PRESS, PUBLISHERS
WESTPORT, CONNECTICUT

The Library of Congress cataloged this book as follows:

Redlich, Hans Ferdinand, 1903–
   Claudio Monteverdi, life and works. Translated by
Kathleen Dale. Westport, Conn., Greenwood Press ₍1970₎

   vi, 204 p. illus., music, ports. 23 cm.

   Reprint of the 1952 ed.
   Bibliography : p. ₍192₎–194.

   1. Monteverdi, Claudio, 1567–1643.

ML410.M77R432 1970   784′.0924 [B]   70–104253
ISBN 0–8371–4003–X   MARC

Library of Congress   71 ₍4₎   MN

Originally published in 1952 by Oxford University Press,
London.

Reprinted with the permission of Oxford University Press.

Reprinted from an original copy in the collections of the
Brooklyn Public Library.

Reprinted in 1970 by Greenwood Press,
A division of Congressional Information Service, Inc.
88 Post Road West, Westport, Connecticut 06881

Library of Congress catalog card number 70-104253
ISBN 0-8371-4003-X

Printed in the United States of America

10 9 8 7 6 5 4 3

AUTHOR'S PREFACE TO ENGLISH EDITION

THE English edition of the volume *Claudio Monteverdi—Life and Works* differs not inconsiderably from the German edition published in 1949 by Otto Walter Verlag, AG., Olten, Switzerland, as Vol. 6 in the series *Musikerreihe* edited by Paul Schaller, Basle.

Several chapters and continuous paragraphs have been specially written for this edition. They are: MUSIC AND SOCIETY IN MONTEVERDI'S LIFETIME; MUSIC IN ITALY AT THE TIME OF MONTEVERDI'S ADVENT; THE POETS OF MONTEVERDI'S MADRIGALS, and the final section of the chapter MONTEVERDI IN THE EYES OF POSTERITY. In order to extend the scope of the chapter THE LAST MADRIGALIST for the benefit of those English readers who are unable to refer back to the author's book on Monteverdi's Madrigals (H. F. Redlich, *Claudio Monteverdi*, Vol. I: *Das Madrigalwerk*, Berlin 1932), six extensive quotations from that earlier publication have been included in this chapter. They have been completely revised before being subjected to translation. A further addition to this English edition of *The Life and Works* is the series of comprehensive quotations from Monteverdi's letters on the subject of his lost opera *La Finta Pazza Licori* of 1627. Explanatory footnotes on the famous quarrel, Artusi versus Monteverdi, have been rewritten, extended and supplemented with music examples so as to afford a clearer insight into the nature of Artusi's arguments. In the discussion on the sacred 'Kontrafaktur' of the *Lamento d'Arianna* several music examples have been added. A separate Glossary explaining unfamiliar musicological terms to the less specialized reader has been incorporated in the Appendix. Finally, several minor corrections and addenda have been included in text and footnotes. All music examples and illustrations used in the German edition of 1949 have been reproduced in the present volume, but two prefaces to the German edition have been replaced by a new one. This volume was completely set up in type when Leo Schrade's new study *Monteverdi—creator of modern Music* appeared in the U.S.A. For this reason no reference could be made to it in these pages beyond an entry in the Bibliography.

The author wishes to express his sincere thanks to Mrs. Dale, not only for her translation, but for the most generous and helpful assistance she gave him in his editorial task. He further wishes to thank Professor Gerald Abraham for his valuable suggestions as to the extension of certain sections of the book, and to Mr. Frank Walker for supplying him with important information on the subject of the libretto of *La Finta Pazza Licori*. He is in addition greatly indebted to Mr. Alec Robertson for his expert advice on points connected with liturgical music. The author's thanks are also due to the late Dr. Alfred Loewenberg for his highly valued advice, especially concerning early Italian Opera.

H. F. Redlich

Letchworth, Herts.

March 1951

CONTENTS

LIST OF ILLUSTRATIONS

Part I

THE STAGES OF MONTEVERDI'S CAREER

CHAPTER I

GENERAL SURVEY

By comparison with the romantic careers of Beethoven, Chopin, Wagner and Liszt, Monteverdi's career presents a modest, not to say uneventful appearance. Indeed, he lacked the stimulus of political events such as make the biography of his great contemporary Heinrich Schütz a reflection in miniature of the period of the Thirty Years' War. He also lacked opportunities for undertaking the numerous and extensive journeys which impart a certain cosmopolitan tinge to the careers of Schütz and Handel, and by comparison with the wide radius of Schütz's sphere of action—which extended from Denmark to Schleswig, and from Saxony to Italy—the provincial narrowness of Monteverdi's life, spent almost entirely in a corner of northern Italy, is the more strongly perceptible.

A second set of circumstances, the sparseness of contemporary sources, puts difficulties in the way of writing a compelling life-story of Monteverdi. As with Palestrina, the most vital biographical documents and dates are missing, and the biographer is continually being referred to supposition and to the conclusions drawn therefrom. In many of the older biographies of Monteverdi the enumeration of demonstrable facts is heavily overlaid by legends, conjectures and unauthorized assumptions. In the following pages these errors will be avoided as far as possible. The story of the master's life, as disclosed by the documents still extant, will be narrated simply, and no attention will be paid to the fictitious hypotheses which have overburdened earlier biographies. The most important of the existing documents are 121 of Monteverdi's letters in the original.[1] In addition, there are certain documents and papers relating to the circle of people most closely connected with him all

B

his life (letters from his nearest relatives and from the princely personages who employed him; petitions, administrative documents, etc.);[2] prefaces and dedicatory epistles at the heads of works which have been preserved; and finally, constant references to Monteverdi as man and artist in contemporary letters, treatises, dedications, obituary notices, etc.[3] Unfortunately, these cornerstones for a life-history of the master are not distributed evenly over the long span of his lifetime of seventy-six years. The original letters such as have been spared to us relate only to the years 1601–34, and thus they leave out of account the whole of his youth in Cremona, the first decade of his service at Mantua, and the last, deeply significant years of his activities in Venice. Thus, in the case of Monteverdi, just as in that of Palestrina, we know every incident of his life during certain periods, but are left in complete ignorance during others. Under present conditions of archival research it seems to be quite impossible to present an absolutely complete biographical calendar of his career.[4] The following contributions to a biography of Monteverdi should therefore be regarded throughout as merely provisional.

Monteverdi's life falls quite naturally into three sections of almost equal length; his youth in Cremona, 1567–90, his years of service at the Mantuan court, 1590–1612, and the activities of his maturity in Venice, 1613–43. One isolated year of freedom from official duties should be noted: from July 1612 to August 1613; for it is characteristic of the spiritual dependence of the musician of those days upon his employer for the time being that, during the year in question, not a single important musical composition can be authenticated.

CHAPTER II

YEARS OF APPRENTICESHIP
IN CREMONA, 1567–90

For the biographer of Monteverdi the documentary uncertainties commence long before the birth of his hero. To begin with, the origin and history of the family are still hidden in the obscurity of archives. Moreover, it cannot as yet be stated with certainty how long his ancestors had been settled in Cremona. Cremonese instrument-makers of the same name cannot be identified as relatives of this family any more than can present-day bearers of the name now resident in Cremona.[1] We do not even know the dates of the births and deaths of his parents! Neither the Christian nor the maiden name of his mother can be traced with any certainty, though Italian scholars assume that she was named Maddalena. We know more of his father, Baldesar.[2] He was a doctor, apparently not without financial resources, and evidently in a position to give his children a classical education under the best teachers. Of his marriage with Maddalena there were five children, of whom Claudio was the eldest. Their names and dates, as far as can be ascertained, are as follows:

Claudio (Giovanni Antonio), baptised in Cremona on 15 May 1567, died in Venice, 29 November 1643.
Maria Domitilla, born 16 May 1571.
Giulio Cesare, born 31 January 1573.
Clara Massimilia, born 8 January 1579.
Luca, born 7 February 1581.

Of the four brothers and sisters, only one was associated at all frequently with Claudio's activities: Giulio Cesare, who likewise pursued a musical career. He was nearly six years younger than Claudio, and first appeared in 1607 as the publisher of his brother's *Scherzi Musicali* and as the author of the *Dichiarazione*, the latter, however, being strongly inspired by Claudio himself. In Mantua he seems to have been his brother's junior amanuensis, and to have held an appointment as deputy maestro di cappella. That he must have been well thought of as a composer is proved by his having participated, with Claudio Monteverdi, G. Gastoldi, Marco da Gagliano, Salomone Rossi and Paolo Birt, in the composition of Guarini's comedy, *L'Idropica* (Mantua, 1608), and by his having composed an opera to a libretto by Ercole Marliani, *Il Rapimento di Proserpina*, for Mantua in 1611. In 1620 his collection of sacred motets, *Affetti Musici Lib. I*, appeared, and from that time onwards, after having held an organist's post in Castelleone, which he certainly did not take up until after 1612,[3] he can be traced as maestro di cappella at Salò Cathedral (Lake Garda). After that year his name disappears from musical history. It is unlikely that he played any more important part during Claudio's Venetian period. The friendship and collaboration between the two brothers during the last years of the Mantuan period must have been particularly intimate. Giulio Cesare's ardent partisanship for his famous brother during the controversy with Artusi, as well as the inclusion of two small original compositions of his in the volume of the *Scherzi*, implies a happy relationship, far above the average, between the two brothers. A date for Giulio Cesare's death cannot as yet be proved with any certainty.

Neither can the exact date of Claudio's birth, though it may, perhaps, be established in the early part of May 1567. The baptismal rolls of the church of S. Nazaro and S. Celso in Cremona,[4] alone, fix the date of baptism as 15 May. In this register of baptisms the surname is spelt 'Mòdver*do*', in complete contrast to the 121 original letters[5] in which Claudio always signed his name 'Montever*di*'. To complete the confusion regarding the correct spelling of the name, printed collective editions of his works display the spelling 'Monteverde'. As the printing of some of these editions was not supervised by Claudio Monteverdi himself, the incontestable evidence of the letters must indubitably take precedence. The spelling *Monteverdi* should therefore be accepted on principle.[6]

Cremona, which with Milan and Pavia became a Spanish possession at the time of the Treaty of Cateau Cambrésis in 1559, had been the centre of a flourishing north Italian culture since the middle of the sixteenth century.[7] It was the home and the sphere of activity of Andrea Amati (1535 to after 1611) the founder of the great family of violin-makers who, with the Guarneri and the Stradivari, were later to spread the fame of Cremonese violins all over the world. Costanzo Porta (1530–1601), the oldest Italian madrigalist, a noteworthy pupil of Willaert's and later the teacher of Viadana, was born in Cremona. Another Cremonese, Tiburzio Massaino (1550–1612) had been maestro di capella of the cathedral in his native city since 1594, while a third, Benedetto Pallavicino, was destined to cross Claudio's path not infrequently.

To what extent these musicians influenced the rising Monteverdi it is difficult to estimate. That Claudio thought highly of C. Porta, but very poorly of B. Pallavicino, may plainly be seen in letters and prefaces written during his maturity. Owing to the perspicacity of his cultured father, Claudio's musical education was entrusted to Marc' Antonio Ingegneri, prefect of music at the Cathedral since 1576, and undoubtedly the most important musician within the boundaries of Cremona. Here, again, we are pursued by uncertainty as to dates. Ingegneri must have been born in Verona between 1545 and 1550 and must have settled in Cremona as early as 1568.[8] The abundant harvest of his compositions[9] begins in about 1570 with his *First Book of four-part Madrigals*. He seems to have been a pupil of, and a singer under, Vincenzo Ruffo (d. Verona, 1587), Maestro di Cappella of Verona Cathedral, and he prided himself on having been personally acquainted with Cyprian de Rore. In 1581 he married a Cremonese noblewoman, Margherita de Soresina, and in 1588 brought out his most successful work, the *Responsoria Hebdomadae Sanctae*, which was for long thought to have been by Palestrina.[10] Ingegneri died in Cremona 1 July 1592.[11] The question, when did Claudio Monteverdi become his pupil, cannot be answered with any certainty. He described himself for the first time as 'discepolo di Ingegneri' on the title-page of his publication, the *Cantiunculae Sacrae* of August 1582, and he repeated this indication four times more: in the *Madrigali Spirituali* of 1583, the *Canzonette* of 1584, the *First Book of Madrigals* of 1587 and finally, the *Second Book of Madrigals* of 1590. The publication of the *Cantiunculae* by the fifteen-year-old boy must have been preceded by a lengthy period of quiet preparation. The work shows the pupil's complete mastery of the strict three-part vocal writing. It is possible that Ingegneri instructed Claudio in viol playing as well as in. counterpoint and composition. He seems to have been a distinguished violist. In any case, the gap of three years between the publication of the *First* and *Second Books of Madrigals* is striking. Did Claudio continue his studies with Ingegneri after the completion of his twentieth year? The sub-title of the publication of 1590 leads to this conclusion. Thus, the connexion between master and pupil must have lasted for quite ten years: i.e. from 1580 until 1590. The dedicatees of the works published in 1582–7 are Cremonese clergy and noblemen such as Pater Caninio Valcarengo, Count Marco Verità, and the patricians Pietro Ambrosini and Alless. Fraganesco, who probably patronized the rising and precocious musician. Before he attained the age of twenty Claudio had already published four works of the most diverse types: *tricinia*, sacred madrigals, canzonettas and secular madrigals, which reveal a composer unusually mature in technique and extremely fertile in imagination. After the date of his last publication he may have looked beyond the confines of his native city for a post which would be worthy of his talents. At least, so we may conclude from the journey he must have undertaken to

Milan, evidently before 1590, during which, as a violist, he came into contact with the President of the Senate there, Jacomo Ricardi. To this manifestly influential man he dedicated his *Second Book of Madrigals* in 1590, evidently hoping for further patronage. The dedication of the next publication is already addressed to his new master, the Duke of Mantua; and now, for the first time, Ingegneri's name is absent from the title-page and never appears again.

When did Monteverdi finally leave his native city to enter the service of the Mantuan court? In a letter dated 2 December 1608, he speaks of nineteen years' unbroken court service, so he must have been installed there in the winter of 1589–90 at the latest. Against this we must place the journey to Milan, which occurred before the beginning of 1590, and the dedication from Cremona of the *Second Book of Madrigals* to Ricardi. These facts are likewise contradicted by a remark of Claudio's in a letter of later date, 6 November 1615, to the effect that 'after twenty-one years' service at Mantua he left with twenty-five scudi in his pocket'. As he was released on 31 July 1612, we may take it that he must have been installed as early as 1591. Perhaps he worked at Mantua during 1590 'on probation', and obtained a permanent post only at the beginning of 1591, as 'suonatore di Vivuola'* in the cappella of Vincenzo I Gonzaga, Duke of Mantua.

CHAPTER III

YEARS OF SERVICE IN MANTUA, 1590–1612

FOR Monteverdi's future as a creative artist, the appointment at the Mantuan court was a stroke of fortune of the highest order. By their numerous intermarriages with the houses of Hapsburg, Este, Tuscany, Farnese and Medici, the Gonzagas were the very finest representatives of the type of art- and splendour-loving sovereigns of the High Renaissance, to whom the history of the fine arts is so deeply indebted—even if these arts were often only

* See Glossary.

Monteverdi in his youth

[*facing page 6*

most highly favoured by them because they served as the most powerful means of self-glorification.

The house of Gonzaga had ruled over the city and the duchy of Mantua, and over the Margraviate of Montferrat, too, from the middle of the fourteenth century. Since the Treaty of Cateau Cambrésis in 1559, at which a large area of the plain of the River Po had fallen to the Spaniards, these independent principalities, and the neighbouring duchies of Parma, Ferrara and Tuscany, had acquired increased political and cultural significance. Mantua itself, one of the strongest fortresses of the Middle Ages and the Renaissance, held a strategic key-position below the passes of the Italian Alps and Lake Garda which was to prove disastrous to it. France and Spain were greatly interested in the little state, and when the last of the Gonzagas, Vincenzo II, died at Christmas 1627, leaving no heir, the Mantuan war of succession started and eventually culminated in the sack of Mantua by the Imperial troops on 18 July 1630. On this occasion many art treasures belonging to the Gonzagas and numerous manuscripts of Monteverdi's operas were destroyed. This was the only time that his creative work was affected by the scourge of contemporary political events, as was so frequently the case in the life of Heinrich Schütz.

Monteverdi was at work during the final golden age of the Gonzagas at Mantua, i.e. under the reign of Vincenzo I (1587–1612), the splendour-loving son of Guglielmo I (1538–87), whose artistic sense had already been of such great importance to the cultural life of Mantua. Guglielmo I, ill-favoured and deformed, but exceedingly gifted, now carried on his ancestors' active patronage of the arts. As early as 1471 Poliziano had written an *Orfeo*, with music by Angelo Germi, for Cardinal Gonzaga; the first play with obbligato musical accompaniment which has been handed down to us. The composers of *frottole*, Cara and Tromboncino, with whom the blossoming of the madrigal of the Italian Renaissance took its rise, were attached to the Court of Francesco II (1466–1519). In Guglielmo's own time the specific interest in music became intensified. He commissioned a Mass and numerous motets from Palestrina, whom he greatly prized and with whom he carried on a voluminous correspondence towards 1570 during the course of which he sent him his own compositions for revision and criticism. He also tried, though unsuccessfully, to attract distinguished musicians such as Marenzio and Orazio Vecchi to his court. At last he engaged Palestrina's pupil, F. Suriano, who worked at

Mantua from 1581 to 1586. He built the church of St. Barbara, founded the ducal cappella, and finally installed the Fleming Giaches de Wert (1536–96) as maestro di cappella to the Mantuan court and the church of St. Barbara. Under the last-named, Monteverdi was to work for more than five years as assistant violist. Guglielmo was a prudent father of his family and an able politician. By his marriage to Eleonora d'Austria he allied himself with the Imperial house of Austria. His son and heir, Vincenzo I, inherited his father's love of splendour and his inclination for music, but not the economical habits of the older generation. During the reign of this gifted but conceited spendthrift, whose Boccaccio-like exploits as a lover were the scandal of contemporary European courts, the Duke's private resources were continually ebbing; a state of affairs which was to result in catastrophic consequences for court officials such as Monteverdi. Vincenzo I dabbled in alchemy; he protected Galileo, freed Torquato Tasso from imprisonment, patronized the poets Guarini and Chiabrera, and had his portrait painted by Rubens and Pourbus. But his passion for music and the theatre surpassed all his other tastes. His play-actors, who appeared in the Louvre and at Fontainebleau in 1608 and 1613, were world-renowned, and the festivals of opera at Mantua during 1608 outdid in splendour even those of Florence—the cradle of opera. Through his wives, Margherita Farnese and Eleonora di Medici, he was united by ties of relationship with the most important of the neighbouring Italian courts.

Vincenzo I seems to have early recognized Monteverdi's genius and to have manifested a certain liking for him personally. Twice he bade Monteverdi accompany him on distant journeys. Later, he gave him express permission to marry, accorded rights of Mantuan citizenship to him and his children and finally settled an annual income upon him. Yet, year after year he preferred the music of mediocre talents to that of Monteverdi, and when the young master was at the height of his fame as an opera composer, requited him with beggarly sums. Reflecting upon this relationship between a great, art-loving sovereign and a secular musical musical genius, one's thoughts turn involuntarily to the bearing of Joseph II towards Mozart and to all its hardly explicable injustices.

When Monteverdi took up his duties at Mantua he came into touch with a group of colleagues who, by asserting the claims of seniority and taking cover beneath the much-favoured device of court intrigue, made life a burden to him. Among these colleagues, whom Monteverdi vividly describes in scathing terms in his earliest extant letter, 28 November 1601, the aforementioned G. de Wert was the leader by virtue of his position as maestro di cappella at the court. He was undoubtedly an outstanding musician—his madrigals had early shown a tendency towards the *concertante* style—but by the time Monteverdi came to Mantua he was already a sick man. Giovanni Gastoldi (1556–1622), too, who had been director of church-music in Mantua since 1582 and who, as time went on, deputized more frequently for de Wert, was the composer of dance-songs (*Balletti*, 1591) which entitled him to consideration as one of the best representatives of this light type of madrigal, itself the outcome of the *frottola* and the *villanella*. Both these men were considerably older than Monteverdi and held assured positions of authority. Benedetto Pallavicino—whom Monteverdi, in the letter of 1601, contemptuously dismissed as 'il sofficiente messer'—had been in the service of the Gonzagas since 1581, and he ultimately succeeded in getting himself appointed over the heads of all the musicians in Mantua as de Wert's successor.

Other musicians at the court of the Gonzagas whom Monteverdi himself mentioned in letters were: Franceschino Rovigo (d. 1597); Al. Striggio the elder (1535–c. 1595), the composer of an Intermezzo, *Psiche ed Amore*, 1565, furnished with a list of instruments for its performance which gives it the appearance of being a forerunner of Monteverdi's *Orfeo* of 1607; his son, A. Striggio the younger, author of the book of this same *Orfeo* and a lifelong friend and patron of Monteverdi's, and lastly, Lodovico Grossi da Viadana (1564–1627), the important 'inventor' of the Basso-Continuo technique of the sacred concerto in few parts, Maestro di Cappella of Mantua Cathedral from 1594 to 1609, and apparently on terms of friendship with Monteverdi. Despite so much competition, Monteverdi was soon promoted from the position of simple 'violist'—as he described himself in the dedication of his *Second Book of Madrigals* of 1592—to that of 'Cantore'.[1]

It was probably at the turn of the year 1594–5 that, with express permission from the Duke,[2] Monteverdi married Claudia Cattaneo, the daughter of a violist colleague, G. Cattaneo, and herself a professional singer. In 1595 he accompanied the Duke on the unsuccessful campaign against the Turks which Vincenzo I undertook as the faithful vassal of the Emperor Rudolph II. Monteverdi made the campaign as temporary maestro di cappella and took with him five musicians belonging to the cappella. The Mantuan contingent marched up through Innsbruck, Linz, Prague and Vienna to Vyšehrad in south Hungary, where the forces of Mahomet II were drawn up. After indecisive battles, during which the ducal troops suffered from dysentery and the Duke himself was tormented by erysipelas, the corps of Mantuans marched back by way of Vienna, Styria, Carinthia and Venice to their Lombardian homeland, which Monteverdi reached in November the same year after an absence of about six months.

On 6 May 1596 G. de Wert died. From Monteverdi's remarks in subsequent letters it transpires that he regarded the appointment of B. Pallavicino, a man of very moderate gifts, as an undeserved slight to himself. Monteverdi's own fame was increasing, as the new edition of the *Third Book of Madrigals* in 1594 testifies. In the succeeding years he had composed the majority of the madrigals he collected and published in the *Fourth* and *Fifth Books of Madrigals* in 1603 and 1605 respectively, copies of which were now beginning to circulate freely. On all sides there were signs of the dawn of a new era. Palestrina and Orlandus Lassus had both died as early as 1594, the very year the members of the Florentine 'Camerata' had started work on the first opera, *Dafne* by Peri-Corsi and Rinuccini,[3] and Orazio Vecchi's madrigal-comedy *L'Amfiparnasso* had appeared in print.

In 1599 Monteverdi accompanied the Duke on another journey, this time of a pacific character. The destination was Flanders. Vincenzo spent a month at Spa, probably to take the waters; met both Rubens and Pourbus; stayed at Liège with his relative, Ernst of Bavaria, and finally made a state entry into Brussels. On this occasion the route lay through the Tyrol, Switzerland and Lorraine to Spa, and then by way of Liège and Antwerp to Brussels, where it terminated. At the bathing establishment of Spa Monteverdi made his first acquaintance with French musicians,[4] and learned to know and admire the type of *Airs de cour* composed by Mauduit, Lejeune and Guédron. The 'a la francese' style constantly recurrent in his later works may be dated from this time onwards. By now his *Scherzi Musicali*, 1607, had probably already been sketched. Before setting out on his journey on 9 June 1599 Monteverdi had sent his wife Claudia, who was with child, to Cremona to his father, Baldesar. Soon after his return she gave birth to his first son, Francesco, early in 1600 at Cremona.

The year 1600 was noteworthy in other respects in our master's career. It was now that the Bolognese canon and musical theorist

Artusi (c. 1540–1613), published the first part of a polemical treatise, *L'Artusi, overo delle Imperfettioni della musica moderna*, in which four of Monteverdi's as yet unpublished madrigals[5] were submitted to cantankerous criticism. Artusi abstained throughout from mentioning the composer's name, although it may be assumed that he could hardly have been ignorant of the origin of these works, which were circulating in private copies. It is not impossible that Monteverdi replied to Artusi's polemic the same year in an open letter by an 'Ottuso Accademico'.[6] In 1603 Artusi brought out a second part of the *Imperfettioni* in which he reprinted certain portions of this reply of Monteverdi's, the original of which has not been preserved, and compared two other madrigals, not yet published, with Venetian street songs.[7] The year 1603 also saw the publication of Monteverdi's *Fourth Book of Madrigals*, which included two of the madrigals attacked by Artusi and was dedicated to the members of the 'Accademia degli Intrepidi di Ferrara'. In 1605 it was succeeded by the *Fifth Book of Madrigals*, in the preface to which Monteverdi announced a comprehensive theoretical refutation of Artusi under the title of *Seconda Prattica overo Perfettione della moderna musica*, which, judging by the details of the prospectus, most probably denotes the *Dichiarazione* to the *Scherzi Musicali* published by Giulio Cesare Monteverdi in 1607. The great work of theoretical and controversial character upon which Monteverdi must have been engaged until about 1634 was never written.[8] Monteverdi had far more important work to do than to come to terms with this Beckmesser of the Early Baroque who took offence, not only at Monteverdi's setting of his texts, but more especially at the (doubtless astonishing) harmonic audacity of his mature madrigal style.[9] In 1606 Artusi replied to Monteverdi's short but striking preface to the *Fifth Book of Madrigals* ('the modern composer takes his stand on the foundations of truth— that is to say—of expressive realism'), with an anonymous polemical treatise *Discorso Musicale di Antonio Braccini da Todi* which has disappeared, whereas a refutation of its criticism in Giulio Cesare's *Dichiarazione* has been preserved.

Despite the brilliant exposition of Monteverdi's critical methods in the *Dichiarazione*, Artusi did not admit defeat, and presently counter-attacked with a fresh controversial treatise (still in existence) entitled *Discorso secondo musicale di A. B. da Todi per la Dichiarazione, etc.*, in which three items from the recently published *Scherzi Musicali*[10] were attacked on account of their complex rhythm.[11] This brought to a close the battle of words which had been waged for over eight years and which, according to Monteverdi's own statement,[12] was settled later in all good humour when this Saul of a musician was converted into a Paul. The Artusi-Monteverdi controversy, which is symbolic of the ever-increasing contrast between the artistic generations of the 'Prima' and 'Seconda Prattica', may be summed up statistically as follows: Artusi attacked Monteverdi in four separate publications: *Imperfettioni I*, 1600; *Imperfettioni II*, 1603; *Discorso I*, 1606; *Discorso II*, 1608.

Monteverdi replied three times in controversial manner: (1) Possibly in the letter from an 'Ottuso Accademico' (before 1603); (2) in the preface to the *Fifth Book of Madrigals*, 1603; (3) in the circumstantial *Dichiarazione* by his brother comprised in the *Scherzi Musicali*, 1607. In the course of the actual dispute nine of Monteverdi's madrigals, from the *Fourth* and *Fifth Books of Madrigals* and from the *Scherzi*, were specifically subjected to criticism.

After this long digression we must return to 1600. It is not improbable that Monteverdi journeyed with the Duke to Florence this year for the nuptials of Maria di Medici with King Henry IV of France. If he did, he will in all likelihood have heard the first performance there of Rinuccini's *Euridice*, with music by G. Peri, in which the principal role was sung by Francesco Rasi of Mantua. Even supposing Monteverdi did not visit Florence, he is almost certain to have received reasonably precise information as to the methods and aims of the Florentine 'Camerata' from this singer who was a friend of his. On 6 May 1601 the maestro di cappella of Mantua, Benedetto Pallavicino, went into retirement.[13] It is conceivable that Monteverdi, who was now thirty-four and had been in the ducal service for the past ten years, considered himself as Pallavicino's rightful successor. Nevertheless, he waited until 28 November of this year before sending a formal petition to the Duke. Was he perhaps expecting a spontaneous nomination on the part of the Duke? Vincenzo I was just then involved in his third Turkish campaign and in the very midst of the siege of Canisa when Monteverdi's petition eventually reached him. In this remarkably malicious document Monteverdi points out with ill-concealed irony that he has waited patiently for the deaths of many of his colleagues, namely, those of his superiors, G. de Wert, A. Striggio sen., F. Rovigo and B. Pallavicino, and that he feels the time has come when he deserves an appointment as 'Maestro di Cappella', 'non per mente e virtute, ma per merito di fedele et singolar divozione'. The letter is so typical of the writer, and so expressive of his situation at the time it was written, that it is reproduced here in full:

To His Serene Highness my supreme Lord
the Duke of Mantua

Canisa.

Most illustrious Lord and Master!

If, on the occasion of Benedetto Pallavicino's* death, I myself made no haste to request from Your Serene Highness's great favour the rank Signor Giaches† once held as a musician, it might perhaps fall out to my regret that envy of the endeavours of my colleagues (by means of rhetoric rather than of music) would be urged against me publicly in such a fashion as would cloud the good opinion Your Serene Highness entertains of me, and would make it appear that my envy originated in anxiety as to my own capacity, or in overweening conceit of my person, and that therewithal my ambition betrayed me into expecting what an unimportant servant such as I am should seek to obtain with especial humility and earnest entreaty. If, likewise, I no longer cultivated opportunities of serving Your Highness, even though Your Grace offered them to me, there would indeed be cause for deploring my absence of zeal in serving you. If, with my moderate ability, I were not fully conscious of the important occasions when I could make my motets and masses acceptable to your exquisitely sensitive ear, it were surely a matter for justifiable complaint. And if, when the world at large has been aware of the continuance of my zeal in your service as well as of Your Grace's favour towards me, in the first place, after the death of the distinguished Signor Striggio,‡ secondly, after the death of Signor Giaches, and, thirdly, after the deaths of the excellent Signor Franceschino§ and of the capable Benedetto Pallavicino; if, indeed, I were still to fail in aspiring to secure appointment to the ecclesiastical post now vacant—(not as a recompense for exceptional proficiency but as a reward for faithful and especial devotion such as I have always displayed in Your Highness's service)—and if, when all is said and done, I were to fail to beseech you ardently and with deep humility for the post afore-named, my default of zeal would then give cause for scandal. Considering all the foregoing, and taking into account such things as are vital to the continued prosperity of my career and such as could be fulfilled through the instrument of your favour; and considering, also, that Your Highness has never disdained to hear my modest compositions, I do most earnestly pray you to vouchsafe me the post of Maestro di Cappella of Chamber

---

* Cf. Pt. II, *The Works*, footnote 25.   † Jacob van Werth.
‡ A. Striggio sen. *c.* 1595.   § Francesco Rovigo (1542–97).

Music and Church Music, which, if in your goodness and grace you deign to bestow upon me, I shall accept with such deep humility as beseems a modest servant if he is favoured by a great prince such as Your Highness. I make obeisance before Your Highness and proffer my most humble tribute of honour, while I pray daily unto God to grant you the most supreme happiness that a loyal and devoted servant can desire with all his heart for his sovereign lord.

This petition did not fail in its effect. After his return from the campaign the Duke nominated Monteverdi as his 'Maestro di Musica'[14] and at the same time accorded him the rights of Mantuan citizenship. The exact date of this appointment cannot be determined, but it may be placed between the end of 1601 and March 1603, the date of the preface to the *Fourth Book of Madrigals*, in which Monteverdi describes himself for the first time as 'Maestro della Musica del Serenissimo Sign. Duca di Mantova'.[15] In the preface to this publication Monteverdi makes reference to his project of performing several of these madrigals before the former Duke Alphonso II (Este) in Ferrara; a project which did not materialize owing to the sudden death of the Duke that year. The preface makes it clear that many pieces in the *Book* had been composed before 1597. Among them are two which, as we have seen, had already been attacked by Artusi in 1600. In the same year, Monteverdi had become acquainted, through the Duke's interposition, with the Roman singer Caterina Martinelli, then only thirteen years of age, who first of all took up her quarters in Monteverdi's house and pursued her studies with him. The friendship which consequently developed between them culminated in *Arianna*, for the title-role of which 'Caterinuccia' was selected by the composer.

In December 1604, Claudia presented her husband with a second son, Massimiliano, who came into the world at Cremona at a time when his father, now thirty-seven years of age, embittered and overworked for many weeks past, had taken refuge there with his own father, Baldesar. The financial position of the couple seems to have become progressively worse, despite Claudio's tireless activity.[16] The year 1605 saw the publication of the *Fifth Book of Madrigals*, dedicated to Duke Vincenzo, which with its predecessor of 1603 was probably the most successful of his publications. Up to 1620 it went through no fewer than eight new editions! It is probable that we owe Monteverdi's first opera and the feasibility of its performance to the Duke's two sons, Francesco and Ferdinando Gonzaga, who had a passion for the theatre.[17] Ferdinando, in particular, who was then studying at Pisa, seems to have been deeply interested in the performance of opera in the adjacent city of Florence. But Francesco, too, the Hereditary Prince, participated so eagerly in the operatic projects in Mantua that Monteverdi could dedicate the fruit of their joint efforts, *Orfeo*, to him with a clear conscience. It cannot be ascertained exactly when Monteverdi began to occupy himself with plans for opera. As early as December 1604 he was entrusted with commissions from Mantua for several ballets. Thus it is safe to assume that during the winter of 1606–7 he was at work on the composition of *Orfeo*, the text for which had been supplied by A. Striggio, jun. The title-role was assigned to Gualberto Magli, a pupil of Caccini's. The memorable first performance took place in the state-rooms of the 'Accademia degli Invaghiti' under the presidency of the Hereditary Prince Francesco, apparently on 22 February 1607. It was followed by two performances at the court itself on 24 February and 1 March. Incomplete performances took place in Cremona,[18] perhaps in February, and certainly on 10 August under the composer's direction, and repetitions of the whole work were given down to 1609. Striggio's libretto, which had already been printed in 1607, was followed by the two authentic editions of the score in 1609 and 1615. These bare facts record the sensational, but at the same time lasting, success of Monteverdi's first operatic work, which was completed during a period of great mental depression.[19]

To the financial troubles of the last few years, increased anxiety was now added concerning Claudia's health which for some time had appeared to be precarious. On 10 September 1607 Claudia died in Cremona after twelve years of married life, faithfully cared for to the end by her doctor father-in-law. She left Monteverdi a disconsolate widower at the age of forty with two sons of seven and two years. Yet he had little enough time in which to give way to his grief. On 24 September he was summoned by Follino, the court historiographer, to return to Mantua, 'che questo è il punto d'acquistarsi il sommo di quanta fama può havere un huomo in terra'.[20] As if the desolated Claudio could possibly have been in the mood for worldly renown just at this moment! The fact was that the success of *Orfeo*, and, moreover, the approaching nuptials of the Hereditary Prince, Francesco, with the Infanta Margherita of Savoy, had created a regular furore for opera. The wedding ceremonies of 1608 reached a climax in a series of memorable first performances which may confidently be described as the oldest opera festival in Europe. Monteverdi was destined to play a dominating part in it and was first of all commissioned to compose the actual festival-opera, *Arianna*, as well as an opera-ballet *Il Ballo dell' Ingrate* for this purpose. The real director of the festival was Ottavio Rinuccini (1560–1621), the celebrated poet and writer of the texts of the oldest operas in the world, Peri's *Dafne*, 1597, and *Euridice*, 1600, who on this occasion furnished the libretti for Monteverdi's *Arianna* and *Ballo*. He was clever enough to smuggle in a third opera which had been composed much earlier to one of his texts: Marco da Gagliano's *Dafne*, which, greatly to Monteverdi's annoyance,[21] was produced as the *first* opera in the festival at the end of January 1608. Monteverdi gave rein to his pent-up bitterness in a long letter to the Duke's treasurer, Chieppo, which must be given here, at least in part. (Extract from Monteverdi's letter to Annibale Chieppo, dated 2 December 1608.)

... To-day, the last day of November, I have received a letter from Your Honour from which I gather that His Highness commands me to hold myself in readiness to return to Mantua as soon as possible in order to tire myself out once again with exacting tasks; at least, so he commands. I reply, that if I do not take a complete rest from the exacting tasks at the theatre, my span of life will be shortened; for in consequence of my tremendous over-exertions in the past I have developed headaches and a severe, maddening rash on my body which neither the cauterizing I have undergone, nor the purgatives I have taken, nor even the blood-letting and other measures to which I have submitted have succeeded in curing more than partially. The *Signor padrone* ascribes the cause of the headaches to strenuous study, but the maddening rash to the air of Mantua which does not suit me, and he even goes so far as to fear that this air will be the cause of my death not long hence. Just think, Your Honour, what it would mean to me if I had to come and to be beholden to His Highness's courtesy and kindness for acts of mercy and favour, as he commands me to do. I tell you, Your Honour, that the fortune I have enjoyed in Mantua throughout nineteen years has given me cause to feel ill-disposed rather than friendly. For even when I rejoiced that the Duke showed me favour by letting me accompany him to Hungary it was nevertheless to my disadvantage; for expenditure mounted up to an extent such as my poor household has been aware of ever since the time of that journey until to-day. . . . And when, at last, fortune seemed to favour me and I allowed myself to believe that by His Highness's favour I should receive a pension of 100 scudi of Mantuan currency from the city Governor, His Highness withdrew his favour from me once again.

And then, after my marriage, it was no longer 100 scudi, but still only seventy; and in addition, I was deprived of the good facilities I had requested and of the payment due for the months gone by. And then it seemed almost as if 100 scudi might have been considered too much. If the twenty scudi which I draw as salary had been added thereto, it would have amounted to about twenty-two golden ducats a month, which, had I received it, I could have spent on my poor children. I do know that His Serene Highness entertains the kindliest intentions towards me, and I know too, that he is a Prince who dearly loves freedom; but I have been far too unsuccessful in Mantua, as Your Honour will see from the following statements. I am fully aware that His Highness easily alters his intentions; for instance, Signora Claudia decided to make a settlement upon me, but when I arrived in Mantua he changed his mind, and to my sorrow, no such provision was made. Up to the present time I have lost about 200 scudi, and I lose more as each day goes by. It was also decreed, as I mentioned before, that I should be given twenty-five scudi; but then His Highness suddenly altered his mind, and to my grief the five scudi were withdrawn from me. Now Your Honour will understand perfectly well how miserable I am in Mantua.

The principal reason for inserting this performance of Gagliano's opera *Dafne* was to give Monteverdi more time for the composition of the 1,114 lines of the text of *Arianna*. That he was suffering from insufficiency of time and lack of quietude during his work on this opera can be seen from the agonized exclamations in subsequent letters; for instance, that '. . . the shortness of time had almost been the death of him while he was at work on *Arianna*', and 'he must have a peaceful time for composition'.[22] Untoward circumstances, such as Monteverdi's precarious financial position and Claudia's illness, had already cast a shadow over the period when *Orfeo* was produced, but the period of preparation for *Arianna* was even more particularly ill-starred. Although the music was ready in all essentials by the beginning of February,[23] the first performance, which had been planned to take place during Carnival Week, had to be postponed on account of the sudden illness of Caterinuccia who was to play the part of Arianna. Caterinuccia succumbed to smallpox, which was to claim many victims at the Mantuan court. She died on 9 March 1608 at the early age of eighteen and was mourned by one and all, but most especially by the Duke and Monteverdi. The part of Arianna was now entrusted to the well-known singer Virginia Andreini (the wife of G. B. Andreini[24] and a member of the famous company of actors, the 'Fedeli'), who had originally been cast for the title-role of Guarini's comedy with music, *L'Idropica*.

c

This work brings us to the fourth opera of that memorable 'Week of Opera' in Mantua. In the meantime, the two Princes had been hatching out fresh operatic plans which were to invest the wedding ceremonies, now finally arranged for the end of May, with even greater splendour. In addition to the Monteverdi-Rinuccini *Arianna*, which after the many tragic delays was eventually mounted on 28 May, and in which, according to contemporary reports,[25] the musical climax of the work, the *Lamento*, moved the audience to tears, no fewer than four more operatic works were performed for the first time. Monteverdi's active participation in two of them necessitated almost superhuman exertions on his part, as a result of which he suffered from a kind of nervous breakdown in the late summer that year. On 2 June Guarini's *Idropica* and Chiabrera's new 'Intermedia' were performed together. The Prologue had been composed by Monteverdi, the 'Licenza' by Paolo Birt, and the composition of the four 'Intermedia' was shared between S. Rossi, G. Gastoldi, Marco da Gagliano and Giulio Cesare Monteverdi. On 3 June came the performance of the 'Torneo',* *Il Trionfo d'Onore*, based on an idea of Francesco Gonzaga's, with text by A. Striggio jun. and music by Marco da Gagliano. This in its turn was succeeded on 4 June by the Monteverdi-Rinuccini opera-ballet, *Il Ballo dell' Ingrate*, and on 5 June the opera *Il Sacrificio d'Ifigenia* (with libretto by A. Striggio jun. and music by M. da Gagliano) wound up this remarkable Festival of Opera which spread the fame of Mantua all over Europe and enabled it from this time on to vie with Florence for the premier position as a city of opera. Admittedly, this victory was not achieved entirely without assistance from the 'Camerata'. Indeed, in surveying the list of participants in the Mantuan opera festival it is no exaggeration to speak of a 'Florentine Invasion' at the court of Mantua. No fewer than three opera texts were provided by O. Rinuccini, the world's first opera-librettist. Marco da Gagliano, too, produced three works, each filling an entire evening, and he was also concerned in a fourth. During his moments of leisure this astute courtier corrected Prince Ferdinando's compositions. Francesca Caccini, one of the vocally gifted daughters of a famous father, and Jacopo Peri[26] established themselves at the Mantuan court. Many of them, like the courteous Gagliano, were highly paid.

This marked preference for the Florentine 'intruders' must have

* See Glossary.

made Monteverdi more acutely aware of the neglect of his own productions. The wounds inflicted on him by the deaths of Claudia and Caterinuccia were not healed as yet, and he seems to have left for Cremona in June 1608 in a state of physical and mental exhaustion and to have taken up his quarters with his children at Baldesar Monteverdi's. He stayed there for over a year (until September 1609) in an angry frame of mind, worn out, embittered, and obstinately resisting the fresh tasks of composition with which the importunate Duke overwhelmed him during his absence from the court. This state of irritability is reflected in Baldesar's still extant petitionary letters to the Ducal couple,[27] and even more strongly in Monteverdi's own letter to the Ducal treasurer, Chieppo,[28] extracts of which were quoted earlier in these pages. The payments due to Monteverdi from the Ducal purse were in arrears, as they had been ever since 1602 or thereabouts. The expenses of Claudio's destitute household had to be borne by the aged Baldesar who, in a letter to the Ducal couple, already mentioned above, gives a realistic picture of the heavy demands made upon him by his son and grandchildren. In his second letter, this time addressed to the Duchess, Baldesar writes as follows:

Illustrious Lady,

My son, Claudio Monteverdi, came to Cremona immediately after the conclusion of the Wedding Festivities in a very bad state of health, in debt, and shabbily clad. Without any assistance from Signora Claudia he was now left, after her death, with the two poor children, who were a burden to him because his resources were only twenty scudi per month. I am absolutely certain that the trouble is due solely to the air of Mantua, which does not suit him, and to the exhausting work he has undertaken, and will continue to undertake, if he remains any longer in service. And all this is combined with the misfortunes that have attended him throughout the nineteen years he has spent in the service of the illustrious Duke of Mantua. For this reason I have latterly decided to write to Your Highness and to beseech you most humbly in the name of Heaven to grant him the favour of release from his duties. For I am sure, noble Lady, that if he returns to Mantua, the strenuous work and the unfavourable air will speedily be the cause of his death, and then these poor children will become a burden to me, who am old and frail, and who have, moreover, had in the past to maintain his wife, children, man-servants and maidservants, and have not infrequently paid out 500 scudi on behalf of the said Claudio, and even larger sums when he was in His Highness's service in Hungary and Flanders, and again when he came to Cremona with his wife and children, a maid, servants and a carriage, and on other occasions which for the sake of brevity I will not mention. And as his wife received no reply to her appeal I have taken it upon myself to beseech Your Highness to beg of your illustrious consort that for God's sake he will grant me this just request; for it is certain that such a favour could only turn out to the said Claudio's advantage. . . .

Given at Cremona, 27 November 1608.

Baldesar Monteverdi.

In the letter Monteverdi himself wrote to Chieppo at about the same time, he compared with great bitterness his own financial position with the far more favourable circumstances of his colleagues, such as Luca Marenzio, Filippo di Monte, Palestrina and others. At last, on 17 January 1609, Vincenzo I took the matter firmly in hand: according to a decree dated the same day he settled a life-annuity upon his still absent maestro di cappella. This doubtless well-intentioned act of the Duke's was to become an inexhaustible source of annoyance to Monteverdi who, from now onwards until the end of Gonzaga rule in 1627, was to address despairing letters to Mantua demanding arrears of payment. The Gonzagas' love of splendour and their mania for squandering could not keep pace with their occasional excellent projects. Alchemists and jewellers, however, could apparently always count upon preferential payments.

In August of the same year the first printed edition of the score of *Orfeo* came out in Venice.[29] At the end of September Monteverdi returned to servitude in Mantua, accompanied by his children. The year 1609 does not seem to have been very fruitful for the composer. The spiritual upheavals of the years 1607–8 had put too much strain upon his nerves, and the headaches from which he now began to suffer were to become the constant companions of his mature life. That the experiences of these recent years had deepened the creative artist in him may, however, be seen from the triumphantly rising curve of his production during the following year, 1610, during which he composed some of his finest works. Large parts of the *Sixth Book of Madrigals*, 1614, were written at this time, among them being the *Sestina* cycle (in memory of 'povera Caterinuccia') and the madrigal version of the *Arianna Lamento*. But the most important works of this year are the great Mass *In illo tempore* and the *Vespers of the Virgin Mary* with the two Magnificats which Monteverdi put together in a volume of impressive sacred music.[30] In the late autumn of 1610 he travelled to Rome, where he hoped, with assistance from cardinals who were his friends, to interest the Pope in the publication of the sacred works dedicated to him, and where he also intended to request a bursary in the Papal Seminary for his elder son, Francesco. But the Roman journey proved disappointing and barren of results, and the Mass and the Vespers dedicated to the Pope were published in Venice,[31] whither Monteverdi had travelled in January 1611, after having arrived just previously in Mantua, on 28 December.

Was the journey to Venice associated simply with the publication of the Mass, or perhaps with the official interest in his person which had been aroused by his previous Venetian publications: the Scherzi, Orfeo and the Mass?

During the later part of the year Monteverdi was employed once again in various musical activities at the court, and there was no sign of the dramatic change which was shortly to be accomplished in the history of Mantua and of its maestro di cappella. In September 1611 the Duchess Eleonora died quite suddenly. The court was still in mourning when her consort Duke Vincenzo I followed her to the grave on 18 February 1612. By the death of the Duke Monteverdi lost his real protector in the house of the Gonzagas. Vincenzo bequeathed to his son, the Hereditary Prince Francesco, empty coffers and a political situation which was perpetually developing threatening complications. Francesco IV ascended the ancestral throne on 10 June 1612 and straightway ordered splendid festivities in his father's style to celebrate the simultaneous accession to the crown of his Hapsburg cousin the Emperor Mathias. One of the first acts of the young Prince, whom Monteverdi had honoured with the dedications of Orfeo and the Scherzi Musicali, was to dismiss the maestro di cappella who had been with him so many years, and his brother Giulio Cesare as well, on 31 July 1612. At present we have no means of ascertaining any motive for this sudden and mysterious dismissal. It is all the more inexplicable inasmuch as Francesco himself, but more especially his brothers and sisters, were later on to do everything in their power to secure him again for the Mantuan court.

Monteverdi left Mantua in the early part of August. He took with him little in the way of savings. Exactly twenty-five scudi jingled in his pocket: the fruit of twenty-one years' activity at the court of the Gonzagas.[32] He returned once more to his native city of Cremona where he was to spend a whole year without any kind of appointment.

CHAPTER IV

MAESTRO DI CAPPELLA OF SAN MARCO, VENICE, 1613–43

Up to the present, little has been discovered concerning Monteverdi's creative activities after his dismissal. It is possible that many church compositions and madrigals in later collective editions may have been written during the transitional year. It is also possible, not to say probable, that the Tasso-fragment, *Lamento di Erminia*,[1] only recently discovered, belongs to this year of interregnum. It forms a spiritual bridge from the *Arianna Lamento* to the scenic oratorio, *Combattimento di Tancredi e Clorinda*, which Monteverdi composed later for Venice, and with which he was to raise an imperishable monument to his predilection for Tasso.

As a practical musician, too, Monteverdi was not entirely inactive. A journey he made to Milan in the autumn of 1612 may very likely have been undertaken with the intention of obtaining a new appointment. The journey culminated in a concert in Milan Cathedral which Monteverdi directed with the greatest success, although Mantuan scandalmongers tried to spread reports to the contrary. Nevertheless, the concert in 1612 terminated just as ineffectually as did the musical exertions of the young viola-player at the house of Ricardi, the president of the Milanese Senate, in 1589.

At Mantua, in the meantime, the mediocre musician Sante Orlandi, had been nominated as Monteverdi's temporary successor. The attempts made by the court to win Monteverdi back must have already begun at about this time. The revival of *Arianna* during the autumn was possibly an attempt to see which way the wind was blowing. It was Francesco Gonzaga's first and last attempt at becoming reconciled with his Maestro di Cappella of so many years' standing. The sudden outbreak of a smallpox epidemic caused his death, and that of his heir, at Christmas 1612. Ferdinando Gonzaga, the 'Cardinal' of the family, ascended his brother's throne. The revolution in the social and political life of the Duchy caused by this sudden accession to the throne, the second within half a year, seems to have entirely suppressed any possible relationship between Monteverdi and the court for about two years.

Monteverdi in middle life

[*facing page 22*

Monteverdi's residence in Venice

Monteverdi's destiny as an artist seemed more uncertain than ever when the death, on 19 July 1613, of the Maestro di Cappella di San Marco, Don Giulio Cesare Martinengo, who had for long been infirm, afforded him a unique opening. The Procurators came to a decision with extraordinary speed. Early in August, Monteverdi was informed through the Venetian ambassador in Cremona of the Procurators' interest in his person. On 19 August he was in Venice at a festival concert given under his direction at San Marco. Immediately afterwards, he was unanimously elected as Martinengo's successor, and appointed first Maestro di Cappella at a yearly salary of 300 ducats and free residence in the 'Canonica' of San Marco. In a flash Monteverdi's position had changed. After the precariousness of service at the Mantuan court, which in recent years seemed to be progressively disrupted by political crises, an appointment had actually come overnight to the forty-six-year-old composer, and one that was more in keeping than any other with his high standing as a musician and with his individual temperament. It was a matchless piece of good fortune in the history of western music, comparable only, perhaps, with the sudden appointment of Richard Wagner to Munich through the intervention of Ludwig II!

The position of a Maestro di Cappella di San Marco had not always been of such great prominence as it was at the beginning of the seventeenth century. The cappella had been reorganized under the Frenchman, Pietro de Fossis (1491–1527), but it first attained world renown under his two Flemish successors, Adrian Willaert and Cyprian de Rore, who superintended its activities until 1565. These two developed the practice of antiphonal singing in double choirs instrumentally buttressed by the two organs of San Marco. With Willaert and de Rore, the progressive elements of the madrigal and the chromatic style made their way into sacred music, too. Andrea and Giovanni Gabrieli had officiated at these organs, as had Claudio Merulo and other specialists of a newly awakening instrumental style. Finally, the great theoretician, Gioseffo Zarlino (1565–90) had directed the cappella's musical fortunes for the long period of twenty-five years. At his passing in 1590, only four years before the deaths of Palestrina and Lassus, the golden age of Venetian church music was apparently waning after having flourished for more than sixty years. During the régime of Zarlino's successors, B. Donati (1590–1603) and Giovanni della Croce (1603–1609) the standard of the choir deteriorated, and its decadence in style and in performing technique was still further hastened under G. C. Martinengo (1609-13). No sooner was Donati dead in 1603 than the Procurator, T. Contarini, pointed out the need for a complete reorganization of the cappella. With a prophetic glance he declared his opinion at the time:[2] 'L'ufficio et carico importantissimo de Maestro di Cappella della chiesa di S. Marco ricerca . . . di essere collocato in persona grave, no solo per età, ma per vita e costumi. . .' He conjured up the spirits of Adrian, Cypriano and the 'dotissimo' Zarlino and concluded: '. . . Vera cosa è che questi tal huomini—no si trovano qui in piazza che siano ricercati . . . in quai luogo si trovano . . .', with which words he must have dealt Venetian local patriotism a heavy blow. But another ten years were to elapse before the ideal personality corresponding to Contarini's far-sighted requirements was discovered in Monteverdi. Monteverdi was probably appointed first and foremost on the strength of his *Missa, In illo tempore*, 1610, which cannot have failed to make an impression upon the Procurators.

It was now his task[3] to lead the deteriorated staff of the cappella back to the half-forgotten traditions of the *canto di chiesa* and to the polyphonic church style of the Palestrina period into which the intrusion of the now fashionable part-writing in a few parts (opera, monody, and *concerti ecclesiastici* in the style of Viadana) had wrought such great havoc.[4] It was a completely conservative ideal as regards style that the Procurators wished to see realized by the efforts of Monteverdi, the revolutionary composer of music-dramas and madrigals. It is one of the finest achievements in Monteverdi's life that, at the very height of his creative activity and as the composer of *Orfeo*, *Arianna* and the downright revolutionary *Vespers* of 1610, he in no way disappointed his employers. He restored discipline and order, and within three years had succeeded in re-establishing the cappella as a first-rate body of performers. He added to the cappella archives many pieces of church music, old, new, and composed *ad hoc*, and so deeply did he plunge into this fresh work to which he was entirely unaccustomed but which was certainly truly congenial to him, that at the end of only seven years[5] he could assert that his service in the church had, as it were, snatched him away from his own type of music for the theatre. On 24 August 1616, after exactly three years' activity, his annual salary was raised by the Procurators' Treasury to 400 ducats without his having even made request for an increase. The harmonious relationship between the Procurators of the still powerful Republic and their maestro di cappella who had for so long been accustomed to agitations and disappointments in the service of princes, was never clouded. Under Monteverdi and his pupils, Venice enjoyed a musical blossoming comparable with that of the decade when Willaert and Cyprian de Rore held sway at San Marco.

An attack by robbers on the return journey from Cremona to Venice which caused Monteverdi and his companions the loss of about 100 ducats formed a none too promising prelude to his Venetian period. His amusing description of this adventure in a letter to Al. Striggio jun. dated 12 October 1613 is printed below in full:

... I beg to inform Your Honour that while I was in the company of the Mantuan courier on my way back to Venice we were set upon unawares by three ruffians and robbed in Sanguanato—or rather, not in the place itself but a good two miles away. It happened on this wise: from a field by the side of the road, one of the rascals, dark-hued, with sparse beard and of medium height, carrying a long musket with the trigger cocked, suddenly emerged, and another came forward and threatened me with his musket, while the third grasped the bridle of my horse—which continued on its way quite unconcerned and without showing resistance—and led it into the field. I was quickly dismounted and made to go down on my knees, while one of the two armed men demanded my purse and the other took charge of the courier and demanded his portmanteaux which, when the courier himself had lifted them out of the carriage, they opened in turn and one robber packed up everything he could find or that the courier gave him voluntarily. As for me, I remained the whole time on my knees, held fast by the other fellow with the fire-arm. Then both of them seized everything they could lay hands on while the third of the rascals, who held a dagger in his hand, turned watchman and kept a sharp look-out lest anyone might come along the road. When they had thoroughly ransacked all our belongings, the man who had searched the courier came over to me and ordered me to undress so that he could see if I had any more money. As I declared I had none, he went over to my maid-servant and would have submitted her to the same treatment, but she resisted with many prayers, entreaties and tears and succeeded in making him leave her in peace. He then went back to the plunder and to the portmanteaux, made up all the best and most valuable things into a bundle, and as he looked round to see if he could find an article of clothing he lighted upon my cloak. When, however, the rascal saw it was too long for him he said, 'Give me another', and grabbed my little son's cloak, but when he found this was too short, the courier took it upon himself to say, 'Sir, it belongs to the poor innocent; give it up'; and he acquiesced. Next, he came across a

suit of the boy's and went through the whole procedure again. He also got
some more things given to him by the maid-servant after much pleading.
Finally the fellows crammed all the remainder into a huge bundle, hoisted
it on to their backs and made off with it. Then we packed up what was
left and went into the inn. The following morning we lodged a complaint
in Sanguanato, and continued on our journey, myself very dispirited,
eventually reaching Este whence we took a ship for Padua which stuck
on a sandbank the whole of the Thursday night and very nearly the whole
of the Friday without anyone even thinking about trying to float her off.
At last, after a delay of almost twenty hours, in a strong wind and heavy
rain, with none other than our courier sitting aft in the open boat, getting
it under way and even exerting himself valiantly with an oar, we reached
Padua and set foot in the city soon after 1 a.m. On Saturday morning we
rose early to prepare for our departure. During our sojourn in Padua the
courier had put his arm into a sling, saying that he did so on account of the
incident with his cloak when he was robbed, although I knew perfectly
well that he had been neither touched nor searched. I felt perplexed, for
the courier's demeanour excited suspicion in all around him; because,
for one thing, we had none of us noticed any injury, and for another, while
we were in the bark at Padua I said to him, 'What sort of a made-up story
is this, brother?' and when I went on to add a few words, certainly only
in fun, he withdrew from the conversation. He was good-tempered,
and enjoyed himself on the boat; and so we reached Venice about mid-
night on the Saturday. He stayed there only about two hours and then
returned to Mantua to make a complaint against me, as he understood me
to have expressed suspicion of the erstwhile courier. But I replied that I
had harboured no suspicion against him and that I regarded him as a man
of integrity. Nevertheless, it is quite possible that he put his arm in a sling
on the Saturday because of an incident that had already occurred on the
previous Wednesday. And yet there was no one there who so much as
touched him, and he had been the whole of the Friday on board the ship.
I beg to inform Your Honour that I did not suspect this man, and if such
an idea had entered my head I should straightway have sent an exact
report to Your Honour. But I do say that the courier's demeanour the
day he put his arm in the sling gives food for thought; and when it comes
to a matter which gives cause for deliberation, I leave it to Your Honour's
sense of justice to form an opinion. For my part, I think nothing. I shall
not pursue the matter further but leave it in the righteous hands of God.
I swear to Your Honour that I was robbed, among other things, of gold
to the value of 100 ducats. When I was in Mantua I had a half-year's
pay to draw by favour of the Lord President, and I can apply for another
when three months have elapsed from that time. I told the President of
my misfortune; and if you would be so good as to put in a favourable
word for me with him—although I know how great is his kindness—
I should be most deeply grateful, for I stand in sore need.

Given at Venice, 12 October 1613.

This distressing incident was, however, for some time to come the last of the series of misfortunes which had pursued the sorely tried Monteverdi ever since 1607. In 1614 he published his *Sixth Book of Madrigals*, the contents of which date entirely from the Mantuan period. In the following year, 1615, the Mantuan court was already resuming the negotiations with Monteverdi which had been interrupted since Christmas 1612. Ferdinando Gonzaga, who for his part had staked so much upon the production of *Orfeo* and the Festival of Opera in 1608, wanted to interest Monteverdi in a new opera libretto, but the master showed little inclination to come to Mantua, even temporarily. This year he started an exasperated struggle for the payment of the yearly pension decreed by Vincenzo I, which was now more than ever necessary for the education of his growing sons, and with which the ducal treasury was more than ever in arrears. He waged this struggle in numerous letters in which the phraseology characteristic of the Baroque courtier gave way progressively to extremely personal and malicious irony. Nevertheless, he allowed himself to be persuaded into composing a little operatic ballet in the style of the *Ballo dell' Ingrate*: *Tirsi e Clori*, which was probably performed there in April 1616. But he entirely rejected the proposal to compose Scipione Agnelli's *Favola maritima*. The operatic plan which Ferdinando had cherished for so long was finally disposed of in January 1617. Most likely his private maestro di cappella, Santi Orlandi, had lent a helping hand by means of the intrigues customary in Mantua from time immemorial.

It was at about this date that Monteverdi entered into relationship with the court of Parma, which was ruled by the house of Farnese. Odoardo Farnese's consort, Margherita of Tuscany, seems to have been a great lover of opera and a special patroness of Monteverdi. Had it not been for manifold commissions for opera and ballet for these two princely courts Monteverdi would have completely lost touch with the problems of music-drama, for republican Venice of 1613 was not as yet interested in court opera! Opera, which had migrated from Florence, its actual place of origin, to Mantua and thence to the mid-Italian centres of Parma and Bologna, but above all to Rome, was for the next quarter of a century to remain the prerogative of the courts of princes.

During the years 1617–19 Monteverdi was occupied with works for the theatre: the opera *Andromeda* for Mantua, and an Eclogue, *Lamento di Apollo*, to words by A. Striggio. Nothing remains of these compositions, nor of the subsequent operas either. The scores fell victims to the plundering soldiery of 1630. December 1619 saw the publication of the *Seventh Book of Madrigals*, entitled *Concerto* and dedicated to Caterina di Medici, Ferdinando Gonzaga's consort. The dedication unmistakably reflects the intensifying of the master's relationship to the court of Mantua; but when Ferdinando made fresh proposals to Monteverdi to return to service in the Mantuan court, he declined politely but firmly. He preferred to stay in Venice, which had become a second home to him despite the unfavourable climate which still further increased his tendency to headaches. 'Wherever I go to make music, whether it be chamber music or church music, the whole city is eager to be there. My duties are extremely agreeable'—so he wrote in a letter during 1620. The same year, Monteverdi visited the composer and theorist Adriano Banchieri, to whom he was bound by ties of friendship, at the Monastery at Bosco (Monte Oliveto) near Bologna where he was received with especial veneration by the members of the Accademia Florida whose president Banchieri was.[6]

Meanwhile, his sŏns had grown up. The elder boy, Francesco, had been studying law in Bologna since 1618, and the younger, Massimiliano, was just beginning to prepare himself to follow family traditions by becoming a doctor. In the summer of 1620, Francesco suddenly decided to abandon his legal studies in order to become a Carmelite friar. This change in the career of his elder son seems to foreshadow the day when Monteverdi himself would be admitted to the priesthood. These family problems necessitated journeys to Bologna and Mantua, and Monteverdi seems also to have visited his aged father-in-law, Cattaneo, in Mantua. The year 1621 was full of anxieties concerning Massimiliano, who became seriously ill and whose professional career was still far from assured. The following year, on his recovery, he obtained a post in the Collegium at Bologna after Monteverdi had galvanized influential cardinals into action on behalf of his son. Continued anxiety over the careers of both his sons, as well as heavy tasks of composition, which included a Mass for the obsequies of the Grand Duke Cosimo II of Tuscany and *una licenza in Musica* for the Duchess of Mantua, were probably the cause of Monteverdi's illness in February 1623 which prevented an intended journey to Mantua. It was for this reason that Ferdinando Gonzaga visited Monteverdi during an 'incognito' journey to Venice in April. The same year,

1623, Monteverdi's elder son joined the Capella of San Marco as a tenor. His abilities as a singer were evidently considerable, if we can trust the opinion of Camberlotti.[7] In 1624 Monteverdi composed the scene from Tasso, *Combattimento di Tancredi et Clorinda*, for Count Girolamo Mocenigo. It was the first of the master's dramatic compositions to come into being as the result of a commission from Venice. The following year he was engaged upon compositions for a Polish prince. On 16 March 1626 Massimiliano graduated at Bologna as a doctor of medicine, and went soon afterwards to Mantua where he began to practise with great success. On 29 October 1626 Ferdinando I of Gonzaga died, and Vincenzo II, the youngest son of Vincenzo I, ascended the tottering ducal throne. He reigned little longer than a year, and died at Christmas 1627. With his death, the male line of the Gonzagas became extinct. During his brief reign the main bulk of the business affairs of the Duchy fell to the lot of Monteverdi's old friend, the Chancellor A. Striggio jun., who had written the text for *Orfeo*. Striggio took advantage of his now almost unlimited political power by getting Monteverdi to write an opera on a grand scale. And thus, thanks to his persistence, the year 1627—the last of the reigning house of Gonzaga—became one of the most notable in the creative production of Monteverdi who was now sixty years of age. G. Strozzi's libretto to *La finta pazza Licori* seems to have completely captivated Monteverdi because of the problems it set in respect of realism and naturalism in the composition of the music. The twenty-three extant original letters dating from this year are concerned for the most part with this opera and contain a whole musical dramaturgy in a nutshell.

The following extracts from these letters give a good idea of the depth of penetration with which Monteverdi scrutinized every libretto sent to him. They also show him far advanced on the road to a system of characteristic tone-symbols, anticipating Gluck's and even Wagner's musico-dramatic methods.*

* Laconic bibliographical references have so far tended to obscure the fact that Giulio Strozzi wrote two different libretti of the same title, each based on similar psychological premises, for two different composers at different times. The *Licori finta pazza inamorata d'Aminta*, written for Claudio Monteverdi (Mantua, 1627), is a comic love story, in which the woman (Licori) is disguised as a man and the male lover (Aminta) feigns madness. Both the libretto and the music are lost. G. Strozzi's second libretto of the same title has, however, been preserved. (Copy in the British Museum.) The title runs as follows:

1 *May* 1627

. . . and now that I have finished the duel between Tancredi and Clorinda* I have been considering a very beautiful and curious little work by Signor Giulio Strozzi from which about 400 lines could be taken entitled *Licori finta pazza inamorata d'Aminta*, describing how Licori, after resorting to a thousand ridiculous devices, succeeds in marrying Aminta by means of cunning deception. These and similar incidents would do for subsidiary episodes . . .

7 *May* 1627

. . . I send your Illustrious Lordship Signor Strozzi's *La finta pazza Licori* as you commanded me in your gracious letter. It has not yet been set to music, nor printed nor performed on the stage, for as soon as it was completed the author gave me this very copy himself. If the said Signor Giulio knew it appealed to his Serene Highness's taste, I am perfectly certain he would instantly be ready and willing to arrange it in three acts or in any way pleasing to his Serene Highness, as he desires above all things to have it set to music by me, liking to see his well-loved creations clothed with my unworthy notes. . . . I have found him to be most willing and reliable in all he undertakes. So if the story is to your Lordship's liking, pay no heed to its present form, for I know for certain that the author will be able to alter it to your complete satisfaction within a very short time. The plot does not seem bad to me, nor its unfolding. It is true that the part of Licori, being very varied, should not be entrusted to a woman unable to play now the part of a man, now that of a woman, with lively gestures and manifold outbursts. For, since the representation of such feigned madness must take account only of the present moment and not of the past or the future, it must consequently be based upon single words and not on the sense of the phrase as a whole. When she speaks of war she must represent war; when of peace, peace; when of death, death, and so on. And as the transformations occur very rapidly, so must the representations. The woman, therefore, who plays this very important part, which moves to both laughter and compassion, must put

---

FESTE THEATRALI PER LA FINTA PAZZA

Drama del signor GIULIO STROZZI

Rappresentate nel piccolo Borbone in Parigi quest' anno MDCXLV

This is a serious opera, based on the story of Achilles, who is living in woman's disguise on the island of Skyros, and of his mistress Deidamia, who later on in the play feigns madness. Thus the roles of the man and the woman in both libretti seem to be exactly reversed. This second libretto was composed by Paolo Sacrati and originally produced in Venice in 1641. The music is lost. This is the first instance of a libretto by G. Strozzi being composed first by Monteverdi and later by Sacrati. The second instance is *La Proserpina rapita*, composed by Monteverdi in 1630 (Venice) and by Sacrati in 1644. This note is based upon valuable information generously supplied to the author by Frank Walker.

   * *Il Combattimento di Tancredi e Clorinda* (T. Tasso).

aside every other kind of representation but the momentary one occasioned by the word she has to say. However, I believe that Signorina Margherita will do excellently. . . .

22 *May* 1627

. . . I have likewise received your Illustrious Lordship's opinion and instructions concerning *la finta pazza*, and I share your Lordship's opinion that on the stage this *finta pazza* will be yet more novel, varied and delightful. But now that I know what you think I will not fail (when the said Signor Giulio comes from Florence in three or four days' time)— I will not fail, I say, to confer with him, and you will see that he will enrich it with still further varied, novel and diverse scenes such as I shall certainly suggest to him. I shall see, too, if he can enrich it in other ways by adding fresh characters so that the pretended madwoman does not appear so often, and I shall see that each time she comes on the stage she is the cause of new delight and new variations in the harmonies* as also in her gestures; and about all this I will give your Illustrious Lordship the most detailed information. In my opinion the work is excellent in several places, but in two others I think it could be improved, not so much in respect of the poetry as in originality. And in another place, too, where (by the addition of a passage) I should be afforded an opportunity of letting Aminta speak to her (Licori) while she is asleep and where I should like him to speak so softly as not to awaken her. For the necessity of his speaking sotto voce would give me a chance of writing harmonies which would be new and different in type from those preceding and which would also lay particular stress upon the varied character of the dance which is interposed. . . .

24 *May* 1627

. . . Signor Giulio Strozzi has not as yet returned from Florence. I await him with eagerness because of the desire I cherish to accomplish all that your Illustrious Lordship has commanded me concerning *La finta pazza*, and I should already have written to you in full were I not still waiting for the author to make further improvements. According to his last letters he should certainly be in Venice within two or three days, God willing, and I hope that the work will be altered in accordance with your Lordship's wishes and that you will be completely satisfied with it. I have already considered it so thoroughly that I know I could set it to music in a very short time. My intention, however, is that every time the pretended madwoman comes on she should arouse fresh delight with fresh variations. In three places I certainly think the effect will be achieved. The first, when the camp is being pitched and sounds and noises are heard

---

* The word 'armonia' is used by Monteverdi in a much wider sense than is implied by the English 'harmony'. In fact, in his letters it rarely denotes the restricted sense of 'chord' or 'chordal progression', but more usually implies 'music' or 'musical organization' in general.

behind the scene in imitation of her words. I think this will not be unsuccessful. Next, when she feigns death, and the third, when she feigns sleep, where harmonies suggesting sleep must be employed. But in certain other places where the words cannot be matched by gestures or noises or other kinds of imitation that may present themselves, I fear the preceding or the succeeding passages may lose in interest. For these passages I await Signor Strozzi. . . .

10th July, 1627

I send your Illustrious Lordship the first act of *La finta pazza Licori* by Giulio Strozzi as you commanded. I particularly wanted to send the original itself so that your Lordship might see not only the verses, but the argument of the story written in the author's own hand, and the characters, too. Two intermediate acts are completed, which the author will give me to-morrow or the next day. He tells me that the feigned madness begins in the third act. As soon as I receive these acts I will send them also. There will be a dance in every act, each one different from the others and all fantastic. I beg your Illustrious Lordship to deign to return me the act when you have read it, for I have not been able to finish copying it owing to the eye-trouble about which I told you in my last letter, which trouble, God be praised, has almost passed away. Signor Giulio tells me that each act will bring forth fresh incidents, so that I am disposed to think it is bound to turn out well. It remains only for Signorina Margherita to become a valiant soldier and completely to master the appropriate gestures, now bold, now timid, without fear or restraint; for I incline towards having the vigorous imitations by harmonies, gestures and changes of time performed behind the stage.* I believe your Lordship will not be displeased, for there will be sudden transitions from vigorous and noisy harmonies to soft and suave ones so that the dialogue may be brought into prominence. . . .†

It is utterly deplorable that the music for this last opera for Mantua should also have disappeared. In spite of eye-trouble, chills and increasing melancholy—the phenomena of approaching old age—Monteverdi finished the work in about five months, and found leisure at the same time to compose many stanzas from Tasso's *Gerusalemme liberata* (the scene between Rinaldo and Armida) which, like all the other works of this fertile year, has not been preserved. *La finta pazza Licori* was completed on the 10th September 1627, and at about the same time Monteverdi received a commission for an 'Intermedium' for Parma. He declined other commissions for the composition of dramatic works.

* The wording of this passage in the Italian original is obscure.
† The translator is greatly indebted to Mr. Frank Walker for much valuable advice and assistance in the translation of these letters from the original Italian.

Vincenzo II, who was probably strongly influenced by the Chancellor, Striggio, also continued the efforts previously made by his family to regain Monteverdi's services for Mantua. Renewed courteous but ironical refusal on the part of the prudent master! He wrote quite frankly to Striggio at the time that he felt much more inclined for a canonry in Cremona which would be the means of supplying him with a certain income for his old age. He did not conceal that he already estimated the future value of the pension granted to him by Vincenzo I in former days at a very low amount.

In the same year, 1627, he also found time to bring out Arcadelt's *Madrigals* in a new edition and to sketch the 'Intermedium' for Parma. He was engaged, too, upon a new opera for Mantua: *Armida* on a text taken from Tasso. In October this year Monteverdi went to Parma and Ferrara to complete the 'Intermedium' on the spot and to discuss the forthcoming performance, which did not, however, actually take place until 21 December 1628. On his way back to Venice at Christmas 1627, he learned of the sudden arrest of his younger son, Massimiliano, by the Inquisition. By a cruel irony of fate, this last great sorrow in a lifetime abounding in agitations of the spirit was inflicted upon Monteverdi, a most loyal son of the Catholic Church, by over-zealous ecclesiastical arbiters. At almost the same time as this blow fell upon the ageing master, the last of the Gonzagas, Vincenzo, II died on 25 December 1627. Thus, the most fertile year of Monteverdi's life ended in tragic gloom. During its course two large-scale operas for Mantua, the 'Intermedium' for Parma, the *Rinaldo-Armida* scenes from Tasso, and the new edition of Arcadelt's *Madrigals* had come into being; and yet, in a letter of 27 September this year, Monteverdi complained that he no longer possessed the youthful powers necessary for composition.

The opening of the new year 1628 was as ill-omened as was the Christmas week of the old. Although Monteverdi's feverish efforts and A. Striggio's energetic assistance led to Massimiliano's speedy release from imprisonment by the Inquisition, the possibility of re-arrest hung like the sword of Damocles over both father and son during the months preceding the actual trial. Monteverdi's acute care for his son eventually secured Massimiliano's transfer to Venice. The successful young doctor had obviously fallen a victim to the jealousy of his colleagues, who had informed against him on account of his being in possession of a book prohibited by

D

the Inquisition. In order to free his son, who was shattered by grief and self-reproaches, Monteverdi had to stand security for 100 ducats which he was about to try to raise by selling a gold neck-chain. Fortunately, his most loyal friends at the Mantuan court, A. Striggio and E. Marigliani, sprang into the breach and paid the whole sum immediately. At the trial held during the summer 1628, Massimiliano was eventually acquitted—after months of agonizing uncertainty during which Monteverdi had to go on working at his operatic plans for Parma. How cruelly he suffered as a consequence of this happening may be seen from the last letter (8 July 1628) he addressed to the Chancellor, A. Striggio, extracts from which are quoted below.

I understand from your extremely kind letter that you have called personally on the worthy Pater Inquisitor, and I feel not a little embarassed that you should have shown me this favour. Your Honour was told that the two days Massimiliano spent in captivity should suffice to restore him to absolute freedom. I doubt it, and Your Honour will excuse me if, in view of your own confidence, I speak so openly. I am afraid, and so is he—I mean, my son is afraid he will be put on the rack and condemned to pay an exceptional fine or to undergo imprisonment for infinitely more than two days; for he will be brought to trial for something he neither intended nor committed. And so this state of uncertainty is producing an entirely contrary effect to that intended. As it is, anxiety so acute fills him with terror. Your Honour will believe me when I tell you that hardly a day passes that he does not weep or that he is not in the depths of despair. By the post which has lately arrived, the worthy Pater Inquisitor has written me, stating definitely that he will consent to letting me have my son back as soon as I wish. As soon as I wish!! I am ready the whole time —I tell Your Honour. But if this is really his firm intention, and if he has examined my son's career a dozen times within the space of six months, why does he not condescend to let him go free and thus spare both him and myself this torture; and why does he not allow him to practise as a doctor to his own, and my satisfaction? If necessary, I would gladly pay twenty or even twenty-five ducats blood-money if only I were no longer obliged to read these paltry and incredible things which are such as to make me feel certain he will never come back without a terrible to-do. Dear Sir, if only this great favour could be granted, may I beg you with all my heart and soul to obtain it for me? I assure you, life would thus be restored to myself and the lad, for this dread care is tormenting my spirit. . . .

On 13 December 1628 the 'Intermedia', with text by Ascanio Pio, were at last produced at Parma, and on 21 December, as already mentioned, they were succeeded by the 'Torneo', *Mercurio e Marte*, with music in the same style by Monteverdi. Meanwhile, the death of Vincenzo II brought the splendid epoch of the Gonzagas in Mantua to an end. Their successor, Charles of Nevers,[8] confirmed Monteverdi's rights of Mantuan citizenship and approved the continuation of the annuity[9] decreed by Vincenzo I, but the political situation of the Duchy darkened apace. The Mantuan War of Succession, which gradually unleashed the forces of France and Spain against Mantua after the house of Gonzaga became extinct, was already casting its shadow before. Monteverdi's connexion with the court was soon dissolved. The last extant letter to his old friend Striggio is dated 8 July 1628 (see the quotation above) and is filled with descriptions of the anguish he was suffering over his son, then *sub judice*. Exactly two years later, 18 July 1630, Mantua fell a victim to the plundering soldiery of the Imperial leader, General Aldringen, who not only laid part of the unhappy city in ruins and ashes (and the scores of Monteverdi's operas of 1613–30 into the bargain), but introduced the plague into northern Italy. The horrors of the Thirty Years War which darkened long stretches of the life of Heinrich Schütz form the tragic background to the evening of Monteverdi's life. The destruction by ravaging troops of so many documents makes it impossible to follow the individual destinies of the people nearest to him. What happened to A. Striggio? What became of the aged father-in-law, Cattaneo? Did Massimiliano return to his practice in Mantua or remain in the security of his Venetian sanctuary? We do not know; neither do we know if, and when, Monteverdi and Heinrich Schütz met in Venice in 1628, although Schütz's creative enthusiasm for Monteverdi's art, and his later remarks concerning him, make it seem very probable.[10]

There are absolutely no extant records of Monteverdi's activities during the following year, 1629. The correspondence with Mantua had come to an end. . . . In 1630, however, in spite of war and pestilence, the master composed two new operas for Bologna, both of which have disappeared: *Proserpina rapita*, on a text by G. Strozzi, and possibly *La Delia e l'Ulisse*, in collaboration with F. Manelli. He seems also to have been engaged in composing sacred music for the Monastery of San Lorenzo.[11]

The sack of Mantua in July 1630 was followed by an outbreak of plague in Venice, where it raged for sixteen months and carried off about forty thousand victims. When it finally died out in 1631, the occasion was celebrated on 28 November with a solemn Mass in the church of San Marco for which Monteverdi furnished the music (now lost). The upheavals of the years 1627–31 decided him to take the step of being consecrated as a priest; a wish he had possibly cherished ever since Claudia's death. Thus, on the title-page of the *Scherzi Musicali* published in 1632, he is described for the first time as 'Reverendo'. In May this year he probably went to Mantua. It must have been painful for him to see the city again after it had been so cruelly afflicted. During the following years, 1632–4, he was occupied in increasing measure with his theoretical work *Melodia*, which was to be a large-scale commentary to his theories upon the 'Seconda Prattica' (sketched in the prefaces to the publications of 1605 and 1607 already mentioned).

In two letters of later date (22 October 1633 and 2 February 1634) to an unknown addressee, Monteverdi described his plan for this book in greater detail. In the first letter, among other things, he writes as follows:

I took this opportunity of adding that I, too, was writing something else, but I feared my feeble powers would not suffice to bring it to the desired conclusion. . . . The title of the book will be as follows: *Melody*, or *Second Musical Practice*. 'Second': by which I mean, 'From the modern aspect'. 'First' denotes 'From the aspect of antiquity'. I divide the book into three parts which correspond to the three divisions of melody. In the first, I speak of expression (representation); in the second, of harmony, and in the third, of the rhythmical element. I am of the opinion that it will not be unwelcome to the public, for during the course of my practical work I discovered that when I was about to write 'Ariadne's Lament', I was unable to find any book which could instruct me in the method of the imitation of nature, or which could even have made it clear to me that I ought to be an imitator of nature. The sole exception was Plato, one of whose perceptions, however, was so obscure that, owing to my weak sight, I could hardly apprehend the little he could teach me. I must say that it has cost me great efforts to complete this laborious work, which it is necessary to undertake in order to make it possible for anyone to do the very minimum of what I have accomplished in the imitation of nature. And for this reason I hope I shall not cause displeasure. If I should succeed in bringing the work to a conclusion, as I so dearly wish, I should count myself happy to be praised less for modern compositions than for those in the traditional style. And for this new presumption I now beg forgiveness.

This book has not been preserved, any more than have the numerous music-dramas belonging to the same period. In May 1637, Monteverdi celebrated his seventieth birthday. A few weeks later, he was grossly insulted in public, on the Piazza San Marco, by a member of his choir. His dignified but spirited letter of accusation to the office of the Procurators (June 1637)[12] is the last personal document in his own hand still remaining. And now we come to the final, unique chapter in the life of this extraordinary man.

At an age when most of the great masters settle down quietly to rest, and when they contemplate the eclipse of their creative powers with more or less philosophical equanimity (consider Haydn, for instance, who at seventy had practically renounced composition; and Rossini and Wagner at the same age!), the veteran Monteverdi plunged once more into the vortex of intensive activity as a composer. The principal work of these years is comprised in the rich harvest of the Venetian period which was gathered into two mighty collective published editions. Both these publications, which were personally supervised by the master —the *Eighth Book of Madrigals*, 1638 and the *Selva Morale e Spirituale*, 1640—are a triumph for the progressive artist who was looking towards a fresh horizon. He dedicated both works to the princely personages who were the last representatives of his close connexion with the house of Gonzaga: the Empress Eleonora Gonzaga, the youngest daughter of Vincenzo I (*Selva*), and her consort, the Emperor Ferdinand III (*Eighth Book of Madrigals*).

In the meantime, after the long delay of ten years, Venice had evolved as a city of opera. As early as 1637 the first public opera-house (that is to say, the first to which the public was admitted by purchasing tickets), the San Cassiano, had been opened with F. Manelli's *Andromeda*. In 1639, this production was followed by Monteverdi's imperishable *Arianna* at the San Moisé, and by a new opera of the master's, *Adone*, with a text by P. Vendramin, which has disappeared. The year 1641 revealed the seventy-four-year-old composer still extremely fertile in the writing of theatre music. His opera, *Le nozze di Enea con Lavinia*, was performed at the Theatre of SS Giovanni e Paolo. The librettist of this now vanished work, Giacomo Badoaro, also wrote the text of the extant, but disputed, operatic piece *Il Ritorno d'Ulisse in Patria* which was produced at the San Cassiano Theatre.[13] The same year, Monteverdi wrote the ballet *La Vittoria d'Amore*, of which only the libretto survives, for the ruler of Parma, Odoardo Farnese.[14] His masterpiece, probably the most magnificent operatic work of the Early Baroque and also the first *historical* opera, *L'Incoronazione di Poppea*, was composed by him at the age of seventy-five with youthful fire, and was performed for the first time at the Theatre of San Giovanni e San Paolo in the autumn of 1642. He revised the score fundamentally after the first performance, and the indelible traces of his self-critical activity are to be found in the extant manuscript of 1642. They are the last strokes of the master's pen. The only authentic musical notation from his hand which has been preserved for us is comprised in these revisions of 1642–3.[15]

After this last lofty flight Monteverdi was aware of the approaching shadows of death, and he yearned to revisit the haunts of his youth. He went to Cremona and Mantua and spent almost six months away from Venice where he was worthily replaced by G. Rovetta. In the autumn of 1643 he must have had a premonition of his end. He returned to Venice, where he died in his seventy-seventh year after a short illness. An impressive funeral ceremony was held for the immortal musician in two churches in the city of lagoons. At San Marco the requiem was directed by Rovetta; at Santa Maria dei Frari, by G. B. Marinoni, and the earthly remains of the 'divino Claudio' were laid to rest in the mortuary chapel of Sant' Ambrogio (in the Frari church). In the following year, 1644, this same Marinoni published his *Fiori Poetici* which contains Camberlotti's eulogy of the departed composer[16] and the sombre portrait of the aged Monteverdi which has handed down the features of the composer of the *Incoronazione* so memorably to posterity. The great bulk of his musical remains: countless church compositions, madrigals and canzonettas of his thirty years' activity in Venice, were issued in 1650–1 by his faithful publisher Allessandro Vincenti. Even far-away Naples ventured upon a new setting of the *Incoronazione* as late as 1651. Thus Claudio Monteverdi's creative power continued for a time to exercise its influence upon a world which now pursued other artistic aims. Not long afterwards Monteverdi and his works became enveloped in the mists of historical oblivion, whence they eventually emerged to enjoy a late but triumphant revival.

CHAPTER V

THE MAN AND THE ARTIST

To determine the converging point of Monteverdi's artistic greatness from the various psychological aspects of his personality remains one of the most important tasks of the musical historian. This task is made the more difficult by two circumstances which commonly attend the artist of this period: the sparseness of contemporary sources (letters, reports, important biographical documents relating to his career), and the transitional nature of his artistic personality which spans two great periods of style.

When attempting to comprehend Monteverdi as an integral part of his cultural environment we are immediately struck by the lateness of his appearance in the arena of his creative activities. His distinctive contributions to the development of the art of music, such as the discovery of orchestral colour; the colourful blending of vocal and instrumental timbres into the combination of novel qualities of sound (*Orfeo*, *Vespers*, 1610, and the late operas of the Venetian period); the evolving of chromaticism for the purposes of expression and the coining of characteristic types of motive (the late madrigals and the 'stile concitato' of the *Eighth Book of Madrigals*) all have their poetic and pictorial correlatives in the artistic phenomena of a much earlier period. Monteverdi's work is certainly not the equivalent of the exuberantly voluptuous and degenerate art of contemporary painters and sculptors: Caracci (1555–1619), the decadent Domenichino (1581–1641) and Guido Reni (1575–1642). It corresponds far more nearly to that of the great generation of Venetian painters whose glowing colouring seems to anticipate the Monteverdian orchestra of 1607–10. The mature, disciplined mastery and unsurpassed realism of Titian (1477–1576), Tintoretto (1512–94) and Paolo Veronese (1528–88) may be cited as the determining factor in Monteverdi's use of tone colour. This one example convincingly proves the profound truth of Nietzsche's aphorism (in *Menschliches, Allzumenschliches*, II, 171) that music is always the swan-song of its own epoch. An excursion into the realm of poetry only serves to strengthen this conception where Monteverdi is concerned. The two poets who, as creators of a new world of unfettered passion and spiritual agitation which they crystallized into poetry, influenced his music most effectively, both belong to the generation of Tintoretto and Veronese. Torquato Tasso (1544–95) died only a year later than Palestrina and Orlandus Lassus, the last exponents of the 'Prima Prattica' of music; but Tasso's masterpiece, *Gerusalemme liberata*, acted as a stimulus to Monteverdi and as a fountain head of subject-matter from the time of the *First Book of Madrigals*, 1587, until the preface to the *Eighth Book of Madrigals*, 1638, with its artistic and psychological appreciation of the poet. The *Pastor fido* of G. F. Guarini (1537–1612), together with Tasso's pastoral play, *Aminta*, was an inexhaustible source of pastoral atmosphere for Monteverdi, the lyrical madrigalist. The melodic clarity of their verse associates both these poets more convincingly with the much younger musician than does the work of his own exact contemporary in the world of poetry, G. Marini (1569–1625), whose mawkish and garrulous lyricism is far more in keeping with the sentimental imagery of Domenichino and Reni.

The autumnal atmosphere which surrounds Monteverdi's whole appearance as an artist is determined, too, by the singularity of his position as a late-comer and a precursor at one and the same time. His work as a madrigalist was creatively at an end towards 1610. On the other hand, the operas of his old age, ranging, let us say, from the *Combattimento* of 1624 to the *Incoronazione* of 1642, penetrate deeply into the period of the Baroque, whose operatic prototypes, historical heroes, *arioso* forms of melody, and the evolution of the string orchestra as the chief vehicle of the musical happenings, he predestined for a whole century to come. Large portions of his life-work, however—for example, the *Sixth* and *Seventh Books of Madrigals*, the *Selva Morale* and the posthumous publications of 1650—awakened no effective echo in their own time because they were produced and published during the depression between two creative periods and generations. Only some works, such as the first five *Books of Madrigals*, appeared sufficiently early to secure willing acceptance by contemporaries, or so late, like the operas of his old age, as to be accepted and promptly trivialized by a new generation of composers. Cavalli's and Cesti's pompous and decorative operas, for instance, are historically inevitable bowdlerizations of Monteverdi's late operas. Considering the matter more closely, we discover that similar conclusions can be drawn from the career and the curve of production of Heinrich Schütz (1585–1672), whose figure is so indissolubly connected with Monteverdi's.

The parallel between Monteverdi and Schütz,[1] which has not infrequently been traced, has never been thoroughly examined, and might extend to an exploration of the similar personal circumstances of their lives. It is exceptionally convincing because both masters are the embodiment of the latest type of universally cultured humanist of the Renaissance still surviving in a world which was then undergoing drastic changes in the sphere of politics, religion and social life. In the immense contrast between their humanity and that of succeeding generations of musicians there is evidence of the spiritual levelling which came into force in music after 1650 and lasted until the establishing of the rationalistic philosophy of classicism after 1750.

Both masters were men of wide culture who were familiar with the learning of ancient Greece, which Monteverdi, in particular, sought to reinterpret while he was engaged on his uncompleted theoretical work, the 'Seconda Prattica', between 1630 and 1640. Quotations from Plato, references to the great poets of the Early Renaissance, theoretical speculations, philosophical investigations of the phenomena of life and art are all to be found in the prefaces both the masters wrote to their works. How limited, how provincial, and indeed, how poverty-stricken do the prefaces, letters and recorded sayings of J. S. Bach, for instance, appear by comparison with the humanistic arguments of Schütz and Monteverdi! In point of fact, Schütz was so deeply absorbed in the university as the representative of his spiritual experience that he did not reach the decision to devote himself entirely to music until comparatively late in life, and even then not without hesitation. Details of this fruitful comparison, now to be given below, reveal the similarities in the careers of the two men from various angles.

Both Schütz and Monteverdi attained a great age, which alone qualified them to span two epochs, the High Renaissance and the Early Baroque. Monteverdi died at seventy-six, but Schütz lived to be nearly eighty-eight.

Despite their immense creative activity and their lifelong preoccupation with the practical side of instrumental music (Monteverdi was employed for many years as 'suonatore di Vivuola' at Mantua, and Schütz, according to contemporary report, won high repute as a fine organist), neither master left a single instrumental composition.

Both found in poetry an inspiration to the writing of music, and both composed exclusively on the basis of the new evaluation of the poetic word. Both began their creative activity with an Opus I which was not to be succeeded by another volume of the same type. Monteverdi: the *Liber Primus* of the *Cantiunculae Sacrae* in 1582, *a cappella* 'Tricinia' of a kind he never wrote again. Schütz: *Il primo libro dei Madrigali*, Venice, 1611, to which no second book ever followed.

The voluminous operatic production of both composers after 1608 was lost, either as a consequence of plundering during wars, or by reason of other misfortunes. Monteverdi: the sack of Mantua by Austrian troops in July 1630. Schütz: the fire in Copenhagen in 1794, during which all his Danish manuscripts were destroyed.

From among Schütz's compositions for the theatre: the opera *Dafne*, Torgau, 1627, the Danish opera-ballet of 1633, the ballet *Orpheus und Euridike*, Dresden, 1638, the Dresden ballet *Die sieben Planeten*, etc., no more has been preserved than has been from among the numerous operatic works which Monteverdi wrote for Mantua, Parma and Venice between 1613 and 1640. The theoretical treatises by both men have been handed down only indirectly! Monteverdi: in the *Dichiarazione* of his brother Giulio Cesare in *Scherzi Musicali*, 1607. Schütz: in the *Kompositionslehre* of his pupil Chr. Bernhard, after 1648.[2]

The late works of both composers aroused no echo in the creative world of their time, for reasons already given above. (Monteverdi's *Eighth Book of Madrigals*, 1638, *Selva Morale*, 1640, and the posthumous publications of 1650; Schütz's late Passion works of 1665–6.)

Both became widowers at the age of forty after brief, happy marriages: Monteverdi in 1607, Schütz in 1625, and both mourned the loss of their partners for the remainder of their lives.

About ten years after their respective deaths, both composers fell into complete oblivion, but both experienced a late revival in the nineteenth century: Monteverdi was rediscovered by C. von Winterfeld in 1834; his biography was written by E. Vogel in 1887, and the reissue of his works was begun in 1881. Schütz: P. Spitta's biography came out in 1894, and the collected edition was begun in 1885.

The similarity between the portraits of the two masters in their old age,[3] wherein aristocratic melancholy expresses, better than any words, the extent of human and spiritual isolation both had attained towards the end of their lives, is yet another proof of their inward affinity.

The comparison could undoubtedly be continued even further, especially in respect of the relationship which existed between the two men and the princelings who employed them. This has already made us familiar with the inmost region of Monteverdi's qualities as a human being, which are not only explicit in his music and in the few extant portraits and the descriptions and eulogies of his contemporaries, but which emerge principally in the master's 121 preserved letters as well. It is not easy for the modern student to grasp these human qualities in their historical hypotheses and in the curve of their personal experiences. Monteverdi makes the impression of being in many ways the child of two contrasted epochs. He is in some respects indebted to the Middle Ages, which even during his own lifetime came to a natural end. Like many flexibly minded men after the age of the great discoveries he took a lively interest in alchemical experiments. This almost Faustian trait was strengthened by his descent from medical ancestry. His knowledge of medicine seems to have been well above the average. On the other hand, his attributes as a man of the Renaissance period may be recognized in his theoretical speculations on classical art, philosophy and aesthetics, and in his naïve Platonism which ascribed to Plato's decisions upon aesthetics the same mystically determining significance as did the medieval philosopher to Aristotle's axioms.[4] How far removed as a speculative thinker does Monteverdi seem from his great contemporary Galileo Galilei (1564–1642), whose father's, (Vincenzo's) *Dialogo della musica antica e della moderna* of 1581 occupied him in so stimulating and exciting manner after 1613 and again towards 1634.[5] Monteverdi the dramatist, however, appeals to us as a modern whose dramaturgic analyses of opera-texts[6] are not inferior in the acuity of their psychological perceptions to the dramaturgic formulations of Gluck and Mozart. Typically modern, too, is Monteverdi's emotional relationship to his poets, Tasso, Rinuccini and Strozzi, and his obvious dependence upon a stimulus for producing the right atmosphere for composing. His despairing cry, 'havere tempo comodo per comporre', runs like a scarlet thread throughout his correspondence. He must have time for composition; haste and hurry in the production of an emotional work such as *Arianna* bring him 'to the point of death'.[7]

It is in his relationship to Church and State that Monteverdi appears most strongly bound by tradition. He is a 'servant of princes' like all his artistic contemporaries and like so many musicians after him right up to Mozart, who for the first time in the history of the arts rebelled against the yoke of artistic servitude (e.g. his break with Archbishop Colloredo in 1781). Monteverdi spent more than twenty-one of his seventy-six years in court service at Mantua, and thirty in the service of the Venetian Republic. His relations with the princely house of Gonzaga, to whom he remained under further obligations from after 1613 until about 1627, recall in many respects Mozart's connexion with the Hapsburgs. Although Vincenzo I (1587–1612) must undoubtedly have recognized Monteverdi's significance early on, he manifested a continued preference for such mediocrities as A. Striggio sen., F. Rovigo, and B. Pallavicino.[8] Who, in this instance, does not think of Joseph II and his unconcealed preference for Dittersdorf and Salieri rather than for Mozart? The sudden and inhuman dismissal of Monteverdi after the death of Vincenzo I by his successor, Francesco IV, immediately brings to mind the hostile treatment by Leopold II, the successor of Joseph II, of his 'Hof- und Kammerkompositeur', W. A. Mozart, during the years 1790–1. A growing feeling of disillusion, not to say an antipathy to the courts of princes, and an increasing scepticism towards aristocratic methods of business become more and more apparent during Monteverdi's Venetian period. This disillusionment even tones down the traditionally elaborate and obsequious style of his letters to the Chancellor Striggio during his later years.

In his relationship to the Church Monteverdi is entirely the child of his own epoch: the epoch of grandiose Roman resurgence as also of the phenomenon of reaction towards the militant Protestantism of the mid-sixteenth century. Counter-Reformation and Inquisition, together with the reforming of church music in the spirit of a conservative ideal of sound, influenced Monteverdi's life and production at many points. As early as 1610 he made an effort to approach the Princes of the Church. His appointment as Maestro di Cappella of San Marco was due first and foremost to the conservative purism of style which distinguishes the *In illo tempore* Mass of 1610. The reorganization of the decaying church-choirs in Venice was carried out by Monteverdi during the years following 1613 in the sense of the Palestrinian ideal of sound. And yet at the same time he accomplished the miracle of bringing out his own church compositions in the revolutionary style of the 'Seconda Prattica' right down to the publication of the *Selva* in 1640! His son's terrible adventure in the dungeons of the Inquisition had no power to shake his faith in the justice of the Church. In 1632 he received the orders of priesthood, thus becoming the forerunner of the Abbé Liszt who, like himself, was the servant of two worlds until the very end. The existing documents relating to the career of the 'divine Claudio' give a fair idea of his inner life, albeit not a very complete one. He mourned his wife throughout the remainder of his days without any thought of remarrying; very much in contrast to the 'clerico' Palestrina, who married again only a few months after the death of his first wife, and even after he had been admitted to the minor orders of priesthood, 20 March 1581. Among the women singers who were closely associated with Monteverdi, the young Caterina Martinelli, whose premature death he celebrated so exquisitely in the *Sestina* of 1610, must have been especially dear to him. His loving fatherly care for his sons, who at the tender ages of seven and two were bereft of their mother, Claudia, surpassed by a very long way the traditional degree of fondness of Italian parents for their children. This solicitous feeling for his sons affected his own life most extensively after 1607 until about 1630. Monteverdi was spared the lamentable fate of Schütz, who lost his only daughter after her mother's death. He steered both his sons through many vicissitudes and past many dangerous rocks until each had reached a haven of security in his career. Moreover, he did not die in utter loneliness as did Schütz at the age of nearly ninety years. His health was none too robust; in early manhood he already suffered from headaches, fever and eye-trouble. Despite colossal industry he seems never to have been able to compose at great speed. He did not lack a certain malicious humour, as we have already noticed in these pages; nor was he deficient in a deeply realistic power of observation. His subservience to princes and cardinals is not more insufferable in its exaggerated phraseology than that of any of the Viennese classicists, and it is certainly far less grotesque than some of Anton Bruckner's petitionary letters. Only a hypocrite could cavil at Monteverdi's insistence upon his own rights in negotiations or at his relentless demands for the fulfilment of his contracts with the Gonzagas. His essential modesty never deserted him, even in the face of an actual affront— as, for instance, by the bass-singer Aldegati in 1637. The image of his personality stands out clearly from the obscurity of the bygone age of the Baroque. His noble conception of the moral aspect of his vocation, his personal integrity and sobriety, his sincere devoutness, his never-flagging industry, his easy mastery of the technical side of his art, but his interest, nevertheless, in experimenting in everything novel in the musical expression of character, and finally his unfailing good taste and judgement in aesthetics and in all matters connected with the theatre stamp Monteverdi as one of the most lovable and most truly exemplary figures in the history of music.

CHAPTER VI

MUSIC AND SOCIETY IN MONTEVERDI'S LIFETIME

THE function of music within the framework of Italian society, as also the position of the professional musician as a member of that society, underwent a tremendous change during Monteverdi's long life; a change only comparable with the swift transition in musical conditions at the outset and close of Richard Wagner's career (e.g. between 1830 and 1883). The colossal transformation in the social, technical, economic and psychological status of music and the musician, manifest in the antithesis between Wagner's youth and old age, had its earlier counterpart in the no less momentous change which musical life in Europe, but most especially in Italy, was to experience between 1567 and 1643, the dates of Monteverdi's birth and death. The change in the social position of the professional musician at that time can be expressed in one word alone: secularization. Throughout the later Middle Ages and the Early Renaissance, official musical positions were regulated almost exclusively by ecclesiastical appointments. Even in Monteverdi's lifetime, his appointment as Maestro di Cappella di San Marco outweighed any secular post. Palestrina, too, preferred to remain attached to ecclesiastical institutions such as the Julian Chapel and St. Peter's rather than to accept any offer of purely secular character such as that made, unsuccessfully, by Guglielmo Gonzaga to engage him for Mantua. But times were beginning to change, and the princely courts of Italy and Austria were gradually developing into centres of artistic activity where special demands were made upon the skill and adaptability of the professional musician. These courts were steadily becoming the arenas of progressive musical activities, in sharp contrast to the strongholds of conservatism maintained by the Church in matters musical. From the early date of 1471, when Poliziano's *Orfeo* with incidental music by Germi was produced at Mantua, an unbroken chain of festival events can be traced as having taken place, principally in the musical focal points of central Italy such as Mantua, Ferrara, Florence, Venice and Rome. Wedding celebrations or other festivities of political character provided the majority of occasions for the performance of 'Intermedia',* 'Tornei', antique Dramas and Madrigal Comedies, in which music played an increasingly important part. This development led quite logically to the creation of opera by the aristocratic dilettanti and cognoscenti who assembled at Count Bardi's house in Florence. This new type of representative musical spectacle, which in a short time was to eclipse all other types of musico-dramatic collaboration, and which was, rather belatedly, to be termed 'Opera in Musica', was at the outset the favourite pastime of the court and the nobility. It was not a popular art-form, as were the Motet and the Mass in churches or the *frottola* and *villanella* on village greens or in private music-rooms. It was music for the select few who could afford to pay for it, and it furnished a heaven-sent opportunity for young musicians to win renown. The Mantuan Opera Festivals of 1607-8, like their forerunners, the Florentine Opera Festivals of 1597-1602, were devised by princes and noblemen such as the Gonzagas, Bardi, Medici and Estes; were organized by Renaissance poets such as Rinuccini and Striggio sen., and composed by courtiers or court-singers—Peri, Caccini, Jacopo Corsi—who themselves took part in the performances. The first professional musician to write an opera was Monteverdi, whose *Favola d'Orfeo* of 1607, composed for the Mantuan court, established the new, and as yet improvisatory, art-form on the firm foundation of a new musical style. Opera continued to be the exclusive speciality of court circles. Only the fact that Monteverdi received a life-pension from the Mantuan court and that he remained attached to the closely allied and well-disposed court of Parma prevented him from losing contact with the world of opera after he settled in Venice. In Rome, opera developed gradually after 1619 under the inspiring leadership of a Prince of the Church, Cardinal Rospigliosi, later Pope Clement IX (1600-69).[1] More than thirty years after the

*See Glossary: 'Intermedium'.

first performance of Monteverdi's *Orfeo* at Mantua, the first public opera-house opened in Venice, the Teatro S. Cassiano in 1637. Thus, at the end of his career, the seventy-four-year-old Monteverdi started afresh as a composer of operas commissioned by public opera-houses which catered for a modern audience who were now for the first time admitted by purchasing a ticket and a copy of the libretto, instead of for select courtiers fashionably disguised as members of poetic 'Academies' and for a retinue of ruling princes. These operas, *L'Incoronazione* and *Ritorno d'Ulisse* among them, were designed for a modern operatic stage with a professional orchestra placed in an orchestral pit, a scanty professional chorus and a group of soloists which already included castrati in some of the leading parts.[2] But whereas Peri's and Caccini's early operas had required a mere handful of accompanying instruments placed somewhere in the wings, and while Monteverdi's *Orfeo* had, on the other hand, required the large and variegated orchestra of the Renaissance 'Intermedium', the master's Venetian operas of 1639–43 were composed for a professional organization very similar to that of our own opera-houses to-day, except that he relied on castrati for most of his principal vocal parts. He did not, however, overlook the natural attractions of the female soprano (Vittoria Archilei, Caterina Martinelli, Virginia Andreini) repeatedly called for in his early Mantuan operas. As regards stage design and production, the setting of Monteverdi's *Combattimento* followed the older tradition of a private court entertainment. The limited stage space was no doubt responsible for the oddity of the scenic arrangement, which comprised two acting singers and an immobile *testo** from the oratorio, all accompanied by a string quartet; and some purely vocal madrigals, 'senza gesto'—without action, which were sung beforehand as a kind of overture. The intricately written four-part open score of this string quartet accompaniment gives evidence of years of earlier instrumental experience.

Like most musicians of his period, Monteverdi was proficient on a string instrument. He was appointed to Mantua as a violist *c.* 1590 when the modern violin had hardly been invented but when consorts of viols were beginning to take the place of human voices and when vocally conceived motets and madrigals were more and more frequently rearranged as tablatures for lute, harpsichord, string ensemble and so forth. By the time Monteverdi produced his last operas in Venice in 1642 the modern violin was everywhere

* See Glossary.

in the ascendant. An original instrumental style had been evolved for keyboard instruments by the English virginalists and by Frescobaldi in Rome, and even the parting of the ways between the organ and the harpsichord had been effected.[3]

Significantly enough, Monteverdi was appointed 'Cantore' in 1594. The extravagant alternative coloraturas in Orfeo's aria 'Possente spirto' (published by Monteverdi himself in two versions: one simple, and the other overloaded with embellishments)[4] prove that he must have been completely familiar with the new ornamental system of 'Gorgia',* which adorned the simple melodic *res facta* with garlands of vocal embellishments (*passagi*,* *groppi*,* trills and shakes) such as had earlier been expounded by the theoretician L. Zacconi (1555–1627) in his treatise *Prattica di Musica*, 1592, and had been exploited by singer-composers such as Luzzasco Luzzaschi (d. 1607), Antonio Archilei (Florence, 1589), Cristofano Malvezzi (1547–97) and by Giulio Caccini in his *Nuove Musiche* (1602). It is possible that Monteverdi's *Vespers* of 1610 was sung in the court chapel at Mantua before his dismissal thence in 1612. But only at the church of S. Marco did he have at his disposal a body of singers capable of fulfilling the choral demands which had culminated in the Mass *In illo tempore*, a work clearly designed with an eye to choral conditions in Papal Rome. While the great tradition of vocal polyphony, crystallized as Palestrina's 'stile antico', continued to exist throughout the whole of the seventeenth century,[5] the supremacy of the madrigal quickly declined. Pietro della Valle asserted in his treatise *Della Musica dell' età nostra*, 1640, that madrigals were then rarely produced because they had become unpopular. People preferred to listen to others singing by heart[6] and accompanying themselves with lutes and theorboes, whereas the spectacle of some five singers seated at a table with part-books in their hands, so familiar to an earlier generation, was then being ridiculed. On the other hand, G. B. Doni declared that by 1635 the polyphonic style of the motet and the five-part madrigal still counted many adherents who considered the monody and the aria ridiculous (*baja*) and insufficiently refined in the artistic sense to suit their taste. The secularization of musical life gradually enveloped all sections of the community. Even ecclesiastical music assumed a theatrical hue. The splendid pomp of the Early Baroque *concerto ecclesiastico* already foreshadowed by G. Gabrieli and L. Viadana attained full

* See Glossary.

E

stature in Monteverdi's *Vespers* of 1610, eventually to reach a
bombastic climax in the mammoth scores of the later Roman
school[7] which not only reflected the propagandist and militant
character of the Roman Catholic Counter-Reformation, but which
at the same time manifested the close spiritual affinity of opera.
With Monteverdi's *Vespers* the operatic orchestra, *recitativo* and
arioso for the first time invaded the precincts of ecclesiastical
music. By the time of Monteverdi's death in 1643 an altogether
new type of musician had arisen: the opera composer. Monteverdi's
former pupil and second organist at S. Marco, F. Cavalli (1602–76)
composed no fewer than forty-two operas, but sacred music only
as a side-line. His chief competitor in this field, Marc' Antonio
Cesti (1626–69), surpassed him with more than 100 operas, some
of which, like the festival opera *Il pomo d'Orò*, Vienna, 1667,
must have been among the most gorgeous dramatic spectacles
ever produced. Other representatives of this younger generation,
such as G. Carissimi (1605–74), concentrated mainly upon oratorio, a
species which was still in its infancy when Monteverdi composed his
Orfeo and *Vespers*. Only the backward-glancing musicians of the
later Palestrinian school in Rome continued to write sacred music
in traditional forms but in an exaggerated manner in accordance
with the acoustical properties of St. Peter's (O. Benevoli),
while the style of the madrigal and the motet, as well as the declamatory finesse of early monody, found a haven in the more stolid and
ponderous art of German composers.

The three great 'S's'—Schein, Scheidt and Schütz—were the
real artistic counterparts of the ageing Monteverdi, whom Schütz
outlived for almost thirty years. Schütz was also the last representative of the humanist type of composer which had originated with
Ockeghem and Josquin, matured with Orlandus Lassus and
Palestrina and reached its zenith with G. Gabrieli and Monteverdi
himself. Interest in the revival of classical drama, poetry and metre
(still so noticeable in the metrical experiments of A. Striggio jun.
in the libretto of Monteverdi's *Orfeo*); in ancient philosophy (Plato,
Boethius) and in speculative and mystical pursuits gradually faded.
The creative musician adapted himself to the new idea of
virtuosity which was then emerging from the vocal 'Gorgia'
and was very soon to invade instrumental music as well. Biagio
Marini (1597–1665), possibly a pupil of Monteverdi's, published
his *Affetti musicali* ('musical emotions') for the violin as early as
1617, thereby foreshadowing the advent of the great instrumental

virtuosi of the subsequent epoch: G. B. Lully and his 'Seize petits violons' (1652) and A. Corelli with the new violin technique he developed from 1671 onwards. Opera specialists such as Cavalli and Cesti and instrumental virtuosi such as Lully and Corelli maintained an attitude towards musical problems which differed completely from the universal humanism of Monteverdi (d. 1643) and Schütz (d. 1672), both of whom lingered on for a time in a new world feeling its way towards a different artistic goal, much as in our own day the octogenarian Romantics Richard Strauss and Hans Pfitzner lingered on in the anti-romantic, neo-classical, dodecaphonic, mechanically rather than emotionally inspired musical world of the present age.

Part II

THE WORKS

CHAPTER VII

MUSIC IN ITALY
AT THE TIME OF MONTEVERDI'S ADVENT

ALTHOUGH Italy was destined to determine the course of European music for more than two centuries, her own musical supremacy did not manifest itself until comparatively late, with the flowering of the Italian madrigalists and the daring exploits of the pioneers of Florentine opera during the last two decades of the sixteenth century. Until that period, Italian music had suffered from exactly the same malady it was later to inflict so unmercifully upon other countries after 1600: namely—foreign invasion. It cannot be denied that, but for the brief epoch of the Italian 'Ars Nova' inspired by Dante's lofty example, influenced by French and German Trouvères and culminating c. 1300–1400 in the exclusively secular *caccie* and madrigals of Giovanni da Cascia (Johannes da Florentia), Jacopo da Bologna and the blind organist Francesco Landino (d. 1397), Italian music played but a humble role in European musical culture in general. Its official, i.e. ecclesiastical music was for centuries organized and dominated almost exclusively by 'oltremontani' (foreigners). The Fleming Dufay composed the famous motet for double choir *Nuper rosarum flores* for the consecration of Florence Cathedral in 1436, and it was another Fleming, Heinrich Isaac, who in 1480 succeeded the famous blind, Italian-born organist Antonio Squarcialupi (1400–80) at the organ of that cathedral.[1] It was the subtle art of the French motet (Machaut, Vitry) that was practised in the churches and chapels of Italy. The courts of central Italian principalities with their artistic centres at Milan (Sforza), Ferrara (Este) and Florence (Medici) and with their family connexions in France, Spain and Austria drew an increasing number of Flemish composers into the

Italian orbit. Obrecht died in 1505 as Cantor of Ferrara, Josquin des Prés remained for many years (*c.* 1484–94) in Rome and Ferrara attached to the Sforzas. At exactly the same time, the Spaniard, Ramis de Pareja published at Bologna his *Musica prattica* with its recognition of the triad and the essential harmonic function of the interval of the third. This constituted the most momentous theoretical advance towards the still distant goal of functional harmony that had yet been achieved on Italian soil. But the 'oltremontani' who carried the tremendous tradition of the polyphonic epoch into Italy received in return equally formative impressions from Italian popular music. Italy was not as yet rich in great artistic personalities but it was contributing anonymously towards a new conception of music by means of its folk music, especially its *frottole, canti carnascialeschi* and *laude spirituali.* This type of music, with its crude harmony and strong emphasis upon a melodic treble-part, was leading up to an anti-polyphonic conception of vocal music and was already anticipating features of the coming madrigal of the Late Renaissance and also of the oratorio. Flemish theoreticians like Ciconia (Padua) and Tinctoris (Naples) began to find Italian counterparts in Gafori (Parma) and Spataro (Bologna). Nevertheless, the fifteenth century had run almost to its close before Italian music ultimately rose officially to the surface. It was in 1498 that the Venetian printer Ottaviano Petrucci (1466–1539) received the first Italian privilege for the printing of music with metal types. His publications of collections of Italian *Frottole* (1504–14) heralded the dawn of a new epoch: Italian music of international consequence.

The Italian *frottola* was the elastic musical receptacle for various poetic patterns such as the sonnet, canzona, *strambotto** and *ottava rima.* By virtue of its structure, wherein a purely vocal and melodically dominating treble-part was accompanied by three lower parts, which must often have been executed instrumentally, it foreshadowed peculiarities of the serious secular madrigal and its derivatives, the humorous *villanella*, with its persiflage of the folk-music characteristics of the *frottola* (such as parallel fifths), and the *scherzo musicale* and the *balletto*, with their dance rhythms and their growing predilection for instrumental ritornelli. The *frottola* had a comparatively short vogue. Its greatest masters were among the earliest native Italian composers: the two Mantuan compatriots and forerunners of Monteverdi's in the service of the Gonzagas,

* See Glossary.

Marco Cara (known to have been in Mantua 1495–1525) and B. Tromboncino (with the Gonzagas from *c.* 1487). The last collection was published in Rome in 1531. Two years later, the first collection of serious five-part madrigals was published, to be followed in 1535 by its humorous counterpart, the *Villote a la Veneziana*. The advent of the Italian Renaissance madrigal *c.* 1533 was only the logical reaction to the tremendous development of Italian Renaissance poetry inaugurated by Petrarch and carried to an emotional climax by Cardinal Bembo, Ariosto, Torquato Tasso, Sannazaro and others. Just as the flowering of German lyricism in the late eighteenth century represented by Goethe, Schiller, Hölderlin, Hölty and their followers found its legitimate musical echo in the composition of the German Lied starting with Reichardt, Zelter and Zumsteeg and culminating in Franz Schubert, the poetic treasury of Italian madrigal poetry found its musical equivalent in the production of five-part madrigals, very often clearly intended for instrumental execution,[2] created by a new generation of musicians who were growing up in Italy proper. This early school of Italian madrigalists was still far from representing a national school of composers. The leading men were still 'oltremontani' from Flanders and the Netherlands. A glance at the decisive musical personalities active in Italy's musical nerve-centres, Venice, Mantua, Florence and Rome, will serve to corroborate this statement.

Venice, in particular, the city of Monteverdi's glorious maturity, with the church of S. Marco as a pivotal point in north Italian musical life for several centuries, seemed to be firmly in the grasp of the northern invaders. A French Walloon, Pietro de Fossis (Deffossès), reorganized the cappella of S. Marco in 1491 and ruled there with dictatorial powers until his death in 1527. His successor was the Fleming, Adrian Willaert (b. *c.* 1480 at Bruges, d. 1562 in Venice), who came from Rome and Ferrara. Willaert prepared for the great epoch in Venetian music with its glowing instrumental colours, thunderous double and triple choirs, brilliant virtuoso organists and experimenting madrigalists. He anticipated monody as early as 1536 with an instrumental tablature of madrigals composed by his friend the Frenchman Philippe Verdelot (b. *c.* 1567) who lived for the greater part of his life in Venice. Willaert was the first to revive and to reorganize the ancient local tradition of antiphonal choral singing. His *cori spezzati** evolved logically

* See Glossary.

from the architectural planning of S. Marco and its two organ-lofts. In years to come these two organ-lofts were to be occupied by the finest flower of Italian organists: the two Gabrielis, Claudio Merulo, Cavazzoni (b. *c.* 1500), Annibale Padovano (1527–75) and many others. But Willaert's importance for the progress of music towards the establishing of modern tonality and the conception of harmonic progressions regulated from the bass rather than from the tenor part went even beyond these achievements. He raised a school of disciples who attempted to establish the supremacy of Italian music in Europe. Among these, his successor at S. Marco, the Fleming Cyprian de Rore (*c.* 1516–65), was the most outstanding personality. In his 'chromatic' madrigals he excelled in subtle rhythmical divisions, but in his truly revolutionary motet for four bass parts *Calami sonum ferentes* (published in 1555 by T. Susato) he used 'Musica ficta' (i.e. accidentals, alien and dissonant with regard to the chosen ecclesiastical mode) in a highly imaginative manner, anticipating the modernist exploits of the later generation of Marenzio and Gesualdo. Other prominent pupils of Willaert's were all Italians. They included two eminent theoreticians, Gioseffo Zarlino (1517–90) and Nicola Vicentino (1511–72), who helped materially to lay the theoretical foundations of modern dualistic tonality (major and minor), and several excellent madrigalists, Costanzo Porta and Alfonso della Viola among them.

No greater contrast is conceivable than that between Willaert's progressive school of Venetian composers and the simultaneously developing Roman school headed by the greatest Italian composer before Monteverdi: Palestrina (*c.* 1525–94). Palestrina was the very reverse of his glamorous, worldly, exuberant contemporary Orlandus Lassus (1532–94), the last of the great Flemings, who by virtue of his truly international outlook and his many-sided personality may be counted as belonging, at least in part, to Italian music. But Palestrina was equally the embodiment of a conscious antithesis to Willaert and the Venetian school. In a way, his music, unique in its technical purity, its self-imposed limitations and its residue of the fading tradition of Flemish polyphony, was just as much an artistic anachronism in 1594 as was J. S. Bach's *Art of Fugue* in 1750. Yet the personality of Palestrina was great enough to enable him to establish a school and a tradition which were to be carried on by G. M. Nanini, the two Anerios, Suriano and Monteverdi's teacher, Marc' Antonio Ingegneri, and which were strong enough to live on into the eighteenth century and to undergo unbroken, albeit thoroughly reactionary development. Monteverdi's own aesthetic category of *stile antico* was made possible only by Palestrina's overwhelming example of musical Spartanism and self-imposed restraint.

The music produced by native and naturalized Italians so far considered in this brief survey has been mainly vocal in conception, even though the accessory participation of instruments was often clearly implied. The younger composers, most of whom were growing up in the artistic rallying-points of central and northern Italy, now concentrated more and more upon the composition of music which was conceived expressly for instruments, and which culminated in the glorious epoch of Italian organists exactly comparable with the early school of organists and virginalists in Tudor England *c*. 1510–1630. With G. Cavazzoni's *Intavolatura cioè Ricercari, Canzoni, Hinni, Magnificat* . . . the earliest specimen of Italian music written especially and exclusively for the organ, published in Venice, 1542, this younger generation of Italian organ composers heralded its birth. It came of age, so to speak, in the works of Willaert's brilliant pupil, Andrea Gabrieli (1510–86), whose daring *Intonazioni* and *Ricercari* for organ were matched only by his revolutionary *Concerti*, 1587, the earliest examples of liturgical music specially designed for collaboration between voices and instruments. It attained full maturity in the sweeping *Toccate* and *Canzoni* of Claudio Merulo (1523–1604), principal organist of S. Marco and successor of Annibale Padovano, himself an early champion of instrumentally conceived 'battaglie' and 'toccate'. It reached its apex in the greatest personality yet to appear in north Italian musical life, a composer of truly ageless grandeur and nobility, Giovanni Gabrieli (1557–1612), Andrea's nephew and editor. Giovanni developed Willaert's technique of 'cori spezzati' and Andrea's tendencies towards the concerto, and in so doing created the design of the Baroque 'Concerto Ecclesiastico' for double chorus and a variegated orchestra. In addition, he originated the archetype of the later symphony in his 'sonate' for orchestra alone.[3]

With Giovanni Gabrieli, Merulo's successor as principal organist of S. Marco and the beloved teacher of H. L. Hassler, G. Aichinger and H. Schütz, we approach the threshold of the period dominated by Monteverdi who, especially in his *Vespro della Beata Vergine* of 1610, was to continue the royal line of *concertante* church-music so gloriously inaugurated by the two Gabrielis.

Meanwhile, *frottola* and *villanella* had been caught up in the irresistible impetus of the madrigal, or transformed into the *Falala canzonetta* and the *balletto* of G. Gastoldi (1556–1662) and Orazio Vecchi (1550–1605); the former a later colleague of Monteverdi's in the service of the Gonzagas, the latter a forerunner of A. Banchieri's, the composer of buffo scenes and the creator of madrigal comedy (*L'Amfiparnasso*, 1594). Gastoldi's *Balletti* (1591 ff.) and O. Vecchi's semi-dramatic madrigal comedies prepared the way for Monteverdi's own *Scherzi Musicali* (1607) and madrigalian opera-ballets of 1608 and 1616. The composers just named, who were little older than Monteverdi himself, formed a natural background to his own creative development during the years between 1583 and 1605, a period that could boast of two characters of outstanding originality and virtuoso technique in the composition of the five-part madrigal: Luca Marenzio (1560–99) and Carlo Gesualdo, Prince of Venosa (1560–1614). With these two men the Italian madrigal reached its peak of tonal splendour, chromatic daring and emotional glamour. Monteverdi, the madrigalist of *Books I–V* (1587–1605), was deeply indebted to their creative spade-work.

Looking back on Italy's musical development throughout the sixteenth century up to the date of Monteverdi's very first publication in 1583, we note that the polyphonic principle in ecclesiastical and chamber music inspired by Flemings and Frenchmen was still active. Despite the pioneer work of Willaert and his Venetian school, and the achievements of English virginalists, especially between 1550 and 1590, and of Italian organists after 1540, vocal music was still the decisive force in the conception of musical patterns. Nevertheless, instruments gradually came into the ascendant, while Italian poetry became increasingly responsible for regulating the shape and contours of representational music connected with the madrigal. But despite all the pomp and circumstance of courtly Tornei, Trionfi, and Intermedia, opera itself was still unborn, while Beaujoyeulx's *Ballet comique de la reine*—the nearest approximation to the Florentine conception of opera—had only just been performed, 15 October 1581. The first generation of great German musicians who were to spring from the fertile furrows of Lutheran soil, M. Praetorius, H. L. Hassler, S. Schein, S. Scheidt and H. Schütz, were either unborn or still in their infancy. Palestrina reigned supreme and undisputed in Rome, as did Orlandus Lassus in Munich, while Vincenzo Galilei's revolutionary dialogue *della Musica antica e della moderna*, 1581, had only just come from the press. Little more than a decade later, this situation was to be completely transformed.

The year in which the twenty-seven-year-old Monteverdi was promoted to the rank of 'Cantore' at the Mantuan court was momentous in that it witnessed the deaths of Palestrina and Lassus and the almost simultaneous emergence of opera with the production of Vecchi's *L'Amfiparnasso* and the start of Peri-Rinuccini's *Dafne*. The fruitful experiments of the Florentine Camerata between 1594 and 1601, the exploitation of a new style in L. Viadana's *100 Concerti ecclesiastici*, 1597–1603, the madrigal comedies of O. Vecchi, A. Striggio sen. and A. Banchieri (*c.* 1590–1610) belonged to Monteverdi's own epoch, in which Italian music was for the first time in history to become the arbiter of taste and style for the whole of Europe until its supremacy was gradually shattered by the Viennese classics. The publication of *Musica Transalpina* in England by N. Yonge in 1588 marked the beginning of Italian musical domination on British soil, just as the complete reprint of L. Viadana's *Concerti ecclesiastici* as an *Opus musicum sacrorum concentuum* in Frankfurt o/M in 1612 and 1620 indicated the beginning of Italian rule *in rebus musicae* in Germany. [In the formative years between the deaths of Palestrina in 1594 and Giovanni Gabrieli in 1612 the patterns of musical thought itself were reshaping under the plastic influence of Italian innovations. The *frottola* and polyphonic motet declined, but the *concerto ecclesiastico*, the orchestral sonata and instrumental ricercare and toccata flourished. The polyphonic (chiefly five-part) madrigal faded, but the symphonic cantata and the *duetto da camera* lived. Madrigal comedy, *Intermedium* and *Sacra rappresentazione* blossomed and withered within a few decades, but opera, ballet and oratorio had come to stay. These new forms arose, still in partly experimental and ephemeral guise, during the years of Monteverdi's early manhood, but only when his own contributions had appeared did the world begin to understand the spiritual import of this second Italian 'Ars Nova'. Vecchi's *Amfiparnasso* of 1594, E. de Cavalieri's *Rappresentazione di anima e di corpo* of 1600, G. Caccini's *Euridice* of 1602 created a sensation, but no new artistic conviction. With Monteverdi's *Favola d'Orfeo*, 1607, *Arianna* and *Ballo dell' Ingrate*, 1608, music and poetry had at last found a new converging point in the innermost recesses of the human soul.

CHAPTER VIII

PRINCIPLES

MONTEVERDI'S creative activity falls into three divisions: madrigals, operas and church-music. Independent instrumental works such as 'sonate' or 'ricercari' of the kind written by Giovanni Gabrieli (*Sacrae Symphoniae I–II*, 1597 and 1615), or the 'battaglie' of Andrea Gabrieli and Annibale Padovano,[1] or even any other kind of original works for organ and keyboard instruments similar to those of his great contemporaries, Claudio Merulo and Girolamo Frescobaldi, have not been preserved, any more than have those by Heinrich Schütz, his German opposite number.

The making of a reasoned historical survey of Monteverdi's operatic works, as also of those by Schütz, is hampered by the loss of so many important scores. But while Schütz the musical dramatist can be assessed by certain dramatic moments in his sacred choral works and Passions, though he remains for ever a shadowy figure, Monteverdi the opera-composer can be conjured up from the available operas, fragments and extant libretti with better prospects of success. By far the greater part of the church-musician's immense output is still in existence, although we know that some of the Masses have been lost.[2] Strangely enough, however, Monteverdi's production of church-music does not begin until his mature manhood from 1610 onwards, and thus it cannot be considered characteristic of the master's period of development. The complete record of Monteverdi's development, so greatly desired by the biographer, is furnished only by the abundant harvest of the madrigalist, which extends over the whole of the composer's life from the early three-part *Canzonettas* of 1584 to the tremendous double volume of the *Eighth Book of Madrigals* in 1638. For this reason, it is only logical that a critical evaluation of the master's entire production should begin with the complete corpus of the madrigals.

The creative stimulus to Monteverdi's music in general is the new-found experience of the poetic word, the fruitful apprehension of the possibilities of interpreting the poetic verbal symbols by means of the equivalent tonal symbols; an art hitherto only faintly suspected. This original experience begins early in the madrigals, where it is consciously at work trying to build up a musical style which should be the emotional counterpart of the poetic expression. This is achieved in the first place by the systematic coining of characteristic musical motives (madrigalian symbols for the purpose of reflecting the human passions[3]), and later on is expanded into the dramatic by the inclusion of monody. The new experience of words led Monteverdi from the polyphonic madrigal, first to the 'solo'-madrigal with a substructural Basso Continuo and also to the dramatic monody; then to the operatic monologue (*Orfeo*, *Arianna*), and finally to the orchestrally buttressed solo-cantata ('Con che soavità', *Seventh Book of Madrigals*, 1619). The new appreciation and revaluation of the poetic word by the spirit of a passionately expressive musical interpretation led him away from Marinism* and from the idyllic pastoral poetry (*Aminta* and *Pastor Fido*) of the early *Books of Madrigals* to the creative reconstruction of the Greek ritual drama as it appealed to the Renaissance temperament (*Orfeo* and *Arianna*). It eventually led him to the creation of a modern style of expression which was convincingly inaugurated in the preface to the *Eighth Book of Madrigals*, 1638; theoretically, as the *stile concitato* which mirrored the various temperaments in music; but musically and poetically, in the scenic oratorio *Combattimento di Tancredi e Clorinda*, 1624, compiled from Tasso's *Gerusalemme liberata* (Canto XII, verses 52 ff.). With the later *Books of Madrigals* (V–VII) and the first operatic works, but no less with the progressive church-compositions like the *Vespers* of 1610 (which had been influenced by the operatic works of 1607–8), Monteverdi had been advancing both theoretically and practically in the direction of an ever-growing antithesis to the earlier conception of music.

With the establishment of the historical antinomy, 'Prima Prattica'-'Seconda Prattica',[4] this antithesis of styles, which had been controversially disputed by Artusi as early as 1603, became a permanent feature in the further development of music.

Since 1605, Monteverdi had undoubtedly been consciously at work on the creation of a new principle of style which was to elevate the psychological conception of words and the emotional conflicts of music and action to a central position among the problems of composition. In the preface to the *Eighth Book of Madrigals* he naïvely justifies the choice of those particular scenes from Tasso, with their specific aptitude for strongly contrasted and antithetic

* See Glossary: Marinism.

tensions, as the most natural outlet for music of the passions, emotions and dramatic changes in the state of the soul.[5]

For Monteverdi, music arose absolutely naturally and without the slightest effort wherever conflicts of this kind occurred. This explains his preference for the first poet of the modern conflict of passions, Torquato Tasso, who had already been his inspiration in the early madrigals.[6] The gradual relegation of the 'Prima Prattica' to the background, which led, in the sphere of the madrigal, to the madrigal-cantata and the solo-monody, takes place in the region of church-music with the astounding experiment of the *Vespers* of 1610, in which the verses of the psalms are composed in the monodic-dramatic style of the Mantuan operas of 1607–8, without, however, coming to any final result.[7] The problem of the relation of words to music and its reflection in a new style of musical expression may also be followed in Monteverdi's late Venetian period,[8] although the loss of almost all the operas written between 1613 and 1640 makes it very difficult to arrive at a convincing assessment of its development.

Whereas Monteverdi in his younger days was absorbed in finding the apt musical interpretation of the individual word, the master as he grew older was captivated by the contrast existing between the emotions, and its presentation in convincing symbolism by means of comprehensive musical atmosphere and characteristic motives. This led to naïve realism and to naturalism, as in the instance of the duel in the *Combattimento*. But it led, too, to an immense deepening in the style of the music to *L'Incoronazione* in which Monteverdi laid the foundations of the expressive style of the High Baroque music-drama.

We have already observed that Monteverdi paid as little attention to the problems of pure, instrumental music as did his great contemporary, Schütz. In the case of Monteverdi this is all the more curious, since, in his capacity as violist at Mantua for many years, he must have had a profound knowledge of the technique of string instruments which enabled him later on to carry out pioneer work in connexion with the modern treatment of strings.[9] But the orchestral ritornelli of *Orfeo*, 1607, which were obviously inspired by the 'Sonate' and 'Battaglie' of the two Gabrielis and other composers, can no more be detached from their dramatic function, nor can they lead any more independent an existence, than can the much more primitively constructed but much more practicable and consistently modern string ritornelli of the late

Venetian operas. They are all dependent upon the poetic-dramatic actions of the plot, just as each separate part of the madrigal is dependent upon the contour of the verse and upon the relevance of the individual poetic word-symbol. The comparison with Heinrich Schütz[10] must needs obtrude itself here; as must Monteverdi's position as a forerunner of Gluck and Wagner who devoted their creative energies exclusively to operas, and finally, of Schubert the lyricist, the music of whose songs was engendered by the very words themselves. The styles of all these men grew out of a new conception of the art of song. The musical interpretation of words is the aim of this music, which springs into life at the sheer bidding of the words, and which employs the diversity of orchestral sounds exclusively for the purpose of evoking poetic atmosphere.

CHAPTER IX

THE LAST MADRIGALIST

THE history of the Monteverdian madrigal reflects within the compass of a specialized musical evolution the tremendous change in the aspect of the madrigalian forms of the High Renaissance to the monody and the *concertante* cantata of the Early Baroque. It is far beyond the scope of the present book to undertake an exhaustive study of Monteverdi's production of madrigals. An attempt to describe the organic change in style of this species of madrigal, and of its kindred sub-species, the canzonet and the *Scherzo musicale*, in all its historical and aesthetic hypotheses has already been made elsewhere.[1] In the same place, too, an effort has been made to comprehend Monteverdi's madrigalian world as the product of its spiritual epoch and of the psychological and aesthetic influences which were brought to bear upon it.[2] The striking of the roots of this kind of madrigal in the soil of a new kind of poetry has also been sketched in outline,[3] even though the correlation between the madrigal on the one hand and opera and church-music on the other, could be treated only cursorily.

An artistic phenomenon like the *Lamento d'Arianna* which, as an operatic fragment, a five-part *a cappella* madrigal and a sacred monodic *Kontrafaktur** (the *Pianto della Madonna* published in the *Selva Morale* of 1640), is at home in all three spheres of composition, proves beyond dispute that the history of the Monteverdian madrigal is fundamentally bound up with the other two types of composition. The 'spiritual madrigals' of the *Selva Morale*, and the extant torso of the early *Madrigali Spirituali* of 1583, no less than the purely madrigalistic episodes in *Orfeo* (Pastoral scenes in Acts I and II), also point to this significant creative association of the three types. That we must regard Monteverdi's madrigal production as the centre of his artistic personality and consider it as the converging point from which every section of his activities as a composer was destined to be fertilized, is clearly implicit in a succession of historico-evolutionary circumstances.

The madrigals comprise the only actually complete section of Monteverdi's production now extant. It is the only one which can be depended upon to afford reliable insight into the problems of his artistic development. Moreover, his works in the sphere of the madrigal extend in an unbroken succession from his earliest youth (three-part *Canzonettas* of 1584) to his old age (*Eighth Book of Madrigals*, 1638). That the master himself knew the madrigals were considered the most representative section of his creative work may be inferred not only from the series of illustrious personages to whom the overwhelming majority of the madrigal publications are dedicated,[4] but still more definitely from the fact that he also included in these volumes the most daring and historically the most significant examples of his musico-dramatic production. By this means alone have such highlights of his operatic compositions as the *Lamento d'Arianna*, the operatic ballet *Il Ballo dell' Ingrate*, the ballet *Tirsi e Clori* and the Tasso-Scene *Combattimento* been preserved for us at all! Finally, Monteverdi the revolutionary in style and the progressive theoretician nowhere revealed his artistic programme save in the prefaces to his *Books of Madrigals*,[5] whereas he confined the introductory notes to his liturgical publications and to the *Orfeo* score simply to personal dedications. The madrigals also reflect Monteverdi's literary taste. His bias for the poetry of the 'divin Signor Tasso', to whom the preface to the *Eighth Book of Madrigals* presents so striking a memorial; his partiality for the idyllic Arcadia of Guarini's *Pastor fido*, and lastly, his sympathetic understanding of deeply-felt lyrics like Scipione Agnelli's *Sestina*-Cycle (*Sixth Book of Madrigals*), tell a tale that cannot be ignored.

*See Glossary: Kontrafaktur.

I may perhaps be permitted to quote the substance of my remarks in an earlier work on the historical performance of Monteverdi the madrigalist.[6] '. . . With Monteverdi, the destiny of the madrigal form was finally settled. In his first four *Books of Madrigals* he integrated the formal evolution of a whole century in order to lead it towards the logical consequence whither its origin had determined its course: that is to say, into the contrast to all motet-like construction; into architectonic conciseness and the melodically unequivocal precision of the monodic cantata. I visualize the peculiar property of the Monteverdian madrigal as consisting in the universality of its style, which alone enables it to alter the conception of the species as such. The special problem of this type of madrigal can be recognized in the phenomenon of the *evolution in style towards monody*, under whose determinant influence all the sub-species of the madrigal were to be, as it were, 'chemically' changed . . .'

. . . . .

A necessarily cursory synopsis of the whole collection of madrigals[7] should now be the means of demonstrating more convincingly the comprehensive appreciation just quoted above. The three-part *Canzonettas* which the seventeen-year-old 'discepolo del Signor Marc' Antonio Ingegneri' published in 1584 as Op. 3, together with the contemporary and nearly related 'Tricinium' movements of the *Cantiunculae Sacrae* and the *Madrigali Spirituali*, form the highly promising prelude to the master's entire production. The *Canzonettas*, like their sacred counterparts, are astonishing in the maturity and skill of their workmanship and in the complete absence of revolutionary experiments in style. The *Canzonettas* grow in the soil of the Italian *Villanella*-tradition. This miniature form beloved by the community was later to attain creative fulfilment in the musically far more important *Scherzi Musicali* of 1607, in which the slender proportions of the canzonetta-verse were extended in significance by the much longer and more interesting instrumental ritornelli. The possibility of an instrumental background (in the sense of the Early Baroque *Zufalls** instrumentation) to the youthful production of 1584 cannot be proved with any certainty, although it can be for the *Scherzi* of 1607 whereto a prefatory note by Monteverdi giving directions for performance presupposes the collaboration of a chamber orchestra comprising two violins, bass and bass-lute or harpsichord to which every now

---

* See Glossary: Zufallsorchester.

F

and again, even within the canzonetta-verse, the composer entrusts little instrumental enclaves[8] whose evolutionary and historical significance was to be increased by the critical-historical argument of his brother, Giulio Cesare, in the *Dichiarazione*.[9]

This fascinating world of song is echoed later in the *Scherzi Musicali cioè Arie et Madrigali in stil recitativo* by the 'Reverendo' Claudio Monteverdi in 1632, in which the song-like thematic style of the polyphonic *Canzonettas* of 1585 and of the instrumentally supported *Scherzi* of 1607 are condensed into the monodic solo song for voice and Basso Continuo. A comparison of three examples of this evolution of the canzonetta, which extends over a period of almost fifty years, elucidates at a glance the tremendous advance from the polyphony of the High Renaissance to the *arioso* melody of the Baroque.

Canzonetta a 3 voci (1584).„Raggi dov' è il mio bene"

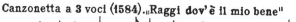

Scherzi Musicali (1607)
(2 Sopr.,1 Basso, 2 Viol.,1 Cello, Cembalo.)

Scherzi Musicali (1632) voce sola col B.C.

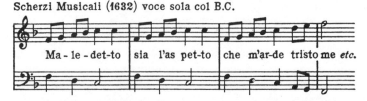

The polyphonic (e.g. five-part) madrigals with which Monteverdi, as the ultimate creative personality, brought the great Flemish-Italian epoch of the madrigal to its close, were produced within the space of just under thirty years between 1587 and 1614. The

First Book of Madrigals, 1587, which he composed while as yet under the supervision of the venerated teacher Ingegneri, still proceeds organically from the balanced sonority of chamber-music peculiar to the motet-like madrigals of Costanzo Porta, M. A. Ingegneri and their Flemish counterparts, Cyprian de Rore, A. Willaert, Ph. Verdelot, Arcadelt and Ph. di Monte. In these works Monteverdi is poles apart from the glowing colouring of Marenzio or the experimental chromaticism of the Prince of Venosa, but in this book, as in the next three, there is a certain prevailing feeling for 'diagonal' harmony which strikes a balance between the pure horizontal thinking and the vertical harmonic structure of later monody. There is still no Basso Continuo, but its advent can be felt in the entire harmonic atmosphere.[10]

Monteverdi's liking for Tasso's poetry is already manifest in two items from this volume[11] which are, however, musically conventional. The *Second Book of Madrigals*, published in 1590 shortly before, or after, his appointment as 'suonatore di Vivuola' at the Mantuan court, shed the conventionality of the early volumes all at once. No fewer than seven of the twenty-one madrigals in this book are based on magnificent pieces by Tasso which call forth Monteverdi's powerfully expressive individual style. In 'Ecco mormorar l'onde' he succeeds in creating a perfect example of madrigalistic landscape-painting in which the musical *pleinairisme* is unsurpassed in the history of the species.

As regards historical development of form, the importance of this composition consists chiefly in its opening section—as so often in Monteverdi's madrigals—wherein a pronounced type of monody, fully conscious of the originality of its material, is already apparent. This opening is one of the first instances of the use of unchanging harmony and of rational utilization by harmonic steps of a fundamental tonality conceived as a dominant. The gently lucent F major of the beginning might be the work of any Romantic, whom the 'murmuring waves' and the 'trembling leaves' could not have affected more powerfully than they did the creator of this magical piece. But the opening is even more remarkable: it is a genuine tenor solo, such as we find more often in the continuo-madrigals of the *Fifth* and *Sixth Books*, with a harmonic, echoing accompaniment by the other parts. The tone-poem-like effect of leisurely repetition of the same notes—the artificial imagery of natural repose—precludes any kind of individual movement, whether it be imitative or otherwise polyphonic.

At this point, the vocal parts have completely renounced their own independence of movement in favour of the overwhelming idea of a harmonic bass, by means of whose driving-power the cohesion of the material is assured. This opening, if written as a tenor solo with obbligato accompaniment, would appear as follows:

It is amazing to observe how, at places where the abstract principle of imitative dovetailing is utilized, the poetically significant idea of echoing voice-parts is introduced. The echo had, of course, for long been one of the most essential means of elaborating polyphonic writing and of achieving a new responsorial style.[12] The piece is clearly divided into three parts. The first is purely impressionistic and descriptive and remains utterly static; the second evokes the gradual coming into being of the morning, musically and dynamically by more forceful development of the motto theme in responsorial rather than imitative style. Finally, after proceeding stepwise over a descending scale in the bass in a sequence of parallel fifths, the composition emerges into a tranquillizing coda which succeeds in establishing a delicate relationship between the whole course of the natural events and the melancholy mood of the poet. It is just these frequently inevitable cross-references from the natural symbolism to the equivalent human condition by means of a recapitulatory coda which enabled Monteverdi to attain a degree of formal and spiritual intensity all his own.[13]

In the deliberate archaism of the last piece in the book, 'Cantai un tempo', Monteverdi says a last farewell to the vanishing world of Flemish polyphony. The next three Books, *III*, 1592, *IV*, 1603, and *V*, 1605, came out in Mantua, and display the ripe fruit of Monteverdi's evolution in style down to the period immediately preceding the era of the figured bass. During the thirteen years in which they were composed, the foundations of musical craftsmanship were transformed as by the violence of a natural phenomenon. The year 1594 saw the deaths of Lassus and Palestrina, but also the births of the Florentine opera, *Dafne* by Peri, Corsi and Rinuccini and of the madrigal-comedy, *L'Amfiparnasso* by Orazio Vecchi. In 1596–7 Viadana's *Concerti Ecclesiastici* for few vocal parts and figured bass were published afar off in Rome, and Marenzio, the last great madrigal composer, died there in 1599.

The development in Monteverdi's style, culminating in monody, the chamber duet, the choral cantata and the *concertante* transitional madrigal in few parts, was accomplished gradually and altogether organically. It shows no perceptible traces either of Peri's and Caccini's experiments in the style of the recitative, or of E. de Cavalieri's and Viadana's method of notation for the new Basso Continuo. Monteverdi continues to employ the five-part imitative texture of the motet as the traditional medium, but the harmonic and melodic material of his music is progressively fermenting through increasing emotionalism and melodies expressive of the passions. In the *Third Book of Madrigals* there is a cycle of madrigals taken from *Gerusalemme liberata* (Canto XVI) wherein the impassioned thematic invention of recitative-like passages[14] matches the dramatic passion of Armida when she is deserted by Rinaldo; while the extravagant polyphonic textures accompanying verses from Guarini's pastoral play, *Pastor fido*,[15] exhibit an ever closer affinity with the world of music-drama as yet uncreated.

The astounding progressiveness of these still only quasi-polyphonic pieces on Tasso's words 'Vattene pur crudel', 'Là tra'l sangue' and 'Poi ch'ella', which often resolve into purely chordal episodes, can nowhere better be recognized than in the structural constitution of their thematic material. Only by comparing the following examples with the thematic style of Monteverdi's

madrigals composed hitherto does one become aware of the powerful tendency towards monodic recitative which now began to
dominate his production.

The typical character and the historical position of this consciously emotionally conceived thematic material is plainly evident
from the examples just given. There is a general urge towards
the unconfined spaciousness of the monodic *arioso*. The protracted lingering upon one harmonic plane within a recitative-
like repetition of notes prefigures the static bass, already present
but not apparent, of the coming monody. By reason of their
homophonic foundation, long stretches of these pieces present
a continuo-like character throughout, as is apparent from the contour of their almost static basses which are now no longer vocal
in type. Two examples will suffice:

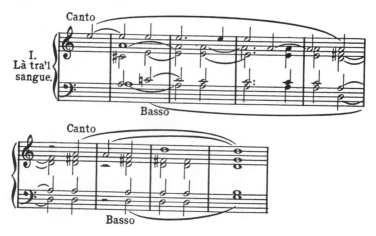

II.
Poi ch'ella.

In the last piece, 'Armida's Lament', the thematic ideas of the later *Arianna* composition are momentously anticipated.

Standing in contrast to the strong emotional tension in the material of the motives is the relaxed diffuseness in the sequential technique of the architectonic structure. Everything is simply in a state of flux.

In the *Fourth* and *Fifth Books of Madrigals* of 1603 and 1605, Monteverdi effectually builds up his system of modern, expressive harmony which does not shrink from any dissonance. More than one of the madrigals in these two particularly advanced compilations had already acquired a certain notoriety even before they appeared in print. They must have been in circulation in manuscript in northern Italy for several years. Otherwise it is inexplicable that the pugnacious Canon Artusi of Bologna should have been able, as early as 1600 and 1603 respectively, to publish his polemical treatise[16] against Monteverdi, in which the madrigals 'Anima mia perdona' and 'Che se tu se il cor mio' of the *Fourth*, and 'Cruda Amarilli', 'O Mirtillo', 'Era l'anima mia' and 'Ma se con la pietà' of the *Fifth Book of Madrigals* were attacked. The points objected to are mostly the effects of false relations, suspensions and *cambiata*-like chromaticism: devices of a young, self-confident musical expressionism doing its very utmost to interpret the 'sorrows', 'torments' and 'sighs' of Guarini's text through the medium of madrigalistic tone-painting. The culminating point of Monteverdi's daring which Artusi call into question may well be the unprepared

ninth at the very opening of the cry of anguish 'Ahi lasso' in
'Cruda Amarilli' (*M.B.V.*, text by Guarini).

'O Mirtillo', too, the text of which, like that of 'Cruda Amarilli',
is taken from Scene II of Guarini's *Pastor Fido*, is in Artusi's list
of proscribed works. On p. 48*b* of *Imperfettioni I*[17] the militant
Canon inexorably condemns this piece, compact as it is of the magic
sounds of a new conception of harmony. He even gives the
opening bars—the *Impertinentia d'un prinzipio*—in musical notation (without the words) simply to render them absolutely ludicrous
by immediately and senselessly appending the concluding bars.
But the point he censures—the beginning on the IVth degree of
F major (i.e. the sub-mediant) and the ending in D major—was the
very one for which Beethoven was severely criticized two hundred
years later. The fluctuating tonality, which has at all times been
the mark of a rebellious genius, must necessarily have seemed an
artistic fault to the pedants of 1600 and 1800. In any case,
'O Mirtillo' proves that the rigid working system of structural
tonality demanded by all theoreticians is ignored again and again
in practice. It was reserved for a later period to discover the more
essential attributes of this revolutionary piece. We are now
approaching the heart of the problem which we consider as crucial
and which we have already designated as the transition of style in
Monteverdi's madrigal production. To begin with, we will
examine the opening of the madrigal in the Basso Continuo
notation by Leichtentritt.[18]

The striking likeness of the structural constitution to that of such works as the madrigal version of the monody 'Lasciate mi morire' (VI, p. 1) is immediately apparent. The formal procedure of the earlier *Arianna* monody was one of retrogression in madrigalistic style. But here, on the other hand, the ostensibly polyphonic layout of the example just quoted has attained a stage of evolution towards the *concertante* madrigal which permits of its reconstruction in pure monodic notation, approximately as follows:

This notation discloses the organic growth of early monody.[19] The expressive leap of a sixth downwards already comes within the scope of the 'emotional'. In the *Arianna-Lamento* we find the same leaping intervals at the same expressive moments. Thus, during the later course of this piece the emotional phrase (*a*) corresponds up to a point to the equivalent phrase in the *Arianna-Lamento* (*b*).

Now follows one of the most remarkable passages in the whole literature of the Early Baroque; one of the few instances, too, which remained in the memories of scholars during the High Baroque. The phrase:

a typical Early Baroque chain of sequences with a trumpet-like up-beat of a fourth, is made by Monteverdi to display itself in a succession of canons such as give rise to the very harshest harmonic clashes. In this passage, early sequential technique, which was still at an experimental stage, furnished one of the most unbridled exhibitions of vitality that succeeded in implanting itself in the horrified recollection of the epoch. Even as late as 1678—that is to say, three-quarters of a century afterwards—G. M. Bononcini, the father of Handel's later rival, recalled this particular passage most emphatically in his famous *Musico prattico*.[20] The passage in question runs as follows:

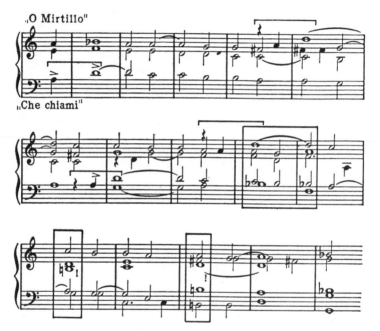

As may be seen, it is a matter of secondary harmonic results arising from strict vocal polyphony. Paradoxical as it may seem, this revolutionary-sounding passage is born of a retrospective *horizontal* sense of sonority, and in the corrosive astringency of its discordant intervals, which are intensified by capricious accidentals, it recalls the audacity of de Rore and Gesualdo. The fact that this particular episode offers no possibility of reconstruction as a Basso Continuo proves the retrospective character of such extravagance. The peculiar harmonies themselves can easily be analysed as the result of passing-notes and suspensions. They are mostly disguised $\frac{6}{5}$ and $\frac{7}{9}$ chords.

Even more striking is the monodic continuo-like tendency in the details of part-writing in the succeeding passage, wherein the alto and the basso proceed harmonically as follows:

In itself, this passage has no justification for its existence; it is simply a means to an end. When the canto is superimposed upon it, the whole thing immediately takes shape and becomes intelligible.

The *Third Book* is already dedicated to his new employer, Duke Vincenzo I of Mantua; on the title-page of the *Fourth Book* Monteverdi now signs himself as 'Maestro di Cappella' (as successor to B. Pallavicino since 1602).[21] The *Fifth Book* is like-wise dedicated to the Duke of Mantua. In this book the outline of the harmonization, which approaches the type of the figured bass, has led to the subsequent addition in new reprints of a later Basso Continuo part, whose authenticity, however, has not gone unchallenged.[22] Yet the new period of style of the Basso Continuo is officially inaugurated in the *Fifth Book*, the sub-title of which expressly refers to the figured-bass technique.[23] This sub-title throws a retrospective spotlight upon the probable style of per-formance of the outwardly extremely vocal first four *Books of Madrigals*. Undoubtedly the majority of these madrigals were actually performed with the support of strings and with harpsichord accompaniment. Monteverdi's long period of service as a viol-player would lose its significance if consorts of viols had not collaborated decisively in this world of exquisitely balanced chamber-music.[24] The last six items in the *Fifth Book*, too, are outwardly indebted to the 'stile nuovo' of the Florentine Camerata and the composer Luzzaschi of Ferrara. In the six-part 'E così poco a poco' and the nine-part 'Questi vaghi' (the last-named provided with an operatic introductory symphony!) Monteverdi finally breaks with the traditional five-part-writing of the motet.

'Questi vaghi' is designed for double-choir (four plus three) after the manner of G. Gabrieli and B. Pallavicino. Nevertheless, the bearing and the contour of the motives are not as yet recitative-like in the sense of the Florentine Camerata, even though occasional alternations between the voice and the Basso Continuo may be considered decidedly advanced.

With the *Fifth Book of Madrigals* the Monteverdian madrigal enters the Early Baroque world of form: cantata, chamber-duet and monody. In the short but cogent preface, the antinomy in the historical style between the 'Prima' and the 'Seconda Prattica' is announced for the first time. Two years later came Monteverdi's first opera, *La Favola d'Orfeo*, which furnishes another example of the blending of the styles of the madrigal, the Florentine recitative, Flemish polyphony and the Venetian orchestral technique into a splendid unity. Then followed in close succession the other music-dramas of the Mantuan period, the mighty feat of the *Gombert Mass* and the *Vespers of the Virgin Mary* in 1610. The spell of the intimate madrigal was broken; the sonority of the new operatic orchestra reverberated above the gentle voices of Guarini's pastoral poetry and Tasso's amorous plaints.

Monteverdi composed his last madrigals, significantly enough, even before 1613 in Mantua, but he did not publish them until 1614 in the *Sixth Book of Madrigals*, on the title-page of which he is described as 'Maestro di Cappella della Ser. Sign. di Venezia in S. Marco'. Considered from the standpoint of the historical evolution in style of the madrigal, this volume is already an anachronism. The madrigal to which the young Heinrich Schütz, while still in Venice in 1611, had paid his tribute with glowing compositions on texts by Marini and Guarini,[25] was beginning to be out of fashion.[26] The two cycles written in pure madrigalian style, i.e. in five-part imitative *a cappella* technique, are the last of Monteverdi's madrigal compositions in the sense of the 'Prima Prattica.' Both were already written by 1610;[27] both are haunted by the spirit of dramatic monody, and both works are thoroughly typical of Monteverdi's new style of expression which had been displayed so convincingly in the operatic works of 1607–8. Although composed without the support of a Basso Continuo, the two cycles breathe the spirit of monody.[28] In their literary origin, too, they are closely related to the nascent music-drama. In this version, the *Lamento** itself represents a transformation

* Cf. also Part II: The First Opera Composer.

of the dramatic monody from the opera of 1608 into the madrigalistic five-part setting, and the *Sestina* is a moving threnody in
six movements (with words by Scipione Agnelli whom we shall
meet again later as the master's presumed opera-librettist) for the
young singer, Caterina Martinelli— 'La Romanina', as she was
affectionately named by her circle of friends—who had been
selected to create the role of Arianna in the first performance
during the Carnival of 1608.

In the *Sestina*, the *a cappella* madrigal form is still only fictitous;
in reality, the piece, like its parallel the *Arianna-Lamento*, is
monodic in type. The procedure equivalent to the madrigalizing of
Arianna could easily be accomplished if the piece were written out
in the notation of Basso Continuo. The difference in species
between the character of the composition and its formal façade
would then be evident. We shall quote this opening in notation
such as will allow the specific bass-character of the piece to be
recognized, too. On closer inspection this supposititious 'Basso
Continuo' proves to be a kind of 'basso seguente'; namely, in its
quality as a synthesis of the bass and the tenor parts. This phenomenon strengthens the hypothesis that these madrigals were
originally sketched in monodic Continuo style and that the lower
parts are, in the main, utilized only for harmonic, not linear-
polyphonic purposes. Here is an example:

The synthesis of the two lowest parts is clearly visible in the
notation, which now for the first time manifests their constructive
homogeneity, or rather, their reciprocity. The new technical medium
of propulsion, the sequence, ensures that the parts balance each
other harmonically and rhythmically once they have been deprived
of every vestige of intrinsic polyphonic and technical connexion.
Monodic notation of the first few bars should reveal the true style
of the composition at its most striking.

No one could deny that the layout is conceived entirely from the aspect of the bass and the primary harmonies, whose individual part-writing seems to approximate to the chamber-music and monodic style far more closely than it does to the madrigalian style of the classical type of madrigal. At the same time, prominence is given to the modernist intention of producing tone-colour, which just at this point assumes a passively dramatic character owing to the use of primitive responsorial effects—here conceived quite clearly in an archaistic sense. The character of the litany, manifest in the leading tenor; the type of the fauxbourdon, inherent in the solemn repetitive singing reminiscent of the liturgy and in the uniform interchange between solo and choir, strengthen the melodramatic intentions of the composition. That Monteverdi was already consciously using tone-colour in this piece is obvious from the unusual style of the whole layout, and also from certain details of colouring which are intentionally archaic: such, for instance, as the typically Palestrinian use of the Phrygian cadence. Here, there are harsh descending parallel fourths such as would be sought in vain in the first five *Books of Madrigals*; needless to say, they occur at the words *Ahi lasso*, which never failed to spur Monteverdi to eccentricities of harmony.

Descending fourths—the intervals of sorrow and mourning—played the same dominant part throughout the work of Monteverdi's maturity as did the chromatic second, for instance, in that of the later Wagner. In the *Sestina*, in which these collective features are to a certain extent prominent, Monteverdi luxuriates chiefly in inventing ingenious disguises for this ominous fourth which, in the work in question, as also at the beginning of 'Lasciate mi morire' (Arianna), is concealed by a long sighing appoggiatura.

Monteverdi's consistent use during a period of fifteen years of the disguised descending fourth as the motive of grief evinces the spiritual consciousness of his artistic production and the great significance which he attached to this much debated musical symbol.

The poetic situation of the next two pieces of the cycle—the invocation of the rivers and dryads by the tormented Glaucos—brings with it an intensifying of the choral character, a more compact, more substantial musical style which presents a certain contrast to the hushed gloom of 'Incenerite' (the first part of *Sestina*). This impression is even further strengthened by the wellnigh intentional harmonic simplicity of the inner parts. The whole structure is integrated by sequential motives and effects of dynamic contrast produced by the abrupt juxtaposition of three-part and five-part episodes in both the 'Ditelo' and the 'Darà la notte' sections. The following bars furnish a splendid example of fourfold sequential progressions:

This example affords an opportunity of observing how strongly the feeling for homophony is supported in its struggle against

hidebound traditional polyphony by the driving-power of the
sequence. In 'Ma te raccoglie' the solo element resumes its
prominence; the tenor solo of the opening makes another appearance. The whole texture becomes more transparent, the five-part
passages make the effect of a *tutti* by contrast to the chamber-
music-like chiaroscuro of the single groups. In comparison with
the madrigalian technique of the first four *Books of Madrigals*,
these final pieces of the cycle produce an impression of unusual
refinement by their texture and by the opalescent effects of
light and shade which are conceived with the utmost understanding. The 'Lamenti' of the unhappy Glaucos are interpreted with
extreme daring:

The chord may be comprehended as the last inversion of a
seventh with the lowered fifth:

In the last two sections, 'O chiome d'or' and 'Dunque amate
reliquie', the solo-continuo elements are increasingly sifted out
from the main choral substance. A particularly good example of
this new chamber style is presented by the following passage:

'Dunque amate' then returns to the solemn tranquillity of the
introductory movement. Tenor and canto play important roles
as soloists; the subsidiary inner voices chant the words in the
fauxbourdon style of the litany. The despairing cry 'Ahi Corinna'
is contested in highly naturalistic fashion by the two topmost

voices. The remaining voices, despite apparent motion, are reduced in status to mere padding. After a climax which is produced by all the resources of monodic rhetoric, the voices subside into a dying murmur. The audacity of the tenfold repetition of a one-bar motive (during the final climax just described), with the change of only one degree of the scale, demonstrates how the musical substance, infinitely loosened by the introduction of the sequence, discovered in this persistent reiteration a new expedient for enhancing dynamic climaxes which was not to be fully developed until the eighteenth century.

With these two cycles of madrigals Monteverdi takes definite leave of a type which by about 1610 was slowly losing ground. He never reverted to the imitative motet-style of the five-part madrigal. From the standpoint of style, even the sacred madrigals of the *Selva Morale* of 1640 belong essentially to the period of the High Baroque. The Basso Continuo numbers of the *Sixth Book of Madrigals* continue the stylistic experiments of the 'stile nuovo' with which we have already become acquainted in the *Fifth Book of Madrigals*. One of them, 'Una donna fra l'altre', must have been published by 1609. It came out the same year as a sacred parody in A. Coppini's *Terzo Libro della musica di Claudio Monteverdi*.[29] The 'Dialogo a 7' 'Presso un fiume tranquillo', like 'Questi vaghi' in the *Fifth Book*, also appears to be influenced by the monumental style of the Venetian double-choir. Despite the interesting conception of the figured bass and its dramatic and dialogic constitution, all these advanced pieces display a decidedly transitional character. As has already been noted, the majority of the pieces in the *Sixth Book* seem to have been produced long before 1614, mostly towards 1610.

The harvest of madrigals during Monteverdi's last thirty years, the period of his intensive organizing and creative activities as Maestro di Cappella at San Marco, is comprised in two publications widely separated in date: the *Seventh Book of Madrigals*, 1619, entitled *Concerto*, and the *Eighth Book*, 1638, which bears the programmatic sub-title, *Madrigali Guerrieri et Amorosi*, and to which the extensive preface announces for the first time the bases of the philosophical thought and of the manner of performance of the 'stile concitato' newly invented by Monteverdi for this purpose.[30] Both publications are far more extensive and copious than any of the earlier books of madrigals; both volumes are dedicated to European princes of the highest rank,[31] and they both

G

contain dramatic culminating points of the species in question. The *Seventh Book*, wherein, as the sub-title indicates, all the items are planned in *concertante* style and are often provided with an instrumental substructure, reaches a climax in the *concertante* vocal ballet *Tirsi e Clori* of 1616,[32] which opens with a dramatic dialogue and closes with a combined choral and orchestral dance. The vast majority of the items in this volume are duets with obbligato Basso Continuo; forerunners, in fact, of the chamber-duet form so much beloved during the period of the High Baroque (Agostino Steffani!). The few monodies are the more interesting from the standpoint of the historical evolution of style. In the solitary experiment 'Lettera e Partenza amorosa', Monteverdi carried the stylistic programme of the Florentines to the point of absurdity. Both pieces—extreme borderline cases of the psalmodic operatic recitative of 1597–1600—must already have been considered anachronistic by 1619.[33] To make up for this, however, 'Con che soavità'[34] offers the first example of an aria with orchestral accompaniment. The piece, which is distinguished by ardent melodic inspiration, is based on three orchestral groups—'per Choros' in the sense of M. Praetorius' theory of colour[35]—and what is more, it makes the appearance of being an early type of modern score-writing.

That we are face to face here with a phenomenon which is unique in the whole literature of the madrigal (no fewer than three independent instrumental groups join forces in accompanying an alto voice) has already been pointed out by Ambros.[36] He was, indeed, obliged to deduce the unique character of the piece simply from the fact that an organ was prescribed as the continuo instrument, for he had nothing to go upon except an insufficient continuo part. Today, however, when G. F. Malipiero's reprint of the original edition is available, this fact must perforce be contested. The direction 'Basso continuo per l'Organo' mentioned by E. Schmitz[37] as occurring in the *Terzo coro*, is nowhere to be found throughout the carefully marked score in the Collected Edition. The stave containing the continuo part of this *Terzo coro* is, however, marked 'Concerto, Terzo coro à 4, Basso Continuo' in contradistinction to the specification of Continuos I and II. This rather obscure nomenclature, which is in lamentable contrast to the absolutely clear directions 'Basso Continuo per duoi Chitarroni e Clavicembalo e Spinetta' and 'Per il Clavicembalo Basso Continuo secondo coro', seems to me to signify essentially the same as the direction to coro II; namely, that here it is a question of four-part *accompagnamento* to the otherwise three-part coro III. The term 'Concerto' can denote many things. The most likely explanation in this instance is that it is fundamentally a tautology of the conception 'Continuo' and that the *concertante accompagnato* character of the group in opposition to the dominating function of the leading, higher-pitched groups is especially emphasized thereby. This explanation would be in accordance with the definition of the term 'Concerto' given in Riemann-Einstein's Lexikon (11th ed., 1929). As the *accompagnamento* of coro III involves the laying on of the ground-colour of the most sombre instrumental hues (gambas, viola da braccio, basso da braccio, contrabassi) it is possible, nay, probable, that for practical purposes the organ was seized upon as an expedient for securing tone-colour equivalent to the dark colour-scheme of coro III, and further, for ensuring a contrast in colouring between the three overcrowded continuo parts. This practical expedient, which may originally have been derived from directions in an old part-book and subsequently legitimized in print, throws an interesting light upon the problem of the multi-coloured continuo part in general, and proves that continuo performing-practice during the first decade of the second 'Ars nova' must already have attained a certain degree of refinement.

Now for the details of the piece itself. First of all we are struck by the division of the melodic line into periods in accordance with modern conceptions. There is already a prevailing symmetry which distributes the segments in the sense of a modern line. Few of Monteverdi's creations are so unpolyphonic as this composition. It is imitative in detail and genuinely contrapuntal on the surface, but in accordance with the contemporary predilection for group-technique it reduces its nine instruments to three orchestral contingents. For this reason, the whole work excels in iridescent interplay of sounds, while in the distribution of tone-colour it discloses an expertness far surpassing that which had established the renown of *Orfeo* in this particular respect. The breaking-up of the melodic line, a problem whose solution is here so closely approached by dividing the line into four- or eight-bar periods and by realizing the charm of inserting telescoped phrases, can best be illustrated by quoting the opening bars of the piece, which may also serve as a shining example of the harmonic sequence upon the second degree of the scale, a favourite device at this period.

The protagonist of the melodic interpolation is mostly the principal instrumental part, which is treated in the main as befits a second violin and only occasionally takes the lead. If it does, however, it is merely as a quasi-imitative foil to the singing-voice. When we come to examine the bass we shall allude to the intermediary function of the 'viola da brazzo'. A noble and dignified coloratura forms the transition to the second large section, which opens with the lugubrious voices of the *terzo coro*. The startling entry of the bass instruments on 'che soave armonia' is ingeniously prepared by the half-bar silence.

Now to the consideration of the bass. Although this is a question of monody with the singing-voice as the centre of gravity, and although—in contrast to 'Tempro* la cetra'—there is no set of variations on a static bass, the bass here, which is no longer motionless but entirely liberated and relaxed, supplies powerful germinative impulses. The entire continuo structure of the piece rests upon two thematic pillars, like two primitive cells, to which everything that occurs later may easily be referred. These are the two rudimentary motives:

They are already completely instrumental in constitution and have cast off the foundationless character of the old vocal bass. (See, for instance, the basses of the 'Lettera amorosa' or of the first monodies in the *Fifth Book*.) At the places where this bass comes to rest it establishes an intentional pedal-point. Sometimes it develops a powerful life of its own, which finds its most striking expression during the great *tutti* passage 'O cari baci' where it

* See Glossary: 'Tempro'.

proceeds as follows while the singing-voice sustains the note D
for four bars:

There will be no difficulty in identifying the motive A at this
point. While the low continuo and coro III execute the whole of
the line, the continuo and coro I support them only during the
first two bars, and the contrabasses of coro III for only one and a
half bars. Episode x is freely imitated by the bass viols, and thus
the single line radiates four complementary colours. The rudimentary motive B appears in the following guise during the course
of the piece:

Only towards the end does the soprano take over this bass motive in
order to submit it to fascinating imitation with the tenor viols,
which gives rise to five bars of a sort of elegant fictitious polyphony.

To round off this protracted analysis, one final example is
given to demonstrate the domination of the kinetic bass:

This also furnishes an example of *concertante* echo-effects such as
were later to develop Baroque *concerto-grosso* style in virtuoso
fashion.

The virtuoso vocal variations on the 'Romanesca' bass well
known at that time, and the six-part choral piece 'A quest' olmo'

(influenced by G. Gabrieli's double choirs) must also be mentioned here.

In considering the 'Romanesca a 2' in four sections ('Ohimè dov'è il mio ben') we find that, with the exception of small, unessential differences, the famous 'Romanesca' bass theme remains constant throughout all four sections. If, however, we examine the two upper parts singing in duet, we recognize that a kind of ideal variation-theme is implicit in all four verses and that we are consequently concerned with something in the nature of a fundamental counter-theme to the rigid *basso ostinato*. In this instance it cannot straightway be asserted that the centre of gravity of the proceedings still rests entirely in the all-important bass, as, for example, in the passacaglia-variation of the Early Baroque. On the contrary, the 'ideal' variation theme is interwoven so persistently in the texture that the 'prima parte' can be regarded simply as the exposition—even perhaps as the theme—and the three other sections as clearly derivable variations! The following condensed sketches in music type of the first ten bars placed side by side as theme and variation should make it quite clear that this is an instance of conscious composition-technique on the part of Monteverdi. It reminds us strongly of 'Tempro', in which exactly the same formal conditions prevail. The only difference between the 'Romanesca' and 'Tempro' is that the commonplace type of variation by means of coloratura has been superseded by an essentially more intellectual factor in the significant use of intervals and in the interplay between the varying tensions of the intervals themselves.

Romanesca a 2 (M.B. VII, 1619)

The primitive line of an immanent variation theme can now easily be construed therefrom.

This example gives rise to two interesting observations. The
limbs of the immanent theme are interchanged. First, in the
second variation, the midway elements are placed at the beginning;
in the third variation (which is not included in the example
just quoted) the salient points of the sequence are not:

but:

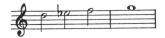

Secondly, the theme itself is constructed on the sequential
principle and is therefore already invested with a certain rudimentary variability: a renewed proof of the importance of the
sequence in the technical system of early monody. The sequential elements A and B form the guiding principle of the organic
variation-development of the later sections. This exceptionally
close integration of the component limbs thus constitutes a
species of 'variation within a variation'! In the 'ultima parte'
of the work there are already rudiments of the imitative relationship between the leading and the auxiliary parts: i.e. between the
canto and the continuo. But the bass theme itself is not constructed without formal concatenation of its individual elements.
The beginning and end of the theme are identical; the final
cadence utilizes the conclusion of the first part as a sort of elliptical reprise as follows:[38]

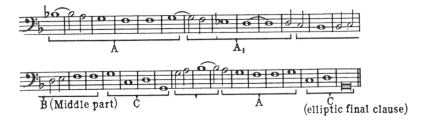

That even this fundamental theme cannot dispense with the sequence is clear from A and A₁. A comparison of the 'Romanesca' theme with the basses of 'Tempro' is very instructive, too. The sequence also takes the place of imitation in both the duet parts further on, and reveals itself as the intrinsic technical agent of the thematic development.[39] The expedient of sequential formation now becomes a leading factor. This may be seen to advantage in an extract from the 'prima parte' which is, at the same time, an example of the architectonic conception of early monody. The C section of the bass theme appears first of all in the elliptical cadential reprise in a manner such as to make it possible to trace the thematic cross-references which impart a tectonic function to the two sections.

From these collective reprises, segments and repetitive units, three-part song form was slowly and continuously coming into being.

The *Madrigali Guerrieri* of the *Eighth Book of Madrigals* reach a climax in the battle-scene in Tasso's *Combattimento* of 1624,[40] in which the whole grammar of the 'stile concitato' undergoes a preliminary trial (tremolo, pizzicato, string quartet texture, motive representing a galloping horse, etc.). In the madrigalian pieces of the half-volume preceding this masterpiece, the whole armoury of motives for the High Baroque martial style of expression is created with ingenious far-sightedness. In 'Altri canti d'amore', and even more in the splendid Petrarch sonnet 'Hor che'l ciel e la terra', quickly-scanning motives such as:

emerge for the first time in a manner determining the new trend of style.

The requisitioning of a six-part choir, first and second violins, viols divided in four and the usual 'fundamental instruments' brings these compositions into a central position among concerted works of the Early Baroque, somewhat after the manner of Schütz's *Symphoniae Sacrae*, the first set of which (1629) appeared *before* the publication of the volume in question.[41] I must forbear to describe the attractive details of the warlike atmosphere which prevails in the choral as well as in the monodic pieces in this book.[42] Elsewhere I have dilated upon the vocal ballet *Movete* which effectively concludes the half-volume.[43]

The *Madrigali amorosi* which, together with the counterpart to *Altri canti d'amore*, *Altri canti di Marte*, start as six-part *concertante* composition, culminate in the enchanting, albeit rather sketchily drafted opera-ballet *Il Ballo dell' Ingrate* of 1608—a far distant date which may, however, indicate the period of origin of the majority of the pieces brought together in this half-volume dedicated to amatory sentiments. The choral madrigals *alla francese* which came into being under the unmistakable influence of Pierre Guédron (1565–1621) may be regarded as the creative echo of the impressions gained by Monteverdi when he accompanied Vincenzo I on his journey to Flanders in 1599.[44] The *Scherzi* of 1607 already betray the influence of the French 'Ballet de Cour'. It is certain that the *Airs de Cour* which Guédron published from 1604 onwards came to be decisive for the bewitching type of the later Monteverdian concert-madrigal. The dialogue character and the style of these pieces, whose sections of monody are answered in block harmonies by the choir, while the melodic line is kept intact, may be observed in the opening bars of 'Dolcissimo Uscignolo':

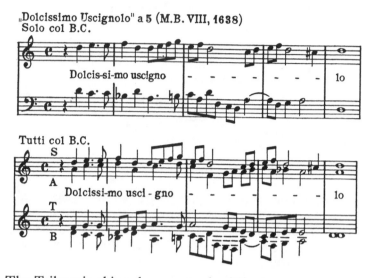

„Dolcissimo Uscignolo" a 5 (M.B. VIII, 1638)
Solo col B.C.

Dolcis-si-mo uscigno — — — — — — lo

Tutti col B.C.

Dolcissi-mo usci - gno — — — — — — lo

The Trilogy in this volume, conceived 'in genere rappresentativo', i.e. in the dramatic sense, soars yet again in the agonizing plaint 'Amor' (*Lamento della Ninfa*) to the solitary peak of expression of the *Arianna Lament*. Like so many compositions of the later volumes, *VII* and *VIII*, it is constructed upon an *ostinato* figure,[45] this time the old Spanish 'Malagueña' theme.

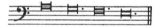

The *Madrigali e Canzonette*, edited and published as an opus posthumum by A. Vincenti in 1651, add little fresh to the actual artistic legacy of the *Eighth Book of Madrigals*; all the less as the two important pieces of the volume, 'Zefiro torna' and 'Armato il cor', had already been published by Monteverdi in the *Scherzi Musicali* of 1632.[46] Besides these chamber-duets, in which the *concertante* style is maintained throughout, the volume contains ten terzets, two of which have only recently been rediscovered in the rather different medium of monodies.[47] Vol. IX of the reprint of the complete works edited by Malipiero includes several other independent pieces found in sundry contemporary collections ('raccolte'), all of which have not as yet come to light. Among them is the cycle of strophic variations 'Ohimè ch'io cado' with its tireless *basso corrente* which has been described as having attained one of the most advanced stages on the way to the High Baroque aria.[48] The piece, which was published in 1624 in Milanuzzi's collection, points in no uncertain manner towards the late *arioso* style of the *Incoronazione* of 1642. It is far removed in conception from the madrigal-cycles of 1610. During the fourteen intervening years Monteverdi had traversed a period in the history of style only comparable in extent with the tremendous distance between the traditional polyphony of his youthful productions from 1582 to 1584 and the revolutionary harmonies of the *Fourth* and *Fifth Books of Madrigals*. In the last three publications by Monteverdi the madrigalist, the motive-power of madrigalian style seems to be dissolved into its elements and to merge into opera and the *concertante* cantata. The last madrigalist could have no successors. The first opera-composer was destined, through the agency of his late operas written in Venice, to lay the foundations of musical-dramatic style for the next two centuries.

CHAPTER X

THE POETS OF
MONTEVERDI'S MADRIGALS

A FEW words on the poets who supplied the verses to Monteverdi's madrigals may not be out of place here. The identification of their poetry still remains a controversial subject among experts. Many of the poems repeatedly used for madrigal-composition were of the type to be found in the so-called 'centoni' (medleys): compilations from different poems. Very often the composer tore part of a longer lyrical poem from its context in order to use it as a 'poetical unit' for his madrigal. During the sixteenth century, authors' rights in literary property seem hardly to have existed. G. B. Doni strongly resented this when he exclaimed that he could not understand why poets did not protest against the systematic suppression of their names in publications of madrigal music.[1] In the notorious collections of poems which were edited for the purposes of madrigal-composition by Barco and Bidelli, every verse was drawn from a different literary source. Sometimes composers even went so far as to supply the necessary verses themselves.[2] In a large number of Monteverdi's madrigals, however, the authors of the respective poems have been identified, thanks principally to Alfred Einstein's scholarly researches.[3]

Among Monteverdi's favourite poets, Torquato Tasso, Guarini and Chiabrera occupy the foremost position. The composer, whose lifelong partiality for Tasso's poems is clearly reflected in many of his letters and especially in the preface to *M.B. VIII*, 1639, used his poetry in thirteen different works. As early as 1587 (in *M.B. I*) Monteverdi composed music to Guarini's famous 'Ardo si' together with Tasso's 'risposta' and 'contrarisposta' 'Ardi e gela' and 'Arsi e alsi'.[4] *M.B. II*, 1590, contains no fewer than nine poems by Tasso, among which is the wonderful verbal landscape-painting 'Ecco mormorar l'onde'. Thenceforward, it was to the inexhaustible treasury of Tasso's epic poem *Gerusalemme liberata* that the composer turned most frequently for the texts of his madrigals. *M.B. III*, 1592; includes a trilogy, consisting of Stanzas 59, 60 and 63 from Canto XVI, giving expression to Armida's grief after she has been abandoned by Rinaldo; a fore-runner, so to speak, of the *Lamento* of Rinuccini's *Arianna* libretto of 1608. Monteverdi seems to have returned to this subject in his later opera *Armida*, 1627, after Tasso, now lost.

His setting of the 'Lamento d'Erminia' (discovered only recently by F. Torrefranca),[5] taken from the episode wherein Erminia finds and mourns the mortal remains of Tancred, killed in battle, probably dates from 1612. The slain warrior of this threnody is the hero of Monteverdi's last and most successful attempt to find the musical equivalent to Tasso's poetry: the scenic oratorio *Combattimento* which he published in *M.B. VIII* in 1638. He had, however, composed this work many years earlier for Count Girolamo Mocenigo in Venice, 1624. It is based on Stanzas 52–8 from Canto XII.

Next to the poetical works of the 'divin Signor Tasso', whose pastoral comedy *Aminta* had already inspired many madrigalists, it was Battista Guarini's 'commedia pastorale' *Il Pastor fido*, 1581–90, which constituted the chief poetical source from which Monteverdi's most emotional madrigals were to spring. In *M.B. III*, 1592, no fewer than seven poems by Guarini have so far been identified, two of them taken from the *Pastor fido*, to which Monteverdi returned in *M.B. IV*, 1603, and *M.B. V*, 1605. In these two last named volumes, ten madrigals are based on stanzas from Guarini's comedy, while nine more are settings of his lyrical poems. Guarini remained a favourite poet with Monteverdi, who composed many of his texts in *M.B. VII* and *VIII*, among them the famous aria 'Con che soavità' with orchestral accompaniment; the *duetto da camera* 'Interotte speranze' and the madrigal *a la francese* 'Dolcissimo uscignolo'.

The artificial and rhetorically complicated style of poetry cultivated by Guarini and even more strongly by G. B. Marini, presents a sharp contrast to the heartfelt simplicity of Tasso's *Aminta*. In Monteverdi's own epoch it was only Chiabrera who kept simple poetry of the folk-tune type alive in his delightful song-like poems which served the composer so well in the *Scherzi Musicali* of 1607, wherein no fewer than eleven poems have so far been identified. Marini's hyperbolic poetical effusions are used in the pronounced emotionalism of Basso Continuo madrigals in Monteverdi's *M.B. VI* and *VII* of 1614 and 1619.

It was only logical that dramatic librettists should gradually have entered the sphere of Monteverdi's later madrigal production, especially as the later volumes were increasingly closely linked with his activities in the world of opera. Rinuccini, the earliest poet of the Florentine opera and librettist of Monteverdi's *Arianna*, 1608, figures as the author of the madrigal version of the famous *Lamento* (*M.B. VI*). Scipione Agnelli, whose libretti Monteverdi later rejected, makes an appearance as the sensitive poet of the *Sestina* cycle, written and composed to commemorate Caterina Martinelli's untimely death.

Among the other poets whose participation in Monteverdi's madrigal publications is beyond doubt, pride of place must be given to Petrarch with his wonderful sonnet 'Hor ch'el ciel e la terra' (*M.B. VIII, Canti Guerrieri*) and other poems in *M.B. VI*, and to Cardinal Bembo, his rediscoverer in the late Renaissance, with 'O rossignol' (*M.B. III*) and 'Cantai un tempo' (*M.B. II*).

M.B. II and *III* also include poems by Girolamo Casone, Filippo Alberti, Ercole Bentivoglio and Ludovico Celiano. The famous 'Romanesca' 'Ohimè dov'è il mio ben' in *M.B. VII* is based on words by Bernardo Tasso; the poems to the lost cycle of madrigals *I cinque fratelli* were the work of G. Strozzi, 1628, the librettist of Monteverdi's opera buffa *La finta pazza Licori*, 1627, also lost.

A. Striggio jun., the poet of the *Orfeo* libretto, provided the words for the lost 'Lamento di Apollo'. Lastly, there are poems by G. Boccaccio, Jacopo Sannazaro, Ansaldo Cebà and Antonio Allegretti, the latter represented by a little trilogy in *M.B. I.* The authors of the poems to Monteverdi's early *Canzonette a 3*, 1584, the fragmentary *Madrigali Spirituali* of 1583 and the sacred madrigals of his last publication *Selva Morale e Spirituale*, 1641, have not as yet been identified. It is to be hoped that the gradual process of literary identification will eventually lead to the discovery of these unknown poets and their stanzas.

Despite the incompleteness of this list, one conclusion may safely be drawn: namely, that Monteverdi was attracted principally by poems abounding in emotional imagery and dramatic situations. His acknowledged predilection for Tasso's *Gerusalemme liberata* and Guarini's *Pastor fido*, as well as for the poetry of Rinuccini and Agnelli which exploited human passions, and his comparative neglect of Marini's empty lyricism at the time of its greatest popularity, clearly emphasize the composer's consciously fastidious and selective taste.

CHAPTER XI

THE FIRST OPERA COMPOSER

OPERA AND BALLET AT THE COURT OF MANTUA

THE title of this chapter is one of those consciously inexact historical abbreviations in which, despite its lack of precision, there is a grain of truth. Of course Monteverdi was no more the first opera composer (still less the 'inventor of opera') than he was the 'last madrigalist'. Operas were composed many years before he made his first contribution to this latest variety of collaboration between music and poetry;[1] just as madrigals were still composed, published and revived later than 1614, after the master himself had definitely discontinued his activity as a madrigalist. Yet both these designations convey a true historical fact. Monteverdi's *Orfeo*, 1607,[2] is really the first opera in the sense of practical music-making; not simply the oldest operatic work which has undergone increasingly numerous revivals since the beginning of the twentieth century, and which is certain to produce an immediate dramatic effect upon modern audiences. Rather is it the first music-drama, in which the poetic words, the dramatic action and the musical construction are held in creative equilibrium. To begin with, the immense distance which separates the *Orfeo* in question from its direct predecessors places Monteverdi's historical achievement in the correct light. The significance of this opera as regards the history of style is comprised in the fact that it was, so to speak, a focus of all the component parts of the monodic and dramatic music-making of the previous decade, now concentrated and welded into an artistic whole. These component parts look back to a long period of preparation. Operatic tendencies can be traced as far distant as the mystery plays of the Early Middle Ages.[3] The Tornei,* Trionfi and Intermedia† of the Early Renaissance with their variegated abundance of orchestral accompaniment,[4] the ostentatious ballets with increasing obligatory vocal interpolations ('Ballets de Cour'),[5] the madrigal-comedies,[6] and finally, the semi-dramatic, sacred 'Rappresentazioni'[7] which tended in the direction of the quasi-dramatic oratorio of the High Baroque derived from the 'Laude spirituali', all collaborated to produce a new art-form which was already in the air and which declared itself in accompanying phenomena, analogous as regards historical style. In all of them, the co-operation between instruments and voices, choir and solo was tried in various ways. By means of the intensive evolution of the Renaissance madrigal from about 1533, the new music became increasingly susceptible to, and capable of reflecting the poetic words. The whole artistic tendency of the time strove towards emphasizing the interpretation of the words at the expense of *a priori* musical texture. Transformations of many-voiced (choral) compositions into soli with accompaniment, or at least into few-voiced variants, were the order of the day.

The experiments of the Florentine 'Camerata', originally archaeological attempts at reviving the hymns and tragedies of the ancient Greeks, led to the same result from a different angle of vision: to composition for a single voice, either singing or reciting, with an instrumental background.[8] From this point it was only a short step to the linking together of several self-contained songs of this character (monodies) into a poetic and logical whole, and the oldest type of melodrama was complete. These first music-dramas, which derived their force from the components already

---

* See Glossary: 'Torneo'.   † See Glossary: 'Intermedium'.

enumerated, are more in the nature of recited plays: pastoral plays with diction elevated by music rather than genuine operas in the sense of the later conception of the species.[9] Their most significant attainment consists in the defining of the zone of the subject-matter. The themes of these first operas are taken either from early Greek mythology[10] or from the contemporary pastoral play,[11] both of which had served as the most important sources of material for the sixteenth-century madrigal. Independently of the Florentine experimenters, Roman musicians had been endeavouring to solve the problems of 'singing-voice versus accompaniment'. Towards 1596, Ludovico Viadana, later maestro di cappella at Mantua Cathedral and a friend of Monteverdi's, composed his first Concerti Ecclesiastici,[12] in which one (or several) singing voices treated as soloists were accompanied by a flowing instrumental bass (mostly unfigured). The epoch-making invention of the 'Basso Continuo' which actually originated from this method of composition was also of consequence to the nascent opera. In Rome, too, Emilio de' Cavalieri, already mentioned here as one of the pioneers of opera, produced his sacred quasi-dramatic Rappresentazione di anima e di corpo, in which the solo songs were accompanied by a minutely figured 'Basso Continuo'. On this occasion the combination of orchestral forces, powerful choral support and dramatically flexible monody was successful for the first time. Precise directions for the constitution of the orchestra, the performance of the obligatory ornamentation and the figuring of the bass clearly defined the individual features of this new style.[13]

The operatic attempts of the Florentines are on a much smaller scale, and the purely musical considerations play a far less important part. Peri's orchestra consists solely of four 'fundamental' instruments,[14] and the deficiencies in the choral forces, in the contrasts between the dramatic situations, in the musical ensemble or simply in the orchestra as an independent unit, condemned these works to crippling monotony. The most significant achievement of the Florentines is that they laid stress upon the creative possibilities of the Orpheus legend and kindred subject-matter as musical stimuli to dramatic music-making. In so doing, they indisputably prepared the way for Monteverdi.

What is the ultimate character of Monteverdi's historical accomplishment in his first opera, La Favola d'Orfeo, which followed the pioneer works just named at intervals from seven to

seventeen years? It consists in the concentration of phenomena
of style (named above) into a complete image of sound, a musical
cosmos which peers, Janus-like, into the past of the 'Intermedium'
as well as into the future of the Gluck-Wagnerian 'Birth of the
drama from the spirit of music'. Glancing at the list of orchestral
instruments in the printed score of 1609, one might be fully
justified in describing *Orfeo* as a belated 'Intermedium' if it
did not also comprise all the other forms of musico-dramatic
evolution of two centuries.

A comparison of the list of the orchestra of *Orfeo* with the
orchestra of the 'Intermedium' *Psiche ed Amore*, 1565 (by
A. Striggio sen, and F. Corteccia), mentioned above will show the
relationship more clearly:

Psiche ed Amore, 1565	*L'Orfeo*, 1607
2 Gravicembali	2 Gravicembali
4 Violini	2 Contrabassi da Viola
1 Liuto mezzano	10 Viole da brazzo
1 Cornetto muto (stiller Zink)	1 Arpa doppia
4 Tromboni	2 Violini piccoli alla Francese
2 Flauti diritti (Recorders)	2 Chitarroni
4 Flauti traverse	2 Organi di legno
1 Leuto Grosso	3 Bassi da Gamba
1 Sotto Basso da Viola	4 Tromboni
1 Soprano di Viola	1 Regale
4 Leuti	2 Cornetti
1 Viola d'Arco	1 Flautino alle vigesima Seconda
1 Lirone	(Piccolo)
1 Traverso Contralto (Alto Flute)	1 Clarino
1 Flauto Grande Tenore	3 Trombe sordine
1 Trombone basso	To which should be added the
5 Storte (Serpent)	following instruments, which are
1 Stortina (Little Serpent)	mentioned only in the inner pages
2 Cornetti ordinarii	of the score:
1 Cornetto grosso	Arpe
1 Dulziano (Bassoon)	Ceteroni (large Zither)
1 Lira	Flautini
1 Ribecchino (early fiddle)	
2 Tamburi (Drums)	
44 Instruments in all	

The shattering toccata for brass instruments at the opening, and
the gay 'Moresca' at the end are still haunted by the courtly
'Trionfo'. The extended pastoral scenes in Acts I and II are the

final echoes of the 'Favola Pastorale' which reached their apogee in Tasso's *Aminta*, 1577, and Guarini's *Pastor fido*, 1585. Moreover, the *Orfeo* libretto of 1607 by A. Striggio jun. bears the significant sub-title 'Favola Pastorale'! The madrigalian parts of the work ('Lament for Euridice', Act II) recall the madrigalian music-dramas of Marenzio and O. Vecchi, and Orfeo's great coloratura aria 'Possente spirto' (Act III) is obviously derived from the *Florentine Intermedia*[15] which C. Malvezzi had already published in 1589. Yet Monteverdi's *Orfeo* surpasses them all in the dramatically pregnant application and the conscious tectonic uniting of all the individual formative efforts (previously enumerated) in the endeavour to produce a unique structure which should serve the musical rendering of the poetic 'affetto'. In this way the composer succeeds in advancing into a new musical territory: the psalmodic recitative of the Florentines becomes accompanied *arioso*; the *arioso* tendencies of Peri and Caccini evolve into arias with variations and strophic songs.[16] *Sinfoniae* for wind instruments, such as originated with G. Gabrieli, acquire the character of leitmotives by means of repetitions inspired by dramatic considerations. Indeed, one strongly marked leitmotive already dominates the scene with the messenger of death. It is the phrase:

which is sung in motivic variants by the messenger, the two shepherds, and later by the choir.[17] In this dramatic unifying of disparate elements of form and in the precise characterization of the dramatis personae and the principal moods resides the stupendous, forward-gazing newness of *Orfeo*. In this work, too, may be found creative understanding in the use of an 'Intermedium'-orchestra which had already gone out of fashion. Monteverdi does not use this 'Instrumentarium' as a chance assemblage of 'Zufallsorchester',* but already as a musical palette in the psychological sense of the later music-drama. The shepherd's music maintains a clear ground-colour with the piccolo flute and piccolo violin; the underworld is portrayed by the regal and by the brass instruments. Orfeo's entreaty is encompassed with the

---

* See Glossary: 'Zufallsorchester'.

strains of the harp; the bearer of ominous tidings sings to the melancholy sounds of the portative organ and the sombre theorbo. Orfeo's passion bleeds to death in the continuous, free recitative of the Florentines; the spirits of the underworld whisper in Flemish counterpoint while paying heed to the exact quantities of the individual syllables. Charon's dark bass is heard in the jarring tones of the regal, and the shepherds sing and play in the rhythm of the 'balletti' of G. Gastoldi, Lejeune and Guédron.[18] In this art of musical characterization, practised here for the first time with the certainty of a somnambulist, lies Monteverdi's appeal to a distant future.

To sum up: *Orfeo* is the product of two epochs. It combines the dramatic aspirations of the Early Renaissance (courtly 'Intermedium' and pastoral poetry) and of Humanism (the atmosphere of Greek Tragedy and the tragic commentary of the Chorus) with the achievements of the Florentine 'Camerata' and of the pioneers of the gradually evolving style of the Thorough Bass. The symphonies for wind instruments in the 'Hades' Act are unmistakable offshoots from the 'sonate', 'dialoghi' and 'battaglie' of the Gabrielis and Annibale Padovano. In Orfeo's dramatic dialogue with the messenger (Act II) the music-drama of later centuries with its elastic 'recitativo accompagnato' technique is foreshadowed in amazing fashion. The vocal ballet of the pastoral scene of Act II and the Charon scene of Act III present operatic surfaces larger in scale than any of Monteverdi's predecessors in the sphere of opera had succeeded in producing. The variegated, 'Intermedium'-like luxuriance of the orchestra soon becomes an anachronism in tone-colour. The future lies in the despairing Orfeo's tragic monologue: the psychological climax of the work is indisputably *not* the superabundantly ornamented coloratura of the 'Hades' Act, but the deeply moving lamentation in Act II, which begins with the typically madrigalistic passion-motive of the falling diminished fourth:

and ends with the passionate outcry of the farewell from the upper world.

Arianna and *Ballo dell'Ingrate*

Although his early operas at Mantua came into being as the result of the impetus provided by court occasions,[19] it was really the elemental, original experience of *das Rein-Menschliche*—to use a definition of Richard Wagner's, the ultimate successor to Monteverdi—dissolved in the delicate sorrow of the early Greek myths which inspired Monteverdi most deeply in his music-dramas, and which he himself came to regard in retrospect as the creative centre of these works. The whole conception of these remarkable early operas precludes both choral splendour and elaborate virtuoso singing, elements of essentially operatic quality which are generally associated with the conception of the Baroque opera. Monteverdi's inspiration to the composition of these and similar texts lay in the inherent possibilities they offered of moulding the original experience of the *human passions* in dramatic fashion by means of symbolical musical sounds. In a subsequent letter to the librettist of *Orfeo*, A. Striggio jun.,[20] in which he declined, with cogent aesthetic arguments, the offer of a *Favola maritima* entitled *Le nozze di Tetide e di Peleo*, he wrote as follows:

How should I, dearest friend, imitate the speech of the winds if they do not speak, and how should I stir the emotions with them? Arianna shudders because she is a woman, and Orpheus was stirred because he was a human being and not a wind! Arianna inspired me to a (dramatically justified) lament and Orpheus to a (dramatically justified) entreaty!

This quotation (here freely translated) lies at the root of Monteverdi's musical-dramatic conviction. It is profoundly significant that in this avowal, the *Lamento* and the *Preghiera* are designated by their creator as the psychological axes of the two music-dramas: and it is clear that *Orfeo* originated in the emotional centre of the entreaty to the gods, just as Arianna grew out of the lament of the heroine so cruelly deserted by Theseus.[21] The passion-laden monody of the heroic principal characters stands, from the purely musical aspect, too, in the very centre of the action. But whereas for *Orfeo* we have at our disposal an original libretto and two printed scores supervised by the composer, when we come to the second opera, *Arianna*, we find that nothing remains but Rinuccini's libretto.[22] The entire music is lost with the one exception of the portion which Monteverdi himself in a later letter to A. Striggio jun.[23] described as 'la più essential parte dell' opera'.

That it was this still extant portion of the opera which was the deciding factor in its success and which imprinted itself so deeply upon the memories of contemporary and latter-day audiences may be seen from manifold contemporary reports. Marco da Gagliano, who was Monteverdi's rival at the time *Arianna* was composed and whose own Rinuccini opera *Dafne* had been performed before *Arianna*, wrote in the preface to this work that the arias in *Arianna* had, 'in point of fact, revived the greatness of early music and in so doing had visibly moved the entire audience to tears'.[24] Authorities such as G. B. Doni, Severo Bonini and F. Follino, the official historiographer of the Mantuan court, also expressed themselves in similar terms.[25] The tremendous impression made by this plaint of a deserted lover is manifested most strikingly in the fact that the *Lamento* was elevated into a 'type' by the musical world of its own and later ages, and was imitated by innumerable composers down to the end of the seventeenth century. The number of operatic (or purely lyrical) 'Lamenti' was legion.[26] Together with funeral-scenes and after-world-scenes it was part of the stock-in-trade of the *opera seria* in all its varied forms until well into the eighteenth century. That the music of the *Arianna Lamento* must have been very dear to Monteverdi himself is proved not only by the relatively numerous excerpts in letters referring to the work[27] and to its subsequent public performances up to 1641, but also by the two important transcriptions to which he submitted the music of this favourite composition. Only two years after its appearance he arranged the *Lamento* as a five-part *a cappella* madrigal which he published in the *Sixth Book of Madrigals* in 1614. The new version is of particular interest musically as an authoritative object-lesson in the interpretation of Monteverdi's type of *continuo* basses. How amply the master himself thought out the harmonic unfolding of the inner parts may be seen clearly by comparing the first six bars of the monodic version of 1608 with those of the madrigal version of 1614.[28]

The fragment of the monody dating from 1608 exists in as many as three different editions, the orthography of which has since caused the student of Monteverdi much anxious thought. They are as follows:

(a) A special print of the *Lamento*, Venice, 1623, made by the printer Gardano (possibly under Monteverdi's supervision).

(b) A manuscript copy in the National Library, Florence, containing many inaccuracies and obvious copyist's errors.

(c) A manuscript copy in a 'Grilanda'* of the copyist F. M. Fuci, first discovered by Torrefranca in 1944.[29]

The second new transcription of the *Lamento* was issued by Monteverdi himself in his last musical publication, the *Selva Morale* of 1640, in which it appears in the scarcely concealed disguise of a sacred 'Parodie' (or 'Kontrafaktur'†) as 'Pianto della Madonna' (Lament of the Virgin Mary).[30]

* See Glossary: 'Grilanda'.   † See Glossary: 'Kontrafaktur'.

The positively incalculable series of *Lamenti* which was inaugurated by Monteverdi's *Arianna* probably begins with a *Lamento* from his own pen. It is the 'Lamento di Erminia' which Torrefranca discovered in 1944, identified and dated as having been written between 1610 and 1612. This composition, which forms a scene from Tasso's *Gerusalemme liberata* (Canto XIX),[31] bears a close affinity in style with the *Arianna Lamento*. The extremely welcome discovery of this offshoot depicting the style of *Arianna* revives the hope cherished by all Monteverdi-lovers that the long-lost music of the entire opera may yet be traced. An unbridgeable gap in the history of the early operas would then be filled.

Within the cycle of the Gonzaga wedding-festivities of 1608 which culminated in the festival performance of *Arianna*, the first performance was also given of *Il Ballo dell'Ingrate* (The Prudes' Ball). This ballet-opera by Rinuccini and Monteverdi followed *Arianna* on 4 June 1608 in the way that a satyric drama follows a tragedy. The court historiographer Follino has narrated in picturesque language the contents of the light-hearted little work with its mythical protagonists, Pluto, Venus and Cupid and the melodic choir of 'prim maidens'.[32] The piece, which is significant in style and produces the effect of being an ancestor of modern operatic ballets (Stravinsky-Pergolesi's *Pulcinella*), is an unmistakable descendant of the French 'ballet de cour'.[33] The centre of action of the work is not occupied by an emotional monody, but on the contrary, by a dance-divertissement in which a motto theme undergoes rhythmic variation.

Preliminary studies to this obvious *Musique mesurée* are to be found not only in Monteverdi's *Scherzi Musicali* of 1607[34] with its numerous instrumental ritornelli, but also in *Orfeo*, the second act of which displays many examples of syncopated dance rhythms patently showing French influence.[35] The lyrical ending of the enchanting work, which has, however, come down to us in a rather sketchy state, comprises the expressive monody of 'Una delle

Ingrate' with the melancholy-roguish choral refrain 'Apprendete pietà, Donne e Donzelle' which cannot have failed in its effect upon the high-spirited ladies of the Mantuan court. Monteverdi published the *Ballo dell'Ingrate* very late, in the *Eighth Book of Madrigals*, together with the *Combattimento* of 1624. Strangely enough, in the long preface to the volume, he made no reference to this interesting minor work 'in genero rappresentativo'.

DRAMATIC WORKS OF THE LATER PERIOD, 1613–39

The event of greatest consequence in Monteverdi's later life, his appointment to the Church of San Marco in Venice, 19 August 1613, straightway removed him from the sphere of musical-dramatic activity. To begin with, opera was merely a whim of the distinguished aristocrat and the princely Maecenas; it flourished at its best in the atmosphere of courts and was for the time being cultivated only in isolated artistic centres in central Italy. From 1597 to about 1613, Florence and Mantua, greatly encouraged by the princely families of the Gonzagas and the Medicis respectively, were the headquarters of opera. In 1620 the production of music-drama shifted more and more to Rome, where Cardinal Rospigliosi, later Pope Clement IX, provided a whole generation of opera-composers with texts and stimulated them to increased creative activity. Democratic mercantile city-states such as the Venetian Republic were not interested in this latest pastime of princes. The Procurators who set their seal upon Monteverdi's appointment regarded him first and foremost as the musician they had commissioned to restore polyphonic church-music and to reorganize the Cappella of San Marco, and also as the serious-minded composer of Masses and Vespers. The fact that during these first twenty-five years of his Venetian labours Monteverdi's activity as a music-dramatist did not languish altogether is due to his having continued to cherish his connexions with the princely houses of central Italy, especially with the Gonzagas, from whom he still drew a salary and to whom he consequently felt especially beholden. Unfortunately, the tangible results of this branch of Monteverdi's Venetian activities have been attended by singular misfortunes. Almost all the operatic works which can be proved as having been composed and performed between 1613 and 1639 have been lost— at least, so far as is known up to the present day. The series begins with the sacred play *La Maddalena*, 1617, to which he composed music in collaboration with two notable Jewish musicians, Salomone Rossi and Muzio Effrem. Only two items of the music (reprinted in Vol. XI of the Collected Edition) have been preserved, both of which betray close affinity in style with *Orfeo*. The year in which the *Maddalena* appeared was particularly fertile in operatic music. Two other operas, *La Favola di Peleo* and *Andromeda*,[36] were produced, but have likewise disappeared. The works of the 'Opera Year', 1627, have fared no better. Nothing remains of *La Finta Pazza Licori* (to a text by B. Strozzi), which is mentioned in so many letters of that year. Gone are the operas *Armida* and the 'Torneo' *Mercurio e Marte*, Parma, 1628, and other operas besides, whose authorship cannot be proved as Monteverdi's.[37] The overwhelming majority of the works mentioned here were written for the courts of princes in central Italy, such as Mantua and Parma. A similar fate was decreed for the operas of 1630, *Proserpina rapita* and *La Delia e l'Ulisse*, the first, composed for the wedding festivities of the daughter of his Venetian patron, Mocenigo, and the second, possibly in collaboration with F. Manelli, destined for Bologna.[38]

Only three small dramatic works, none of which pertains completely to the sphere of opera, have been preserved from among Monteverdi's operatic production during this quarter of a century. They are the operatic ballets: *Tirsi e Clori* (libretto by A. Striggio jun.), composed in 1615, performed in Mantua, 1616, published in the *Eighth Book of Madrigals*, 1619;[39] *Il Ballo*[40] ('Movete al mio bel suon'), published in the *Canti Guerrieri* of the *Eighth Book of Madrigals*, 1638, conjointly with the *Combattimento*; and finally, the oratorio with scene and action, *Combattimento di Tancredi e Clarinda*, to words from Tasso's *Gerusalemme liberata*, which had already been performed at the Palazzo Mocenigo in 1624. Of these three works, the two ballets must be considered as minor compositions in which Monteverdi manifestly enjoyed responding to the stimuli he had received from the French dance music he had heard during the journey to Flanders in 1599. Yet one of the letters already mentioned as having been written by Monteverdi to the librettist of *Tirsi e Clori* contains an extremely enlightening indication as to the flexibility of his printed list of orchestral instruments.[41] The ballet bears the indicative sub-title 'Concertato con voci et instrumenti'. In the score itself, mention is made of two chitarroni (bass lutes) which can be replaced by two spinets. The actual ballet section bears the necessary indication 'Seguita il Ballo a 5 con instrumenti e voci, Concertato e Adagio'. Monteverdi's letter amplifies the 'instrumentarium' of the work and supplies convincing proof that his compositions called for a colourful assembly of orchestral instruments, even in instances where the scoring was apparently for very modest forces. In this letter, Monteverdi demanded a chitarrone and a clavicembalo as accompaniment for his sung and danced ballet; but where the women singers played the instruments at the same time (note the eventual implications and the many possibilities of these avowed experimental directions!), harps instead of bass lutes might be used for accompanying. For the 'Ballo' section of the ballet, described as 'istrumenti a 5', Monteverdi required eight viole da brazzo, one contrabass, a small spinet, 'and if there could be two small lutes, it would be beautiful'. Thus, no fewer than twelve instruments were needed, none of which is listed in the original score.

Despite its small proportions, the Tasso-Scene, *Combattimento*, may well be highly valued as one of Monteverdi's most vital new creations in music-drama. It deserves an exhaustive appreciation, even within the limited scope of this cursory survey of his complete works. It is significant that Monteverdi builds up the paradigmatic example of a new style of musical expression upon the words of a poet who,[42] in unique manner, 'esprime con ogni proprietà et naturalezza con la sua orazione *quelle passioni* . . .'.[43] In his programmatic foreword to the *Eighth Book of Madrigals* of 1638, wherein the *Combattimento* of 1624 first appeared in print, Monteverdi draws attention to the creative importance in style of this work inspired by Tasso, which places the 'stile concitato' (the musical expression of passionate agitations) for the first time side by side with the type of 'stile molle e temperato' (the gentle and tempered style) already employed by earlier masters. According to Monteverdi, these three varieties of style correspond to the fundamental passions of the soul: 'Ira, Temperanza e Humiltà' (Anger, Equability and Humility). The passion of anger, which Monteverdi considers to have been neglected by his predecessors, demands new symbols in sound and a new basic rhythmical character. On the score of aesthetic considerations derived from Plato and Boethius he finds the last-named in the 'tempo veloce' of the pyrrhic metre of classical antiquity. Expressed in the rhythmic proportions of his own period it becomes:

In the substitution of the sixteenfold, agitated repeated notes for the slow semibreve ○ Monteverdi perceives a representation of 'the agitation of anger'. This new effect of rapidly repeated notes, which he dignifies as the symbol of passion is, however, nothing more than the string *tremolo* so well known to us to-day as to be hackneyed ♪; the commonplace of dramatic situations in any type of music. With this device, to which Monteverdi alludes with justifiable pride, and which, as originally interpreted, caused more hilarity than it won appreciation, a second device is associated; one no less important, but to-day likewise a commonplace: the *pizzicato*, which emerges for the first time in practical composition to illustrate the clashing sounds of the two warriors in the *Combattimento*.[44] Monteverdi explains the choice of verses 52–68 of Canto XII of *Gerusalemme liberata* on the grounds of their adaptability as the basis of a musical interpretation of two opposing passions 'War—Prayer and Death'.[45] In the preface issued together with the actual score in 1638 Monteverdi describes the details and the practical conditions of the original performance during Carnival, 1624, which was given before a selected audience that was deeply moved. According to this prefatory note the first performance took place in a gallery of the Palazzo Mocenigo.

The singers acted in costumes and masks and Tancred dismounted from a 'Cavallo Mariano'. The 'testo' (narrator), upon whom devolved the principal vocal part, stood outside the field of dramatic action, like the evangelist in the Baroque Passion. The orchestra was composed of a quartet of viols supported by contrabass and harpsichord, and the string parts were written out by Monteverdi for the first time in a complete, continuous quartet texture which embodied many original directions for performance. It was the birth of the modern string-quartet score and of the violin-technique of a new age!

The action of this strange, hybrid creation—half opera, half oratorio, intermingled with elements of the cantata style—is briefly as follows: Tancred, the renowned crusader and hero of the campaign against the infidels, meets Clorinda, the wild, heathen amazon, beyond the ramparts of the city. A fierce altercation leads to a twice repeated combat. Clorinda sinks mortally wounded to the ground, and dying, acknowledges Christ as her saviour. She forgives her vanquisher and begs him to christen her before she expires. She dies a Christian with the words, 'The heavens are opening, I go hence in peace'. The two combatants have to sing only a few characteristic passages, which Monteverdi selected with unusual dramaturgical skill and understanding from Tasso's narrative verses. His free, but conscientious treatment of Tasso's original text affords an opportunity of looking thoroughly into the opera-dramatist's workshop. It is also indicative of the advanced position of the work that Monteverdi expressly forbids the 'testo' all arbitrary ornamentation (with the exception of one purely contemplative stanza) so that the poetic word may be rightly apprehended in its relationship to the music. In other respects, too, the *Combattimento* is a mine of information regarding the grammar of a new, revolutionary style of expression. For instance, the galloping of the horses as the combatants approach is implicit in the tonal symbols of a rhythmical leitmotive, 'Motto del Cavallo'. For every phase of passionate emotion, from the interpretation of warlike fury to ecstatic mystical transports, Monteverdi's music coins apt sounds for their symbolic expression. Even to-day, we still find them profoundly stirring. It is in this respect, rather than in the interesting novelties in 'Aufführungspraxis',* that the imperishable worth of the composition resides.

THE LATE VENETIAN OPERAS, 1639–42

Monteverdi's manifold operatic production which has, however, come down to us in such fragmentary condition, falls easily into three creative periods clearly divided from one another and each standing under the aspect of a completely different style.

The first period, with *Orfeo*, *Arianna* and the *Ballo dell'Ingrate*, represents the last constructive synthesis of the Renaissance 'Intermedium' with the results of Florentine monody. The second, extending from about 1616 (*Tirsi e Clori*) until 1630 (*Proserpina rapita*), stands under the aspect of the momentous change in style from the 'Zufalls' orchestra of the humanistic period to the well-balanced accompanying orchestra of strings associated with the Baroque opera. Only one single work, the Tasso-Scene *Combattimento* remains. Its four-part texture of viols forms the basis of sonority for the approaching period of enhanced opera production. From 1630 until 1639 no operatic work by Monteverdi can be authenticated. The master withdrew, as he says,[46] further and further from the environment of the theatre by reason of his occupation with the liturgical works he was commissioned to

* See Glossary: 'Aufführungspraxis'.

write. He was engaged upon his great theoretical work, *Melodia,* the outcome of which has been preserved in the revolutionary conception of style in the *Eighth Book of Madrigals,* 1638.

Monteverdi's third period as a composer of operas owes its existence to the impetus afforded by Venetian delight in opera, which was evidently influenced by Roman taste for the theatre and which found easily perceptible expression in the opening between 1637 and 1650 of the first public opera-houses in Europe. In 1637 the Teatro Tron di San Cassiano was inaugurated, as the first opera-house open to the public, with a Roman company in a performance of B. Ferrari's *Andromeda* with music by F. Manelli (*c.* 1595–1670).[47] During the following years, the opera-houses of SS. Giovanni e Paolo (Grimano) and S. Moisé came into existence. Monteverdi, now seventy-two years of age, appeared once more before the Venetian public, as the powerful rival of his gifted pupil, F. Cavalli, with five operas, among which, unfortunately, only the last two have survived: *Il Ritorno d'Ulisse in Patria,* 1641, and *L'Incoronazione di Poppea,* 1642. In these late works Monteverdi appears on a level of style which differs entirely from that of the *Combattimento.* The important reduction of the Renaissance orchestra to the nucleus of strings supported by theorboes and harpsichord has been accomplished, and the pathos of the early Roman operas, the buffo elements of Roman and Venetian musical comedy, the heroic essays of Cavalli and Ferrari-Manelli have visibly influenced the ever-young and resilient veteran. Monteverdi's late style bears the marks of the da capo aria which had shed its *arioso* elements; the buffo duet; the concise orchestral ritornelli; recitative of a freer, more declamatory style and finally the reduction of the operatic chorus and of the *akzessorische Pointenkolorit.**[48] The opera *L'Adone* (libretto by Paul Vendramin after the poem by G. B. Marini),[49] first performed on 21 December 1639 at the Teatro SS. Giovanni e Paolo, and several times repeated during Carnival, 1640,[50] and the revival of the Mantuan *Arianna* at S. Moisé, 1639–40, were succeeded by three important works: *Le nozze d'Enea con Lavinia* (libretto by G. Badoaro)[51] at SS. Giovanni e Paolo; *Il Ritorno d'Ulisse* (libretto likewise by Badoaro) at S. Cassiano, and the ballet *La vittoria d'Amore* composed for the wedding celebrations of the Duke Odoardo Farnese.[52] Lastly in the autumn of 1642, the original performance of *L'Incoronazione* (after the text by G. F. Busenello) took place at SS. Giovanni e

* See Glossary: 'Akzessorisches Pointenkolorit'.

Paolo. Hardly a year later Monteverdi died at the age of seventy-six. In 1644 his *Proserpina rapita* (now lost) was reinstated in the repertory at S. Moisé, as was the *Incoronazione* at SS. Giovanni e Paolo in 1646. After 1650 Monteverdi's name disappeared from the annals of Venetian dramatic history.

.   .   .   .   .

Il Ritorno d'Ulisse in Patria, the first of the two late operas still extant, has remained the despair of Monteverdian research until the present day. Having up till 1881 been regarded as lost, like the majority of the music-dramas of the master's Venetian period, it was identified that year by W. Ambros in a manuscript in the Vienna State Library[53] as a presumable work by Monteverdi[54] on the grounds of certain earlier statements by R. G. Kiesewetter. As the manuscript lacked both title-page and author's name it had been classified as an 'unknown opera'. The great divergence between this manuscript and the extant libretto by Badoaro (the Vienna MS. has three acts, but Badoaro's libretto five) led E. Vogel[55] to declare that the Vienna MS. was not identical with the opera by Monteverdi which had been performed during Carnival in Venice, 1641, at the Teatro San Cassiano. On the other hand, H. Goldschmidt[56] acknowledged the opera as an indubitable work of the composer. From then onwards the *Ritorno* was considered genuine, an opinion which resulted in two important reprints of the Vienna manuscript.[57] Renewed doubts as to the authenticity of the work have been alleged in recent years by Italian scholars. Thus, D. de Paoli (in a letter to the present writer) maintains that the Vienna MS. dates from the eighteenth century and cannot therefore be considered either an autograph or a contemporary copy. On the contrary, he associates it with the (lost) *Ulisse* opera of 1630 by Monteverdi and Manelli[58] and mentions the possibility that fragments of the music of this older *Ulisse* composition might have been transferred to the score for Venice. This argument is all the more plausible, as between 1639 and 1642 Monteverdi completed no fewer than five new operatic works, an almost superhuman feat for a man in his seventies, which encourages the supposition that the master may have wanted to lighten his tremendous task by taking over material from earlier compositions. Perhaps one may go even further than de Paoli and surmise that the Venetian *Ulisse* of 1641 (provided that the Vienna MS. really reflects Monteverdi's conception) came into being with the assis-

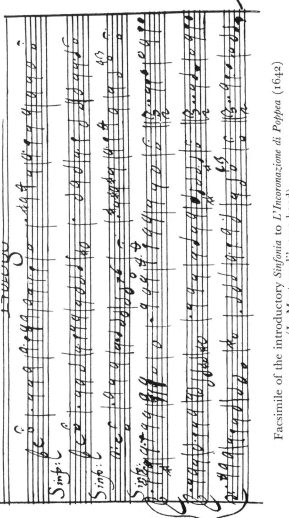

Facsimile of the introductory *Sinfonia* to *L'Incoronazione di Poppea* (1642)
(In Monteverdi's own hand)

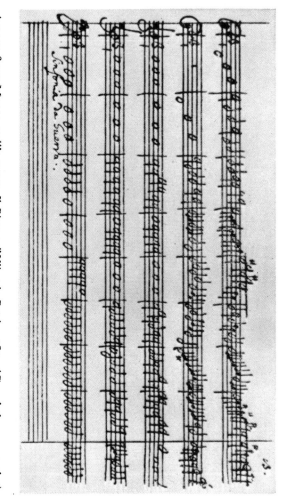

A page from Monteverdi's opera *Il Ritorno d'Ulisse in Patria*, 1641 (Copyist's manuscript)

tance of a younger colleague. That would furnish an artistic and psychological explanation of the inequalities in style which inevitably obtrude themselves in the Vienna MS. During the course of this survey we have often had occasion to observe that Monteverdi composed in conjunction with other musicians. In the instance of *Arianna*, G. Peri's collaboration has for long been (wrongly) presumed; in Andreini's *Maddalena*, that of Salomone Rossi, Muzio Effrem and A. Guivizzani[59] has been proved, and in the instances of *Adone* and *Delia e l'Ulisse*, Manelli's active participation, if not exclusive authorship, is a possibility. It is therefore not out of the question that Monteverdi allowed a younger assistant to complete parts of the Venetian *Ulisse*. In this connexion one's thoughts turn involuntarily to Süssmayer who, at Mozart's wish, completed the secco recitatives for *La Clemenza di Tito*.

In opposition to this, there is the theory put forward by G. F. Malipiero,[60] that the variants in the Vienna MS. represent alterations which may even have been undertaken by Monteverdi himself for a performance in Vienna (which cannot, however, be proved as having taken place).

In view of the doubtful authenticity of this work, a detailed analysis is probably unnecessary.[61] The conventional aspect of Badoaro's libretto, which is based on Cantos XIII to XXIV of the *Odyssey*, recalls other Venetian libretti of this period (lifeless mythological characters who delay, rather than hasten the action; burlesque figures such as the clown, Iro), but it is lacking in the constringency and the concentrated climax of a work like Busenello's *Incoronazione* libretto. The musical workmanship so strongly recalls that of the *Incoronazione* in all the diversity of its melodic inspiration that a minute description can be dispensed with in these pages.[62] Here and there one finds a highly developed recitative which often approaches pure *arioso* (with almost *un*figured basses); now and then, musical climaxes in dramatic monologues (such as Penelope's solo in Act I with the refrain *Torna, torna*, of leitmotive character, and Ulisse's first monologue in Act I, Scene 7); occasionally, short, pregnant symphonies and ritornelli, which culminate in the *Sinfonia da Guerra* indebted to the *Madrigali Guerrieri* of the *Eighth Book of Madrigals*, and are mostly written in five-parts. More exact directions for the scoring are lacking in the Vienna MS. as completely as they are in the manuscript of the *Incoronazione*.

The recent performance of the *Ritorno d'Ulisse*, during the

'Maggio Florentino' in 1942, in a new practical arrangement by
L. Dallapiccola[63] and under the direction of M. Labroca,[64] has
reopened the arguments for and against the authenticity of the
work. In particular, an article by G. Benvenuti, the excellent
Monteverdi specialist recently deceased,[65] which sets out to prove
the spuriousness of the work by means of intrinsic, aesthetic and
psychological reasoning, makes it difficult to maintain the uncritical
attitude of earlier Monteverdian research. And yet it is just as
difficult not to associate Monteverdi's creative fancy with such
pieces as Penelope's monologue (quite obviously a worthy descendant of the *Arianna-Lamento*), or frankly popular little songs, like
Iro's solo (Act III, Scene 1), which recall the canzonettas of the last
Books of Madrigals, or colourful arias as, for instance, Minerva's
solo 'Fiamma e l'ira' (Act III Scene 6) which all contain the same
kind of 'motive-ideogram' (to use Dallapiccola's apt term) as do
so many of Monteverdi's illustrative madrigals, e.g.

Fia - - - - - - ma e l'-ira

A proof of the authenticity, at least of Iro's comic air 'O dolor'
(Act III, Scene 1), may be seen in the quotation by Monteverdi of
his own *ciacona* bass from the duet 'Zefiro torna' (also used by
Schütz in *Symphoniae Sacrae II*), which dominates portions of this
scene and accompanies Iro's tragi-comic outburst 'Chi lo consola'.

„Ritorno d'Ulisse" (1641) Act III/i

etc.

Nineteenth-century music historians scheduled *L'Incoronazione
di Poppea* as lost. Not until 1888 was the score discovered by Taddeo Wiel under the deceptive title *Nerone,* and after comparison
with Busenello's printed libretto, identified beyond doubt.[66] The
Library of San Marco owns two versions of Busenello's libretto:
one, in manuscript, which Monteverdi ostensibly used while he
was composing the work, although it differs in many decisive points
from the text comprised in the written copy of the score; the other,

a printed edition of 1656.[67] Only one scenario was already in
print in 1643.[68] In a brief note, entitled 'argomento', the contents
of which do not tally exactly with the actual sequence of events
listed in the index to the printed edition of 1656, Busenello mentions the *Annals* of Tacitus as his historical source.[69] The Venetian
manuscript score was never printed.[70] A second manuscript of the
music was found by G. Gasperini in Naples in 1930.[71] This
manuscript differs from the Venetian manuscript in many respects,
principally in including a large number of additional new instrumental symphonies as well as new versions of several important
vocal items.[72] The contents of Busenello's libretto,[73] apparently
taken from Book XIV of the *Annals* of Tacitus, places the Emperor
Nero's love for Poppea, the wife of Ottone, in the centre of the
plot. Their mutual passion passes the bounds of convention.
Ottone is dispatched by subterfuge to Lusitania (this is one of the
foregone conclusions of the plot); the position of Nero's rightful
wife, Ottavia, is seriously threatened. During the course of the
action Poppea finally rejects the love of Ottone who has returned
secretly, and forces Nero to the decision to put away his wife on the
grounds of her childlessness. Admonitions which Nero's former
tutor Seneca dares to utter, result in a tyrannical command to
commit suicide. Ottavia incites Ottone, whose feelings of love and
honour are outraged, to murder Poppea. With the help of Drusilla,
a confidante of Poppea's who loves Ottone, the latter creeps into
Poppea's garden at night, disguised in the former's clothes.
The sleeping Poppea is protected by Amor (a *deus ex machina*)
from the fatal stab of the dagger. Drusilla, Ottone's accomplice,
is at first taken captive, but Ottone saves her from the death sentence
by acknowledging his own and Ottavia's guilt. Nero pardons
Ottone and Drusilla, repudiates Ottavia and on the very same
day has Poppea crowned Empress in the midst of his court. An
impassioned love-duet between the Imperial couple concludes
the work, in which the often sensational happenings in the plot
are interwoven with entries of allegorical personages and figures
of deities, as well as with burlesque interludes of comic minor
characters.

The peculiarities in Busenello's poem[74] which strike us in
particular may be recognized to-day as concessions to the very
definite taste of Venetian theatre-goers. First and foremost, the
bulk of the interpolated scenes of gods and allegorical personages
(Fortuna, Virtù, etc.), which, as descendants of the Euripidean-

Roman tragedy, are already well known from the humanistic
environment of Striggio's and Monteverdi's *Favola d'Orfeo*. But
the last-named operatic mystery, the action of which takes place in a
mythical past, had already afforded an opportunity of establishing
that Monteverdi's realistic fancy was beginning to show signs of
being ill at ease in the company of divinities. The same holds
good in greater degree in this last work of the composer's old age,
in which the mythical scenes have become a stumbling-block to
his inspiration. But mythical and slumber scenes (*Incoronazione*,
Act II) were indispensable to the enjoyment of Venetian opera.
The abrupt introduction, too, of burlesque minor characters into
the course of the drama, the obvious method of securing amusing
improvisatory acting in the sense of the traditional 'commedia
dell' arte' (exemplified here in the scene with the page and the dam-
sel, the 'comic' old woman, the mocking of the philosopher Seneca
by the impertinent page), is due essentially to the dictates of contemporary taste. Whether the example of Rospigliosi's and Landi's
Roman opera *San Alessio* with its comic interludes, or that of
the contemporary Spanish theatre should be held the more responsible for this phenomenon must remain undecided. It may be
taken for granted that the disguise-scene of *Poppea* in particular
is derived from Spanish models. The singing of the men's parts
by male sopranos (and at that time, women's parts, too, were sung
by men) and the deception it necessitated in the timbre of the
singing voice were also highly favourable to the expedient of
disguise in the clothing of the opposite sex. As an ever-growing
antipathy towards 'madrigalism' was making itself felt in the 1620's
the madrigal element took refuge in the ample folds of the libretto's
robes. Kretzschmar calls attention to the borrowing of whole
sections, word for word, from Petrarch and the Renaissance poets
as well as from Virgil and Horace in Busenello's erudite libretto.[75]
Another significant factor in the contemporary history of the Venetian opera is to be seen in the increasing lack of enthusiasm for
the chorus which, in *Poppea*, results in the almost complete exclusion of this element of sonority. If older observers, like Kretzschmar, are still inclined to ascribe these facts to aesthetic
considerations by alluding to the increasing unpopularity of the
madrigal and the invasion by comic elements, and by regarding the
allegorical figures as a kind of substitute for the chorus, modern
opinion inclines to the view that economic difficulties in the running
of this first private theatrical enterprise must have been primarily

responsible for the reduction of the chorus. The Teatro SS. Giovanni e Paolo seems to have been the first to dispense with the chorus,[76] whereas the San Cassiano and the San Moisé were still employing choruses at the beginning of the 1640's.

The essential alterations to which Monteverdi submitted Busenello's libretto while he composed the music comply throughout with the conditions just mentioned as existing during the period in question. He omitted to compose six sections of the libretto, two of which were complete scenes. Particularly characteristic are the manifold alterations in the closing scene which culminated, in the libretto of 1656, in an apotheosis of the pair of lovers by Venus, Amor and a chorus of cupids. Monteverdi wrote music only for the words of Amor and Venus (with cuts), but left the choral parts uncomposed.[77] He subsequently changed his mind and eliminated the gods altogether from the closing scene. In their place he put the magnificent final duet 'Pur ti miro', the words of which are not to be found in Busenello's libretto and are apparently attributable to Monteverdi himself.[78]

The music of the *Incoronazione* has been subjected a number of times already to thorough critical appreciation in respect of the creative quality of its form, its wealth of harmony, its melodic diversity and original ingenuity in utilizing the technique of the leitmotive.[79] As regards its relationship to the libretto, the precise distinction between recitative, ritornello and aria is already unequivocally accomplished. The aria displays a marked preference for the *da capo* form with clear-cut demarcation of the verses by the insertion of the orchestral ritornello, by which means Riemann's 'Devise'* (the opening of the verse artificially interrupted by the repeat of the ritornello) and ₁rhythmical variation (triple time disguised as $\frac{4}{4}$ in Amor's 'O schiocchi, o frali', II, 13) are already demonstrated. The duet, which occurs with great frequency (and the aria, too), shows a decided predilection for the support of passacaglia basses or basses evolved in *ostinato* style. The buffo-duet 'Valletto-Damigella' ('Sento un certo', II, 5), the Mozartian quality of which astonished Kretzschmar, is music of the definitely four-bar *Lied* period and clearly anticipates the style of the later Neapolitan opera. In strophic songs, as, for instance, in the duet between Poppea and Ottone at the end of Act I, Monteverdi produces an abundance of contrast by means of melodic variation over a ground bass which remains unchanged. The *basso corrente*

* See Glossary: 'Devise'.

of the later elaborately figured music of the Handelian period is foreshadowed in the amazing section 'Chi professa virtù' (Prologue to Act I). By comparison with the composer's earlier music-dramas, the lack of choral and madrigalian parts (an exception being Seneca's death-scene, II, 3) is particularly noticeable, as is also the extreme moderation in the use of coloratura, which is restricted to gods and allegorical personages.

In both the manuscripts, the extent of the orchestral collaboration is left in doubt. The same absence of orchestral indications is noticeable here as in the *Ritorno d'Ulisse*. The exact collaboration of any 'fundamental instruments', too, can merely be conjectured.[80] The Venetian manuscript of the *Incoronazione* contains only fourteen *sinfoniae* or *ritornelli*, mostly written in two- or three-parts. Compared with the consistent five-part writing in the orchestral symphonies of the almost contemporary *Ritorno*, such economy seems to indicate that Monteverdi felt a certain creative antipathy towards this province of sound which may have been exaggerated by the meagre instrumental resources now known to have been available at the Teatro Grimano. In the Naples manuscript, however, all the symphonies are carefully written out in four-parts, and while retaining the fundamental bass of the 1642 score, often give rise to fresh realizations.

As regards the authenticity of the Venetian manuscript, G. Benvenuti's valuable researches[81] make it quite clear that no fewer than four copyists were engaged upon it and that Monteverdi himself made emendations to their work. The master's numerous interpolations, the longest of which is probably the introductory symphony, have been painstakingly identified by Benvenuti and recognized as having been made after the performance of 1642. Those corrections by Monteverdi which he particularly specifies, therefore represent the master's 'last words', and make it impossible to continue to give credence to the drastic alterations in the Naples manuscript. The fact that the manuscripts of both Monteverdi's late operas, after having for many years been considered as his original autographs, must now irrevocably be acknowledged as copyists' productions, is one of the disappointments called forth by the more reliable and practical methods of present-day musicology.[82]

CHAPTER XII

THE CHURCH MUSICIAN[1]

COMPARED with the organically continuous evolution of the madrigals and the opera, the works Monteverdi composed in the category of church-music at first sight present an irreconcilable dissension in the fundamentals of their style. Whereas the madrigalist strove unceasingly to achieve his aims in remodelling the cantata on monodic lines and in creating the dramatically expressive solo-song which had thrown off the yoke of motet-like polyphony; and whereas the opera-composer led the newly created 'Dramma per Musica' out of the experimental uncertainty of the Florentine 'Camerata' and the improvisatory atmosphere of the Renaissance 'Intermedium' into the closed dramaturgic circle of the Venetian opera, the liturgical composer's production displays the problematic aspect of an absolutely implacable contradiction in style, a stylistic duality which must be a unique phenomenon in the history of art. If one glances at this work of a whole lifetime in the sphere of church-music (still almost intact, in acute contrast to the operatic works which have been handed down in such fragmentary condition), one discovers that, as a liturgical musician, Monteverdi composed to the end of his days in *two* species of style which were, by intention, widely divergent from one another. In conformity with these two categories of style which he named 'Prima' and 'Seconda Prattica', the church compositions may be divided into two completely opposite halves which, in point of their antitheses in Monteverdi's life-work, never succeeded in becoming conclusively reconciled in a creative compromise. By 'Prima Prattica' Monteverdi understands the older art of polyphonic music-making which was inaugurated by Ockeghem and brought to its highest pitch by Adrian Willaert: the splendidly enhanced linear art wherein 'music was not the servant, but the mistress of the words'.[2] In the 'Seconda Prattica', however, the long suppressed emotional content of the enslaved words breaks through with elemental force. It is the art of psychographical understanding of the words in the manner already foreshadowed in the *Musica Riservata* of the sixteenth century:[3] it is the modern style which began with Cyprian de Rore and reached its climax in the representatives of the Florentine 'Camerata' who aimed at the consummation of the 'melodia' and made poetic speech the mistress of the music.[4] In the historically important preface to the *Fifth Book of Madrigals*, 1605, Monteverdi announces the appearance of a theoretical treatise, *Seconda Prattica, ovvero Perfettione della moderna Musica*, which title, alone, expresses a clearly defined programme of the politics of art. The writing of this treatise did not come to fruition, any more than did that of the treatise, *Melodia*, on the philosophy of music, which he planned towards 1630.[5] But in the *Dichiarazione della Lettera stampata nel V Libro de' suoi Madrigali* published as a supplement to the *Scherzi Musicali* of 1607 Monteverdi proffered, through the pen of his brother, Giulio Cesare, a commentary on musical history and the psychology of style which proved how profoundly conscious he was of his unique historical position as an intermediary between two epochs. For the first time in the history of music a great creative genius realized that an epoch of style was historically definable. From this point originates the conception, so familiar to us moderns, of 'stile antico', sensitivity to archaic music and conscious reversion to periods of evolution long since terminated. But whereas Monteverdi the madrigalist, adopting the programmatic motto 'Il moderne Compositore fabrica sopra li fondamenti della verità',[6] strove to attain a musical art of interpreting words which was to find ultimate fulfilment only in Gluck and Wagner; and whereas the opera-composer (in the psychological conception of the expression of temperament in the terms of music) added the revolutionary stylistic elements of the 'stile concitato' to the earlier stylistic category of the 'stile molle e temperato',[7] the church-musician remained captive in the permanent duality of two opposing styles, and to the end of his life composed works for the church both 'da cappella' (i.e. in the archaistic style of the Flemish-Palestrinian polyphony) and 'da Concerto' (i.e. in the sense of the modern stylistic principle of *concertante* instrumental co-operation and free monodic part-writing). It is difficult to find a satisfying explanation of this phenomenon of a division in creative consciousness and a permanent ambivalence in the style of one definite sphere of Monteverdi's production. D. de Paoli's purely historical argument,[8] that the Venetian Procurators had explicity entrusted him with the re-organization and restoration of the 'Canto polifonico' which had fallen into decay, and had thereby succeeded in intensifying his interest in liturgical music rooted in tradition, is certainly attractive in itself; but taking into consideration the dates of production of the church compositions, it does not hold good. For, as early as 1610, i.e. three years before his appointment to the Church of San Marco and while still in Mantua, Monteverdi had written two of the most strikingly contrasted compositions of his entire liturgical production and had published them in one volume: the archaistic Mass *In illo tempore* and the ultra-revolutionary *Vespers*, in which the 'stile concitato' of the Mantuan opera for the first time invaded the sacred precincts of the liturgical tradition in style. The creative disunion which this publication symbolized was therefore already in being before his position as Maestro di Cappella at San Marco obliged him to write church-music of the traditional kind. Monteverdi, who in the Mass of 1610 evinced his unrivalled skill by ingeniously assimilating the already obsolescent style of the early Flemish composers, must have been painfully aware of the results which would ensue from the penetration of theatrical and emotional elements into the sphere of pure church-music. He may have foreseen that the intrusion of the 'Seconda Prattica' and the 'Concerto' style into church-music would lead to the inevitable decay of the last-named. And he may at times have been of the same opinion as the great conservative and purist in style of a later date, Padre Martini, who in his famous *Treatise on Counterpoint*, 1775, reprinted the *Agnus Dei* from this Mass of Monteverdi's as an illuminating example of the fact that 'the great masters of music always endeavoured to write church-music in a style completely different from that of secular music'.[9] In Padre Martini's own time this aesthetic requirement was hardly more than a pious wish, far removed from reality during a period in which church-music could vie with any opera buffa in the matter of 'Galanterie'.[10] Can it be that Monteverdi shrank from the consequences of his own revolution in style, and that he was anxious to maintain the traditions of the venerable 'Prima Prattica', at least in liturgical music? The solution of this problem will still call for great exertions on the part of artistic and psychological research for many years to come.

Monteverdi's church-music, apart from the works of his early youth, was assembled and issued in three large collective publications: in the publication of 1610, which contains the Mass *In illo tempore*, the *Vespers of the Virgin Mary* consisting of twelve separate movements, and the two Magnificats; in the *Selva Morale e Spirituale* of 1641, an important compilation of forty compositions of liturgical character and of the most diverse types of style, the last publication to be supervised by the master himself; and lastly, in the *opus posthumum* entitled *Messa a quattro e Salmi* by the editor, A. Vincenti, Monteverdi's printer, who in 1651, seven years after Monteverdi's death, brought out this volume containing fifteen important liturgical works, differentiated widely in style and in date of composition, which were now published for the first time.

In addition, there are nineteen pieces of church-music which were issued during Monteverdi's lifetime by other musicians in various collections, mostly between 1615 and 1627. Only in the instances of the youthful sacred works and the publication of 1610 do the dates of publication correspond at all closely with the period at which the compositions themselves were produced. The later collective volumes of 1641 and 1651 bring together works which can be authoritatively assigned to the most contrasted periods of Monteverdi's production.[11] For this reason it seems more appropriate to discuss the composer's church-music according to its structural type than to follow the deceptive chronological order of the complete publications. The principal categories of his liturgical works which will now be referred to are as follows:

1. Masses.
2. *Concertante* movements for the Ordinary of the Mass.
3. Other liturgical compositions of cyclic character (*Vespers, Magnificat*).
4. *Concertante* Psalms and Hymns.
5. Motets in many parts.
6. Solo-Motets (sacred Monodies) and 'Duets'.
7. Sacred Madrigals.

Monteverdi's earliest sacred works, composed and published at a long distance of time from the main body of his liturgical music, will be treated first of all and made the starting-point of this whole survey of the compositions from the aspect of style-criticism.

Two collective publications of this type may be named: the *Sacrae Cantiunculae* of 1582 and the *Madrigali Spirituali* of 1583 which, together with their secular sister, the opus 3 of 1584, *Canzonette a tre voci*, represent the youthful beginnings of the creative musician. Only two of these three publications are preserved intact. Monteverdi's opus 2, the *Madrigali Spirituali a 4*, is lost except for the part-book of the 'Basso', and for this reason must be excluded from an analysis of its style until such time as the other three part-books may have been recovered.[12] Nevertheless the extant bass-part, which contains a preface and an index of contents, affords a certain degree of insight into the type of layout of this work, which originated in a style very similar to the other two early works and is much the same in extent.[13] Even superficial consideration obliges one to reflect that these early works signify much more than the needlessly modest titles the young composer bestowed upon them lead one to surmise. Far from being 'immature and insipid first-fruits',[14] these youthful works of the 'egregii Ingegneri discipulo' display an amazing degree of technical maturity within the bounds of the traditional technique of composition, and in this respect they need fear no comparison, for instance, with the works of the fifteen-year-old Mozart. With the three-part *a cappella* motets of the *Sacrae Cantiunculae* of 1582,[15] composed to texts from the scriptures and from the *Breviarium Romanum* young Claudio perpetuated his precocity of thought and his good judgement in the finest manner conceivable. As yet there was no trace of revolutionary propensities in the direction of new regions of monodic, colourfully expressive 'Musica moderna'. The youthful works of the years 1582–4 came into being at the midday bloom of the Renaissance. Palestrina and Orlandus Lassus dominated the scene with their prodigious musical creations, Marenzio and Giovanni Gabrieli were just beginning to penetrate the surface, and Ingegneri and Costanzo Porta were at the zenith of their creative powers. Opera and monody were as yet unborn. Ten years later everything was to change, and the superb musical structure of early Flemish polyphony was to be shaken to its foundations.

The same year, 1594, that saw the deaths of Palestrina and Lassus also saw the birth of the Florentine 'Camerata'[16] and the rise of Monteverdi, the Mantuan violist and author of the *Third Book of Madrigals*, to the position of 'Cantore'. Of this multitude of events, the *Cantiunculae* foreshadow as little as do, apparently, the kindred *Madrigali Spirituali* of the succeeding year. The constructive principle of imitative, interlocking part-writing, as expounded by Marc' Antonio Ingegneri in his sacred and secular compositions published not long before,[17] dominates the twenty-three numbers in this volume almost in their entirety. The same kind of traditional, motet-like technique in the dovetailing of the vocal parts, which so convincingly forms the opening of No. 1, prevails in the greater number of the pieces of this publication,

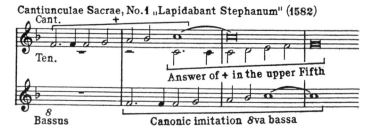

Cantiunculae Sacrae, No. 1 „Lapidabant Stephanum" (1582)

Only seldom, as in No. 10, 'O magnum pietatis', does one come across a half-hearted attempt to build up the tonal structure in chordal, homophonic style. Similar enclaves of harmonies only are already to be found in the sacred music of Palestrina, Jacobus Gallus (Handl) and Ingegneri, and Monteverdi's bars can therefore hardly be appraised as indicative of future innovations in style. Between the publication of the *Madrigali Spirituali* in 1583 and the composition of Monteverdi's next piece of church-music there is an interval of twenty-seven years. This figure is no approximate assumption, but is demonstrable by means of biographical facts. From about 1590 Monteverdi was in the service of the Duke of Mantua as violist, cantor, and after 1602, as 'Maestro della Musica'. His preserve was the court, whereas Ludovico Viadana, the founder of modern General Bass technique, was Maestro di Cappella at Mantua Cathedral. Practical stimuli to the composition of liturgical works hardly presented themselves to Monteverdi who, from 1607 onwards, was overwhelmed with commissions for operas, and who had to accompany the Duke on his campaigns in Hungary and Flanders between 1595 and 1599.[18] The master evidently did not feel drawn to the composition of church-music until he had passed through the inferno of the years 1607–8. From a contemporary letter[19] we know that he was actually engaged during 1610 in composing the Mass *In illo tempore* and the *Vespers of the Virgin Mary*, and that he took the manuscript with him to Rome, hoping it might be instrumental in securing the interest of Pope Paul V in his own career. The outward impetus to the resumption of liturgical composition may have been the thought of the future influential patron—who was, however, so bitterly to disappoint him. The inner prompting is undoubtedly to be sought in the spiritual emotions attendant upon the deaths of those dear to him; emotions which rendered the master, always inclined to melancholy, particularly susceptible to religious experiences.

Henceforward, the threads of Monteverdi's liturgical music were never again to be severed.

THE MASSES

Taking the three monumental works in this category into consideration, it is no longer possible to-day to support the opinion still expressed by P. Wagner[20] that Monteverdi applied himself only incidentally to the writing of Masses—an opinion which echoes the harsh judgement on Monteverdi first expressed by C. v. Winterfeld in 1834,[21] then by a remark of G. Verdi's in a letter dated 1887,[22] and perpetuated up to the present day.[23] These three Masses:[24] (A) *In illo tempore*, 1610, (B) *Messa a 4 da cappella*, 1641, and (C) *Messa a 4 da cappella*, 1651,[25] must be accorded the same central position in his lifework as must, for instance, Anton Bruckner's three Masses in his. They bear witness for Monteverdi as the guardian of powerful traditions. The Mass that undoubtedly goes furthest in this respect is the first, (A), intended for the Pope in 1610, which may be classed as a 'Parodie' Mass,* a type fast becoming antiquated at that time. The work, which clings fanatically to an Ionian C major, except for two startlingly effective sections in the remote key of E major which intensify the mystical character of the words 'Et incarnatus' and 'Benedictus', is constructed upon ten motives (Monteverdi called them 'fughe') from the motet *In illo tempore* by the Fleming Nicolas Gombert (d. *c.* 1560). It is written for six-part choir, a number which in itself precludes the technique of the Venetian double-choir after the manner of the two Gabrielis and B. Pallavicino but which is ideal for strict polyphonic writing. The only concession to the 'Zeitgeist' is the added seventh part of the Basso Continuo, which lacks any independent function and is simply an organ accompaniment representing the lowest vocal part at any given time. But even in this austere work, haunted by the spirit of the early Flemings and abounding in canonic imitations and contrapuntal combinations, Monteverdi the magician in tone-colouring produces remarkable contrasts in colour-effects with the four-part *Crucifixus* (evidently to be sung without the organ accompaniment), as he does also with the seven-part *Agnus Dei* of the final section.

The other two Masses (B) and (C) are more modest in the vocal

* See Glossary: 'Parodie Messe'.

texture but no less sublime in the effect of their archaism and the polyphonic treatment of the voices, which are amazingly blended. Both works are kept as simple as possible, and they could be performed without difficulty even by a very moderate choir. They are obviously the outcome of the master's long practical experience as director of the Cappella at San Marco and they necessarily embody the wishes of the Procurators who insisted that Monteverdi should revive the traditional ecclesiastical style. That Monteverdi felt the principle of the 'Prima Prattica', here in the ascendant, constituted something of a danger to the work as a whole may be seen from the curious footnotes to the original of (B), according to which, certain movements of the Mass might be 'substituted' by *concertante* insertions (set to the same words and available in the complete collection of the *Selva* published at the same time).[26] Ch. v. d. Borren has already drawn attention to the modern character of the tonality of the whole work, especially the final *Agnus Dei* which is markedly in F major.[27] The harmonic sequence in the concluding bars of (B) might be found in any church composition of the eighteenth century.

The 'insertions' proposed by Monteverdi: a *Crucifixus a 4* and an *Et resurrexit a 2* with I and II Violins obbligato,[28] both represent the 'affetuoso' style and are full of chromaticisms. The instrumental parts of the second item abound in picturesque touches of operatic character.

The third Mass (C), which was published as an opus posthumum nearly seven years after the composer's death, displays exactly the same procedure in style as does (B). Nevertheless, it is less simply laid out and it calls for great assurance in singing technique from the boys' choir for which it is quite obviously conceived. In the grandiose sweep of its flowing lines it recalls (A). The splendid climax at the words 'suscipe deprecationem', and the peculiar cross-bar rhythm of the *Amen* and *Gloria*, in particular, remind one of the sacred works which had come into being more in the spirit of the 'Seconda Prattica'. (C) is composed syllabically, just as strictly as is (B)[29] (except for the traditional vehicles of the embellishments of the Mass, such as the *Eleison* and the *Amen*): a type of setting very much in contrast to the archaistic treatment in (A). Like (B), (C) solidifies at psychological moments into harmonic sequences which run counter to the archaizing outline of the musical texture. Places such as

Messa a 4 (1651)

Ho-san - na in ex-cel - sis in ex-

would be difficult to find in the Masses of an older generation. The shaping of the Basso Continuo organ parts in all three Masses and their relationship to Viadana's innovations will be more fully discussed elsewhere.

CONCERTANTE MOVEMENTS FOR THE ORDINARY OF THE MASS

These works may be mentioned briefly at this point. They are all included in the collective volume of the *Selva*, 1641. It is necessary to refer to them, even within the bounds of this enforcedly hasty general survey, for they typify in the most striking degree the permanent state of ambivalence in style so characteristic of Monteverdi the church musician. The movements are all conceived more or less as *Offertories*; that is to say, as additional *concertante* insertions in the principal work of this publication, the *Missa a 4 da cappella*. In the instance of the *Et iterum*, a footnote of Monteverdi's[30] expressly indicates that the piece is intended to serve as an 'alternative concert-insertion' within the framework of the Mass. In accordance with an original direction as to performance, this work, as well as the three other Mass-Offertories, is to be accompanied by four trombones *or* four viols (at discretion). Such alternation in respect not only of separate portions of the Mass, but also of whole groups of instrumental instruments of different timbres, recalls the 'Zufallsorchester'* and the practical

* See Glossary: 'Zufallsorchester'.

combinations arising therefrom proposed by M. Praetorius in his
Syntagma Musicum, III, 1619.[31] The observations of H. Schütz
relating to the subject, printed in the prefaces to his oratorio
compositions,[32] must be mentioned, too, in this connexion. The
most pretentious of Monteverdi's works of the type under discussion
seems to be the long *Gloria a 7*[33] which, in addition to the fundamental support of the 'Zufallsorchester' consisting of two
violins, four viols or four trombones (and basso continuo instruments), also requires a large choir. The list of instruments for this
piece, which is composed in the stately style of the *Eighth Book of
Madrigals*, recalls in every detail the show-piece of the 'Canti
Guerrieri' printed therein: the *Altri Canti d'amor*. (Vol. VIII, 1.)
The two lists are given here side by side for comparison:

Gloria a 7 (Selva 1641)	*Altri canti d'amor* (1638)
Canto I/II	Canto + Quinto
Alto	Alto
Tenore I/II	Tenore I/II
Basso I/II	Basso
Violino I/II	Violino I/II
4 Viole da brazzo	Viola I/II
(ovvero 4 Tromboni)	Gamba
B.C.	Contrabasso
	B.C.

The use of 'curved' Baroque motives such as

Gloria a 7 (1640)

Glo - - - - - - ri-a

in both these works leads one to the conclusion that they were
composed at the same time, probably towards the date of the
completion of the *Eighth Book of Madrigals*.

OTHER LITURGICAL COMPOSITIONS OF CYCLICAL CHARACTER
(*Vespers, Magnificat*)

The revolutionary masterpiece of Monteverdi the composer of
church-music is incontestably the *Vespers of the Virgin Mary*,
which he issued in 1610 in the same publication as the Mass *In*

illo tempore.[34] Whereas the *Missa da cappella a 6 voci* upon motives from Gombert's *Motet* looked back to the formal structure of early Flemish polyphony and embodied the *a cappella* motet which towards 1610 was already considered reactionary, the *Vespers* represents the imposing attempt to fill the traditional form of the old antiphons, hymns, and canticles with the disturbing contents and revolutionary devices of the then novel, passionately expressive monody; of the operatically conceived type of instrumental music and of the new psychological treatment of music as a projection of the words. Despite the semi-official liturgical character of the work as specified in the original title, a large part of this tremendous musical creation goes far beyond the scope of the traditional liturgical composition based on motives of plainchant. First of all, the enormous length seems to break through the recognized limitations as to size. The *Vespers* itself comprises no fewer than fourteen pieces, among which are the 'Magnificat' in two versions, an 'Orchestral Sonata' of extensive dimensions, a set of choral variations on 'Ave Maris Stella', an almost operatic solo-monody 'Nigra sum', and in addition, nine more movements, the formal and instrumental constitution of which proves to be the most variegated imaginable. The exorbitant demands made by the instrumentation may also be considered a revolutionary factor in the style, even at an epoch when there was a passion for magnificence in musical sound.

'In addition to the six-part or seven-part choir which must, however, be of sufficient numerical strength to divide into an eight-part double choir in 'Ave Maris Stella', and even into a ten-part double choir in 'Nisi Dominus', the following instruments also participate: two cornetts (Zinken), three trombones, flutes, and oboes (shawms), organ and a number of differentiated groups of strings which comprise violins, viols, gambas and contrabasses. With regard to these instrumental requirements, Monteverdi had only to follow in the footsteps of his great predecessor, Giovanni Gabrieli, who with his *Sacrae Symphoniae* of 1597, had produced the model of the species.[35] In another, far more important feature of this work Monteverdi stands out as a revolutionary innovator: in the consistent employment of the orchestral ritornello as an instrumental counterpoise to the purely vocal, fauxbourdon, and choral parts of the composition. The *concertante* character of the many vocal parts also deserves to be especially mentioned. For instance, the monody 'Nigra sum' (*a voce sola*) is kept throughout in the style of the *Arianna Lamento*, and the solo part of 'Audi coelum' goes so far as to evoke the coloratura of the aria in Hades, 'Possente spirto' from *Orfeo*, 1607. Lastly, in 'Duo Seraphim', all the different methods of performance current at that time in the up-to-date *Gorgia** are in evidence in scale passages, vibrato on one note, trills, bleating trills and *groppi.**

The collective title of the original unites two entirely independent liturgical works. The addition of the 'nonnulli sacri concentus' clearly betokens the elastic character of the whole arrangement, whose fortuitous grouping together as a unit implies no further mutual obligation with regard to performance. Rather, as so often in Baroque music and its collective publications, a selective principle dictated by liturgical needs seems to have been at work here, as may apparently be deduced from the circumstances that the Magnificat appears in two (thematically related) versions.[36]

The a dacities in the instrumentation of this *Vespers*, however, appear to be surpassed in both the Magnificats, which are appended to the *Vespers* publication as an *obbligato* liturgical conclusion, and which are both founded upon the same basses and similar nuclei of motives, but with the difference that the first piece is intended for a large body of singers and players and the second for an essentially smaller number.[37] The 'Magnificat septem vocibus et sex instrumentis', whose use of plainchant motives within the framework of an entirely *concertante* operatic orchestral apparatus, and of a choir treated as a vehicle of colour-effects rather than as a polyphonic texture, stamps this piece as a culminating point in Monteverdi's entire production, is designed for a much larger body of performers than the sub-title seems to indicate. In point of fact, the original calls for many more instruments, namely: I and II violins, viola, organ and three cornetts; and in addition, two 'fiffari' (that is, shawms, forerunners of the oboe), two flutes, two trombones, two solo violins and an unspecified wind instrument (probably of the trombone type) for sustaining prolonged notes (in the 'Deposuit' section). This whole collection of instruments, evidently only sketchily indicated, needs to be sorted out into instrumental groups in a new edition for the purposes of performance.[38] The extent of the original orchestration, the boldness of the formal layout and the passionate intensity of the interpretation of the text[39] all render this Magnificat the most radical manifestation of Monteverdi's ceaseless exploration of new musical

* See Glossary.

regions within the sphere of church-music. The little *Magnificat* '*a 6 voci*', merely with organ accompaniment, the registration of which was carefully marked by Monteverdi, is a simplified 'pocket edition' of the preceding large Magnificat. It contains enchanting details, principally in the lyrical 'Sicut locutus', and deserves to be revived just as much as does its more magnificent sister-composition.[40]

Echoes of the two Magnificats published in 1610 were to be awakened much later on in Monteverdi's production by two further compositions based on the text of the 'Hymn of praise', both published for the first time in the *Selva* of 1641. Of this pair, the *Magnificat I* ('a 8 voci et 2 Violini et 4 Viole overo 4 Tromboni') proceeds in no uncertain manner still further down the path of the 'Seconda Prattica' which had been opened up in the works of 1610. Nevertheless, a difference in principle immediately distinguishes the works of the two periods. The seven-part writing of the earlier work still pointed in the direction of the polyphonic technique of the six- and seven-part writing of the archaistic Mass *In illo tempore*, whereas the eight-part writing of the later work called for the 'Al fresco' treatment of G. Gabrieli's 'cori spezzati'.* It was not for nothing that the later work originated in Venice. In it, contrapuntal antitheses are limited to the contrasting forces of the two semi-choirs, each of which is laid out independently in syllabic, chordal style and not in linear polyphony. This tendency towards the creating of large surfaces is further emphasized by a five-part body of strings which supports the alternations of the double-choir in a completely modern *concertante* manner. The superb details of workmanship in the compositions of 1610 have been fined down to a more schematic 'blanc-et-noir' style of buoyant tutti- and *concertante* 'solo'-episodes. This is a work which must have exerted a profound influence upon the Schütz of the later *Symphoniae Sacrae*. The *Magnificat II* 'a *4* voci in genere da cappella' (also included in the *Selva*) represents the contrasting type of archaistically conceived church-composition already well known to us, this time carried out entirely in the style of the *Messa a 4* in the same volume. Here and there we find the same syllabically monotonous and evenly poised linear treatment of the words, the sparse continuo part, the archaistic reduction of the vocal parts to four, the renunciation of a colourful orchestra, the absence of impassioned motives and a delight in pure Palestrinian diatonicism.

*See Glossary

K

The lack of any kind of *concertante* impulses in this work is as astonishing as is the fact that, despite its consciously archaic mien, it never produces a feeling of monotony but is, on the other hand, always touching in effect. That Monteverdi did not shrink from characteristic harshnesses, even in this lyrically contemplative sphere, is proclaimed by the parallel sevenths in the following example.

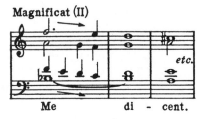

CONCERTANTE PSALMS AND HYMNS

The works in this category, which are contained in the two big publications of 1641 and 1651, are strongly reminiscent of the *concertante* Psalm-Antiphons of the *Vespers* of 1610. They are conceived much in the style of the 'sacred concertos' (in which respect they resemble the corresponding works by H. Schütz) and they call for the obbligato assistance of a three-part string orchestra and the accessory collaboration of fourfold viols or trombones in the sense of the 'Zufallsorchester' of M. Praetorius. The two eight-part 'Dixit' of the *Selva*, orchestrated in this manner, are quite obviously closely related to the splendid 'Dixit Dominus' which inaugurates the series of Psalms in the *Vespers* of 1610, except that in the pieces composed later, the intrinsic technique of composition based on 'Canti fermi' (i.e. the thematic spinning-out of actual plainchant quotations) gives way to an interpretation of the text, conceived in the spirit of the Baroque music drama.

A fivefold bass sequence such as the following, which occurs at the words 'implebit ruinas' in the first 'Dixit'

Dixit (I) (1640)

and which does not even quail before the prohibited tritone chord, demonstrates how far .Monteverdi had already advanced by this time towards an emotionally theatrical style in ecclesiastical music. Terse choral entries such as the dramatically explosive 'Tu' in the second 'Dixit' must have been decisive for the style of H. Schütz's 'Saul, Saul, why persecutest thou me' (*Symphoniae Sacrae, III*, 1650) and similar dramatic outbursts. The contrasts between the 'f' and 'p' in the original obviously influenced Carissimi. A striking fact in all three works is that all the *dramatic* words in the text, such as 'conquassabit', 'confregit', etc., are scanned according to operatic usage and are portrayed in picturesque fashion; not treated with philosophical detachment as they are, let us say, in the *Vesper Psalms* of 1610 which employs the same text. It seems to me quite certain that these compositions must have originated as *concertante* works of a later period in the same spiritual environment as the *Madrigali guerrieri ed amorosi*, i.e. in about 1638. The same holds good for the three *concertante* 'Confiteor' of the *Selva*. In the first of these pieces, strong contrasts in dynamics are obtained by the division into three *cappella* and five *ripieno* parts; in the second, the obbligato violins *divisi* in two recall sacred concertos, similarly laid out, by Schein, Scheidt and Schütz. The third piece bears the stylistic indication 'a la francese', and in its dependence upon the style of Guédron's *Airs de Cour*, is twin sister to the 'a la francese' concert-madrigals of the *Eighth Book*. It may, however, like the latter, have been written *before* 1611.[41] The exorbitant coloratura passages on 'Gloria' bring this piece into the closest possible relationship with the 'Duo Seraphim' and 'Audi Coelum' of the *Vespers* of 1610. Both the 'Beatus vir' of the *Selva*, too, are indebted to the style of the madrigal work, as is also the 'French' 'Confiteor'. The first 'Beatus' is constructed over an irregular *basso ostinato* divided into two cell-like bass motives which follow one another in irregular sequence.

„Beatus I" (1640)

As regards the technique of interlinking motives, this piece
recalls the Vesper Psalm 'Laetatus sum' of 1610. The themes of
the movements for the three-part string orchestra (including the
basso ostinato already mentioned) are identical in *every respect* with
the *concertante* Madrigal 'Chiome d'oro' (*VII Madrigal Book*, 1619),
of which this 'Beatus' appears to be an offshoot. Compare the
first four bars of the bass of each composition.[42]

„Chiome d'Oro" (1619)

„Beatus I" (1640)

A comparison of bars 9–11 in the obbligato violin parts of each
piece, too, should prove convincing as to the close correlation
between madrigal compositions and progressive liturgical music in
Monteverdi's production.

„Beatus I"

„Chiome d'Oro"

The voice parts of the two pieces, as well, reveal great similarity
in the melodic line. In the instrumental parts, however, it is a
matter of complete identity, which leads to the conclusion that
this 'Beatus I' was most probably composed before 1610.

According to directions given in the original, the five vocal parts
in the more polyphonically designed 'Beatus II' can be doubled
and sung *forte*. It is impossible in this rapid survey to discuss the
details of the other *concertante* Psalms of the *Selva*; this must be
reserved for thorough treatment in a special study.[43] But an eight-

part 'Credidi' divided between two typically Venetian semi-choirs should at least be mentioned here.

Even more copious is the yield of *concertante* Psalms and Hymns in the posthumous publication of the *Messa a 4 e Salmi* of 1651. Almost the entire volume, with the exclusion of the Mass itself and two sacred monodies, is devoted to this type of composition, to which Monteverdi obviously gave the preference while in Venice. The 'Dixit Dominus' for double choir in the *concertante* style of the *Selva* recalls G. Gabrieli in respect of its blocks of harmonies, but as regards the theatrical scansion of the declamatory rhythm in the many 'Fusae' it is related more closely to the *Madrigali Guerrieri* of the *Eighth Book*. In these particular surroundings, a *Dixi a 8 voci alla breve*, whose consistent semibreve notation and archaic texture recall the *Messa a 4* of the *Selva*, gives every appearance of being an erratic boulder. Similar tendencies of 'Prima Prattica' origin dominate sublime conceptions such as 'Laudate pueri a 5 da cappella' and 'Laetatus sum a 5', whereas in pieces like the 'Beatus Vir' and 'Laetatus sum a 5 instr. e 6 voci' which are conceived in the style of the High Baroque, all the spirits of the 'stile concitato' seem to be let loose. This is particularly so in the last piece, the thematic relationship of whose bass to that of the *Vesper Psalm* of the same name composed in 1610 I have described in full elsewhere.[44] The many ♪ and ♪ in the strings, as also the fact that it is the only piece requiring the obligatory use of the bassoon, mark it as a typical representative of the 'Seconda Prattica' in Monteverdi's church-music. The 'Nisi Dominus a 3', whose light-hearted melodic invention of dance-song type is obviously influenced by Guédron's *Airs*, can only be characterized as a sign of decadence in a church-musician before 1650. The extent of the disintegration of ecclesiastical style under operatic influences may be seen from the following picturesque passage in the madrigalian manner with the typical Baroque touch of the rising melodic line on the word 'surgite':

„Nisi Dominus" a 3 (1651)

sur-gi-te, sur-gi-te, sur-gi-te,   sur-gi-te, sur-gi-te, sur-gi-te,   *etc.*

B.C.

It is impossible to investigate all the other pieces of the post-humous volume. Nevertheless, this six-part 'Nisi Dominus' must not be left unrecorded, for its trumpet technique on 'surgite' brings it into relationship with the style of the *Madrigali Guerrieri* of 1638:

Lastly, in 'Lauda Jerusalem a 3', the leitmotive character of the harmonic progression employed conveys the effect of being very much in the manner of Schütz.[45]

Here, as elsewhere in this volume, the fascinating tone-painting on words like 'nebula', 'sparsit', increasingly supplants the poly-phonic tension of the decaying Palestrinian style. Among the pieces of motet-character first published as *Frammenti pubblicati in varie raccolte* in the Supplement to Vol. XVI of the Collected Edition, one at least should be mentioned: a six-part 'Cantate Domino', 1620, which even at this date is still built upon the typically madrigalistic progression of parallel fifths of the picturesque madrigal 'Ecco mormorar l'onde' of 1592.

MOTETS IN MANY PARTS

The works of this type which are to be found in the *Selva* of 1641 may be included here. The *Himnus* (!) 'Deus tuorum militum', wherein the wonderful interchange between the vocal and instrumental parts endows it with the character of the Baroque concerto, must at least be mentioned. The scale motive:

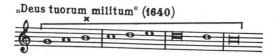

runs through the whole piece like the theme of a chaconne.

SOLO MOTETS

Two other works in the *Selva* may be included in this category. Although, in the main, they are conceived as duets, they partake essentially of the character of the concert-monody and belong to a group of compositions of which the most important are not included in the two large publications of 1641 and 1651 but are to be found as valuable independent pieces printed in collective volumes by other publishers. Of the few monodies in the *Selva* of 1641 and *Missa a 4 e Salmi* of 1651; the bass-solo 'Ab aeterno' (*Selva*, 1641) is conspicuous by reason of the tremendous leaps across wide intervals such as

Laudate Dominum (1640)

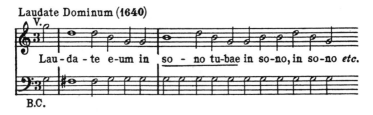

Lau - da - te e-um in   so - no tu-bae in so-no, in so-no *etc.*

B.C.

and of the coloratura passages which are indebted to the contemporary 'Gorgia' and are neck-breaking in the most exact sense of the word. The same applies to the bass-solo of the *Missa*, 1650, 'Laudate Dominum', which, with the exception of a slight alteration by means of variation in the final bars, is absolutely identical with the bass-solo of the same name[46] published in Vol. XVI of the Collected Edition among the *Frammenti pubblicati in varie raccolte*. Two 'Confiteor' of the monodic type (each a variant of the same fundamental creative idea) are of interest in respect of their obligatory parts for violin. The dynamic markings 'f-p' indicating obbligato echo-effects at the end of the second piece, especially, are among the most personal characteristics of Monteverdi's style.

Amid the eighteen sacred monodies originally printed separately and first published together by G. F. Malipiero in Vol. XVI of the Collected Edition, a few compositions stand out on account of their extreme melodic beauty and their startlingly passionate expressiveness. The others are mostly pieces of the same chaste ardour and restrained ecstasy as 'Nigra sum', 1610, the earliest of these monodies which constituted a spiritual climax in the *Vespers* of 1610. Only the 'sacred chamber-duets', 'O beatae viae', 1620, 'Venite, venite', 1624, and 'O bone Jesu', 1627, will be mentioned here, as also the Baroque *arioso* for tenor solo, 'Salve Regina', in which the range of colour depicting the emotions is derived from operatic passion (*Arianna*, 'Nigra sum'). Another tenor-aria, 'Currite, populi', 1625, comprising a refrain in dance-like triple-time with verse-sections in duple-time, might be described as a 'sacred canzonetta'. A two-part 'Sancta Maria', 1627, is based upon the same hymnal quotation as the famous 'Sonata sopra Sancta Maria' of the *Vespers* of 1610. Perhaps the most magnificent examples of the Monteverdi solo song are the two *Motetti a voce sola*, 'Jubilet, jubilet' ('a voce sola in Dialogo') and 'Laudate Dominum', both included in the *Selva* of 1641. The 'warlike' types of motive from the *Madrigali Guerrieri* force their way into the other-worldly regions of these hymns, as, for instance, at the passage:

"Ab aeterno" (1640)

e - rant   a - bis - si

and in the chromatic ecstasy of the final climax of the 'Salve Regina a 2 voci' (*Selva*, 1641):

"Salve Regina" a 2 (1640)

Monteverdi attains a climactic point in the musical shaping of the emotions, which was to be reached again by Schütz later on.[47]

The High Baroque technique of echoing rhymes and the expressive coloratura in another 'Salve Regina' ('a voce sola risposta d'ecco et due violini') recalls the 'Audi coelum' of the *Vespers,* 1610. A number of *Hinni* for solo voice and *concertante* strings, evidently composed for specific liturgical purposes, must be passed over here. They should be treated within the framework of a later specialist study, as should other sacred compositions by Monteverdi.[48]

SACRED MADRIGALS

After the prentice work of the *Madrigali Spirituali a 4* of 1583 Monteverdi did not return to the composition of sacred madrigals until later. This phenomenon may perhaps be explained by the fact that A. C. Coppini[49] had already published the master's favourite secular madrigals transformed into sacred 'parodies' in three collections (1607, 1608, 1609). That Monteverdi must have acquiesced in a practice which strikes us as both strange and aesthetically controversial is proved by his having published his own secular 'Kontrafaktur' of the *Arianna Lamento* as *Pianto della Madonna* in 1641. With the exception of one accidental[50] it corresponds exactly to the monody of 1608, and breaks off at the very same bar as does the madrigalistic version of 1614 (*Sixth Book of Madrigals*): 'a parli la lingua si ma non il core'. It thus pays no more attention to the last fourteen bars of the original monody (from 'Misera' until 'e troppo crede') than did the madrigal version of 1614. Both these transcriptions give preference to the earlier ending and thus curtail the opera-fragment by the omission of the entire final section. The text of the 'Kontrafaktur' rigidly maintains Rinuccini's assonance and pattern of rhymes. Thus 'Lasciatemi morire' becomes 'Iam moriar, mi Fili'.

„Pianto della Madonna" (1640)

If this piece belongs intrinsically to the sacred solo-motets, then only the first five numbers of the *Selva* of 1641, which are conceived in the style of the 'Concertato' madrigals of the

Fifth, *Sixth* and *Seventh Books of Madrigals* and are designed for three to five voices with obbligato violins, can claim to be considered as genuine sacred madrigals in the sense of Monteverdi's madrigalistic development. They bear a particularly close relationship to certain experimental pieces in these volumes, and in so doing, they lead to the conclusion that they were in all probability composed between 1605 and 1610. It was not in vain that these pieces appeared in a half-volume together with the very 'Confiteor Terzo alla francese' that M. Praetorius was able to incorporate in his *Hymnodia Sionia* as early as 1611. The *Canzonetta morale*, 'spontava il dì', based upon the principle of the refrain and expressing the sentiments of Schiller's poem *Nänie*, 'Auch das Schöne muss sterben', strongly recalls the rhythm and thematic structure of the 'Lamento della Ninfa' (*Eighth Book of Madrigals*), as it does also of certain later canzonettas among the posthumously published *Madrigali e Canzonette* of 1651. 'Chi vol che m'innamori' for three voices, two violins and Basso Continuo closely follows the style of the *Scherzi Musicali* of 1607, with obbligato instrumental ritornelli and an instrumental postlude of singular expressive power. 'O ciechi, ciechi a 5 voci e 2 Violini', like 'Voi ch'ascoltate', too, is composed wholly in the *stile concitato* of the *Eighth Book*, with orchestral *tuttis* forming climaxes and 'emotional', that is, strongly emphasized, syllabic treatment of the text. If these sacred motets add nothing essentially new to the full-length portrait of Monteverdi the church-musician, they nevertheless strengthen us in the conviction that, despite all the differences in aim, a concealed connecting link formed of a common stylistic purpose and based upon creative verbal interpretation, spans the gap between the madrigal production and the sacred compositions. A particular significance attaches to these *concertante* Psalms, sacred Monodies and Madrigals as exponents of Monteverdi's 'Seconda Prattica'. They hold the balance between the two magnificent polyphonic creations of the *Masses* and *Magnificats* (in the two large collective publications of 1641 and 1651) which are bound to a musical ideal then already in process of ossification. They oblige us to recognize the creative ambivalence of Monteverdi the church-musician as a definite and determinative psychological phenomenon in the history of music.

CHAPTER XIII

THE MUSICAL INVENTOR

IN popular musical textbooks one still occasionally finds Monteverdi described as the 'Father of Opera'. This erroneous and inexact priority, which has continually been accorded to the composer who never claimed it for himself and which may perhaps be accounted for by the wide circulation of *Orfeo* during the last fifty years, has hindered the just appreciation of his actual musical innovations, whose revolutionary nature stamps their creator as the ancestor of what he himself termed 'Musica Moderna'.[1] If we let the whole of his abundant, even though incompletely preserved, lifework pass before our inward eye in chronological succession, the following innovations strike us as being the most fundamental characteristics of his inventive genius.

First should be mentioned the numerous risky chromatic harmonies in the *II–V Books of Madrigals*, 1590–1605, which culminate in the unprepared ninths in 'O Mirtillo' (*V Book*), the chord of the dominant seventh in 'Era l'anima mia' (*V Book*) and the excessive chromaticism of the madrigal version of the *Arianna Lamento* (*VI Book*).

Next come the Mantuan operatic works of the years 1607–10, in which the relationship of the singing-voice to an obbligato instrumental ensemble is for the first time submitted to a definite ruling in respect of form, and thereby succeeds in becoming the most important element of style in a new type of musical expression. This novelty reveals itself: (*a*) in the madrigal style, in the *Scherzi Musicali* of 1607, wherein verses of *villanella* character alternate with ritornello dances played by a three-part string orchestra; (*b*) in the structural interpolations of symphonic ritornelli (in *Orfeo*, 1607, and in the *Vespers* of 1610) into the vocal sphere of the opera and the liturgical psalm.

This leads in turn to the complete autonomy of the instrumental accompanying body which, in *Orfeo* and the *Vespers*, is often meticulously elaborated after the manner of an orchestral score.[2]

In the solo-motet 'Nigra sum', 1610, the dramatic recitative style of the Florentines (in its special Monteverdi *arioso* pattern) seems for the first time to be transferred to the region of the *sacred*. The new invention of the *stile concitato* (the 'agitated style') as a supplement to the earlier type of the 'stile molle e temperato' was considered by Monteverdi himself to be the culminating point of his creative activity.[3] The creation of this style inaugurates the following significant technical and structural innovations: (a) the homogeneity in the part-writing of the movements for four-part strings (*Combattimento, VIII Book of Madrigals*); (b) the first use of the 'tremolo' and 'pizzicato' in the strings (*Combattimento*).

Both these devices lead to the intensifying of the dramatic expression.

Next, the introduction of typical, characteristic motives which were thenceforward to become the indispensable adjuncts of every kind of operatic music. They may be found principally in the *Madrigali Guerrieri* of the *VIII Book of Madrigals.*

Among them are rhythmical 'picturesque' motives which are particularly striking: for instance, the 'Motto del Cavallo' in the *Combattimento,*

"Motto del Cavallo" (Combattimento)

and the typical 'Guerra' motive of the *VIII Book of Madrigals.*

ar - mi, ar - mi *(etc.)*

Unexpected harmonies, such as the mystical passage,

"Lauda Jerusalem" a 3 (1650)

from the 'Lauda Jerusalem a 3' (*Messa a 4 e Salmi*, 1650, Collected Edition, Vol. XVI), anticipate Heinrich Schütz's most daring chord progression in the *Dialogo per la Pascua*:

Schütz „Dialogo per la pascua"

Ma - ri - a   Ma - ri - a

How strongly Monteverdi's precedence in all the details of the evolution of style relating to the *stile concitato* was perceived by his contemporaries is shown in the *Kompositionslehre* by Ch. Bernhard, a pupil of Heinrich Schütz, which was written *c.* 1649 and in which Monteverdi was expressly described as the *inventor* of the 'stylus luxurians communis' (vocal pieces for church and chamber; sonatas) and was also described as the leading representative of the 'stylus luxurians theatralis' (operatic style).[4]

Whether he may be adjudged the first to introduce the distinguishing rhythmical peculiarities of the *Stilo francese*[5] into Italy cannot be decided here and now.

Conscious attempts at the da capo aria,[6] which was to become traditional in later years, occur for the first time in the operas of Monteverdi's Venetian period. Their most decisive impetus towards modernization is, however, the radical simplification and reduction of the superabundant *Orfeo* orchestra of 1607 to a flexible ensemble of strings and 'fundamental instruments' which became the effective centre of the musical events in the opera for the next 150 years. In these late operas, as also in the few extant dramatic works of the period between 1608 and 1640, there may be found important attempts at two- and three-part arias, elaborately varied arias, *concertante* chamber-duets and variations of the passacaglia type.[7]

G. Benvenuti has already drawn attention to the unique fusion of the historical, the mythological and the comical which occurs for the first time in the *Incoronazione*.[8] Similar experiments in the combination of dramatic and epic elements of style, likewise appearing for the first time, may be found in the 'Oratorio with action' based on Tasso's *Combattimento*, 1624, which evolves logically within the compass of a Baroque 'Teatro da Camera'.[9] The stabilizing of the relationship of the dramatic singing-voice to the accompanying orchestra, as it is first attempted within the sphere of chamber-music in the *Combattimento* and finally manifested in all its perfection in the late Venetian operas, was to form the basis of every kind of serious operatic music-making from Cavalli to Gluck.

Special credit should also be given to Monteverdi the musical colourist, for having as early as 1607 laid such particular emphasis upon the installation of the violins (Violini piccioli in *Orfeo*!), and for having thereby dealt the effective deathblow to the old consort of viols.

This doubtless incomplete survey of the most important musical innovations associated with the name of Monteverdi may perhaps, despite its cursory nature, succeed in persuading the musician of modern times how profound is the debt of gratitude he owes to the 'divino Claudio'.

Part III

MONTEVERDI IN THE EYES OF POSTERITY

WHEN Monteverdi closed his eyes in Venice on the 29th of November 1643, he was at the zenith of a personal renown extending all over Europe. Nevertheless, the interest which was willingly accorded by the representatives of the younger generation to the tireless champion of a new and realistic ideal of musical expression already considerably outweighed the actual popularity and circulation of his music. There were good reasons for this. Monteverdi had composed a large portion of his most valuable music indubitably as the last of the line of great madrigalists: that is to say, as the exponent of an art-form which had reached its peak at about the time of the appearance of his *First Book of Madrigals*, 1587, and whose catastrophically swift decay began very soon after 1600, even before the appearance of Monteverdi's most important contributions to this species of art, the *Fourth* and *Fifth Books of Madrigals* in 1603 and 1605 respectively. The publication of the last three *Books of Madrigals*, *VI* in 1614, *VII* in 1619 and *VIII* in 1638, took place during a period when public interest in the madrigal and its allied forms was rapidly declining. The dates of the reprints of his *Books of Madrigals* are eloquent in this connexion.[1] After 1621, interest in his madrigal production faded. The theoreticians of that time, however, entirely ignored the inexhaustible problems of *Books VII* and *VIII*.[2] The tremendous effect of the great liturgical publications of 1610, *Missa 'In illo tempore'*, the *Vespers* and two *Magnificats*, awakened a speedy echo in the production of the Early German Baroque.[3] Yet the master's second publication of ecclesiastical music, the *Selva Morale e Spirituali* of 1641, was already too late in appearance to impress the generation for whom it was primarily intended.

Monteverdi's operatic works were singularly ill-starred. *Orfeo*, 1607, with its two published scores of 1609 and 1615, was the only one which managed to penetrate to far distant circles in Europe. Nevertheless, this work, despite the revolutionary ingenuity of its total conception, is indebted in parts to the experimental declamatory style of the early Florentine chamber-opera of 1597, whose actuality waned after 1608, more especially from the moment when Roman operatic production was inaugurated.[4] The other operas of Monteverdi's Mantuan period (*Arianna, Ballo dell'Ingrate*, etc.) acquired European fame either much too early, or else far too late, to exert any decisive influence upon younger composers. His abundant operatic production between 1613 and 1639 was destined almost exclusively for the princely courts of Parma and Mantua. The majority of these manuscripts were destroyed at the sack of Mantua in July 1630. Thus, Monteverdi's European reputation as an operatic composer would have ceased to exist as early as 1639 had not his production of music-drama experienced a grandiose, if late resurgence with the Venetian operas of his closing years, 1639–42. With the *Ritorno* and the *Incoronazione* he engaged once more in the process of renewing the music of the age. The *Incoronazione*, in particular, became the prototype of the opera in the grand style with a historical rather than a mythological subject, and the starting point of the High Baroque specialization of the problem of the dramatic representative aria. The increased effective radius of these last works (possibly a performance of the *Ritorno* in Vienna, and an authenticated new setting of the *Incoronazione* in Naples in 1651) shows yet again how ready was the age to receive Monteverdi's message, provided it was couched in the language of the day and not clad in the anachronistic raiment of declining artforms (madrigal, Flemish polyphony of the 'Prima Prattica', declamatory style of the Florentine 'Camerata'). The pompous Venetian operas of Cavalli, Sacrati, Rovetta, etc. are unthinkable without this late pioneer work of Monteverdi the composer of music-dramas.

In this respect, Monteverdi's fate in the remembrance of posterity is different from that of J. S. Bach, who at the time of his death in 1750 was already considered out of date as a musician, and whose music had to wait for eighty years before being rediscovered by Zelter and Felix Mendelssohn. During the decade following Monteverdi's death, he continued to be regarded as an integral constituent of its artistic culture. In the years 1641 to 1646 many sacred 'Kontrafakturen' of his madrigals, as well as single liturgical works, appeared in Profius' Collections.[5] In 1647 the *Second Part* of Heinrich Schütz's *Symphoniae Sacrae* came out, and with it that unique document of the same composer's personal homage to our hero, the sacred concerto *Es steh' Gott auff*, in which Monteverdi's madrigals 'Armato il cor' and 'Zefiro torna' were presented in fresh and recreated guise.[6] Monteverdi the man and his work were still the focus of theoretical discussion and biographical interest. In Christoph Bernhard's *Kompositionslehre*, a work probably inspired by his teacher H. Schütz about 1648-9 but possibly only partially completed about 1680,[7] Monteverdi is cited as the exemplary master 'of the "Stile luxuriante communi"', of which same style he was certainly the inventor and which he developed to a high degree'. In the 'Stylo Luxuriante Theatrali', too, 'he had shown what remarkable things he could do'. It is deeply significant that[8] the compilation of this section of Bernhard's *Kompositionslehre* which mentions Monteverdi, and which was never published during the author's lifetime, can be established as having been undertaken during the years before 1651 when Monteverdi's name was still held in remembrance in civilized Europe. Christoph Bernhard's testimony is the strongest possible evidence of the dominant position still occupied after his death by Monteverdi in the world of Heinrich Schütz, as it is of the availability of Monteverdi's published compositions at this period. For the composers whom Chr. Bernhard explicitly mentions and among whom Monteverdi twice occupies a first place, are those 'whose works are easily acquired'. After 1650, a statement of this kind would hardly be in accordance with the facts. M. Camberlotti's official obituary notice of Monteverdi, an enthusiastic panegyric with many interesting biographical details, appeared in 1644 in G. B. Marinoni's *Fiori Poetici*.[9] G. B. Doni's important discussion regarding the *Arianna Lamento* and the early madrigals must have originated before 1647.[10] In 1642, the Dutchman Bannius extolled the works of the *Eighth Book of Madrigals*, which demonstrate the 'Seconda Prattica', above all the master's earlier compositions.[11] The interest shown in Monteverdi by the general public as late as 1651 must have been sufficiently great to warrant the issue of the two great posthumous publications of that year: the *Messa quattro e Salmi* and the *Madrigali e Canzonette* (both printed by A. Vincenti). This interest was demonstrated no less conclusively by the revival of the late Venetian operas after 1643: *Proserpina rapita*, 1644, and the *Incoronazione*, 1646, both in Venice, and the *Incoronazione* yet again in 1651 in Naples. On the other hand, after 1651, Monteverdi's name rapidly disappears from contemporary annals. The

L

fact that he is mentioned in the *Musica Poetica* published in 1673 by G. Maria Bononcini (b. *c.* 1640) is only of value as a rarity. Thenceforward, a whole century was to elapse before the greatest musical theorist of the eighteenth century, Padre Giambattista Martini (1706–84,) was to recall the forgotten master with admiration.[12] The discerning appreciation shown by Martini in his analyses of three of Monteverdi's compositions, and his skill in differentiating the revolutionary harmonist from the archaizing church-musician, were merely incidental and produced no practical result, any more than did C. v. Winterfeld's rediscovery of *Orfeo*, the *Ballo dell'Ingrate* and the *Combattimento* fifty years later in his book, *Gabrieli und sein Zeitalter*, 1834, which was designed to lay the foundations of a modern type of musical research. The fragments of Monteverdi's compositions reprinted for the first time in these two important works did not, however, succeed in promoting any deeper interest in circles where sensitivity to the historical aspect of music was cultivated. (The German Bach renaissance had begun in 1829!)

The year 1881, which saw the foundation of modern musicology with the first appearance of the *Vierteljahrschrift für Musikwissenschaft* and the first series of *Denkmäler*, was the decisive turningpoint in the appreciation of Monteverdi. This year, the first modern reprint of *Orfeo* was published.[13] During the following years, Emil Vogel scored the complete *Madrigals* from the rare original editions, and in 1887 published the first biographical study of Monteverdi.[14] In 1888, Taddeo Wiel discovered the manuscript of the *Incoronazione*.[15] In 1904, the *Ritorno*, about which Ambros, Kiesewetter and E. Vogel were still in doubt, was identified as a work of Monteverdi's by H. Goldschmidt, who also published the text and music of the *Incoronazione* in an almost complete edition.[16] Henceforth new reprints and practical performing editions of Monteverdi's operas increased and multiplied. For a long while *Orfeo* occupied the central position in the newly awakened interest,[17] but both the late Venetian operas, too, began to engage the pens of modern editors to a constantly increasing degree. The *Incoronazione* had already made a preliminary appearance with a selection of scenes prepared by V. d'Indy. These were followed by new editions of the complete work by Ch. v. d. Borren in 1914 (MS.) and J. A. Westrup in 1927 (MS.). In 1937 alone, three completely new editions of the work were brought out by E. Křenek, G. Benvenuti (MS.) and H. F. Redlich, while in 1931 the complete reprint of the Venetian and Neapolitan manuscripts had been published by F. Malipiero in Vol. XIII of the Collected Edition. Finally, G. Benvenuti issued a facsimile reprint of the Venetian manuscript of the opera, at Milan, in 1938.[18] The controversy over the authenticity of the *Ritorno* began to die down after 1904. An abbreviated stage-version was published by V. d'Indy in 1927, but the work had already first appeared in a scientifically complete edition as Vol. 57 of the twenty-ninth annual publication of the DTOE (R. Haas). It was followed in 1931 by the complete reprint in Vol. XII of the Collected Edition (Malipiero). The new practical edition completed by L. Dallapiccola in 1942 and performed at the Maggio Fiorentino that year under M. Labroca's direction was violently attacked by G. Benvenuti who declared the work to be unauthentic in every section.[19] Monteverdi's smaller music-dramas likewise succeeded in gaining publicity in the modern musical world.[20] On the other hand, acquaintance with the madrigals was for long restricted to a few individual items.[21] A change in this state of affairs was first accomplished by the complete reprint of all the *Books of Madrigals* in Vols. I–X of the Collected Edition (Malipiero, 1926–9). This invaluable publication formed the basis of the present author's specialist study *Cl. Monteverdi, I. Das Madrigalwerk*,[22] which was the first to undertake an analysis of the madrigals of 1584–1650 from the point of view of their historical evolution.

It was Monteverdi's church-music that had to wait the longest for its final, inevitable disinterment from the dust of library shelves, although C. v. Winterfeld, W. Ambros and other scholars had already drawn attention to the beauties of the *Missa* and the *Vespers* of 1610.[23] The only works which had acquired any publicity were isolated fragments such as the 'Sonata sopra Sancta Maria',[24] the 'Missa a 4 a cappella' from the *Selva* of 1641, edited by v. d. Borren and Tirabassi in 1914, and the *Cantiunculae Sacrae* of 1582,[25] edited by Terrabugio at Orvieto in 1910. Not until 1932 were the publications of 1610 issued in a complete reprint.[26] On the basis of this memorable new edition the author of the present study undertook a fresh revision for practical purposes of the *Vespers* of 1610 in 1934. It was performed for the first time in 1935 and has led to important results.[27] A direct outcome of this new revision was the re-editing for practical purposes of the little *Magnificat* of 1610[28] on the same basic principles. In 1940 and 1942 respectively the *Selva* of 1640 and the posthumous 'Missa a 4 e Salmi' were published in Vols. XV and XVI of the Collected Edition. The appearance of these important concluding volumes in the very midst of the Second World War has as yet delayed the fulfilling of their usefulness in the modern concert-room. The numerous new editions of Monteverdi's original works fall into two completely different categories: (1) trustworthy *reprints* of the originals, either as facsimile reproductions of the first editions, as, for instance, *Orfeo* (A. Sandberger, Nuremberg, 1927); or as a facsimile reprint of the manuscript, as in the instance of the *Incoronazione* (G. Benvenuti, Milan, 1938), or also as *transcriptions* in modern notation as in the case of the Collected Edition carried out by G. Malipiero; (2) practical new editions which often deviate from the *res facta* of the extant originals.[29]

Specialist biographical studies of Monteverdi, which made a most promising start with E. Vogel's monograph in 1887, culminated in the valuable biographies by L. Schneider, Paris, 1921, H. Prunières, Paris, 1924, and G. F. Malipiero, 1930.[30] A welcome synopsis of all the specialist studies devoted to Monteverdi by earlier Italian scholars such as Caffi, Davari, Sommi-Picenardi, Ademollo, etc., together with a valuable survey of the results of the most recent investigations, is provided by Domenico de' Paoli's biography, Milan, 1945.

It remains to add a final word on the effect of Monteverdi's musico-dramatic conception upon later composers of operas. It cannot be proved with any certainty that the frequent operatic revivals and resuscitations of the Orpheus legend are the direct consequence of the paradigmatic example of 1607, although some of the Italian operas on this subject composed in the Early and Middle Baroque were undoubtedly inspired by Monteverdi's *Favola d'Orfeo*.[31] The type of dramatic Lament created in Monteverdi's *Arianna* in 1608 was perpetuated far into the eighteenth century. But as time went on, Monteverdi's humanistic conception of opera, so eloquently expressed in his letter of 9 December 1616 to A. Striggio, sank into ever deepening obscurity as the tyranny of castrato and prima donna gradually turned the regenerated Greek drama of 1607 into a vocal contest with orchestral accompaniment. The two great reforms of opera undertaken in the following two centuries are certainly nearer to this humanistic conception of inherent dramatic truth, human dignity and deliberate limitation to the 'purely human' (Rein-Menschliche). Gluck's famous remark, 'When I compose an opera, I forget that I am a musician', is, in effect, a revival of Monteverdi's dictum, 'L'oratione sia padrone della armonia e non serva' (*Dichiarazione*, 1607). The restitution of the elementary rights of poetry to their original supremacy over the demands of virtuosically exuberant music, and the new regulation of the relationship between words, music and scenic action as conceived by Gluck in his 'Reform Operas'[32] with their rejection of coloratura and concert elements in favour of a truthful reflection of the dramatic essentials in the mirror of music, were also at the basis of Wagner's reform,[33] which was as strongly inspired by the lofty dramatic conception of classical tragedy as were the operas of Gluck-Calzabigi and Monteverdi-Striggio in their own day.

Monteverdi's conception of drama which, even in his latest operas composed at the dawn of the coloratura style, retains its firm grip on dramatic essentials,[34] must have continued to exercise a kind of occult influence throughout the two centuries when it was apparently forgotten. While it is almost certain that neither Gluck nor Wagner had any knowledge of Monteverdi's operatic work, the last few decades have shown how strong has been the influence of the 'divine Claudio' upon composers of our own time. This influence is noticeable even in the works of the latest German Romantics, Strauss and Pfitzner. In the former's *Ariadne*, 1912, not only the choice of subject, but the general outline of Ariadne's beautiful first soliloquy strongly suggest that the composer was not unfamiliar with the extant Fragment of 1608. In his later opera *Die schweigsame Frau*, 1934, Monteverdi's *Incoronazione* is several times quoted note for note with explanatory footnotes in the vocal score. In the First Act of Hans Pfitzner's musical legend *Palestrina*, 1916, the antithesis of styles between Count Bardi's 'Camerata Fiorentina' and the Palestrinian world of Papal Rome is expounded in the music and constitutes the mental background of the whole drama. Features of Monteverdi's idiosyncratic passages may frequently be detected in the musical language of his modern editor, G. F. Malipiero (b. 1882), who, particularly in his operas dealing with the subject of Venetian history (*Il mistero di Venezia*, *Torneo Notturno*, *Il finto Arlecchino* and others), has integrated characteristics of Monteverdi's style in his own music. The synchronized combination of singers, narrators, actors and dancers in one dramatic enterprise, as exemplified in Monteverdi's scenic oratorio *Combattimento*, in his opera-ballet *Il Ballo dell'Ingrate* as well as in the improvisatory buffo scenes of *Il Ritorno* and

L'Incoronazione, has led to very striking revivals in recent musico-dramatic works such as Stravinsky's Pergolesi-inspired *Pulcinella* ballet, 1924, D. Milhaud's *Christoph Colomb*, 1930, Stravinsky's *Oedipus Rex*, 1926, and his primitive scenic oratorio *L'Histoire du soldat*, 1918. Monteverdi's formative influence is also noticeable in Benjamin Britten's *Rape of Lucretia*, 1947, which is a genuine instance of definite re-creation of Monteverdi's descriptive ideas. The music of Tarquinius' ride to Rome accompanied by the excited narration of the Chorus resuscitates 'Il Motto del Cavallo' and the description of the duel in Monteverdi's *Combattimento*. In this opera of Britten's, the male and female Chorus, whose narrations interrupt or accompany the dramatic action, are exact replicas of the 'testo' in Monteverdi's Tasso-Scene. It is equally obvious that Monteverdi's operatic conception must have tinged the weird, primordial atmosphere which surrounds Carl Orff's own musico-dramatic creations such as *Carmina Burana*, 1937, *Der Mond*, 1938, and *Antigonae*, 1949. Orff devoted many years to German adaptations of Monteverdi's principal operas,[35] a labour of love and self-effacement which has borne rich fruit in the recent harvest of his own operatic conceptions, and which has materially helped to popularize the name and the cause of Monteverdi among German-speaking audiences.

Many more composers of our own period could be enumerated as having been affected by Monteverdi's timeless art to the benefit of their own development. That this influence, which is also noticeable among young Italian composers and has led to a purification of Italian music in general under the leadership of Alfredo Casella (1883–1947) and G. F. Malipiero, may become as powerful as that of the Bach-revival during the past hundred years, must be the wish of every sincere believer in Monteverdi's spiritual message.

Part IV

THE PROBLEMS OF EDITING
AND PERFORMANCE

PRINCIPLES

The preparation of scientifically sound new editions of Monteverdi's works suitable for performance under modern orchestral conditions is rendered especially difficult by the lack of authentic original manuscripts. As in the instance of Palestrina and other composers of the High Renaissance, only a minimum of Monteverdi's works have come down to us in their manuscript state, and even the few manuscripts which the late H. Prunières[1] considered authentic have now been discovered to be the work of copyists; and not always even contemporary copyists. According to current opinions among musicologists, only very limited authenticity can be conceded to the extant manuscripts.[2] The manuscript of the *Arianna Lamento*[3] and also that of the *Ritorno* have been unanimously classified as being not the work of Monteverdi's own hand. In the manuscript of the *Incoronazione* at the Library of San Marco, Venice, G. Benvenuti has discovered the writing of several contemporary copyists who were engaged upon the work. This manuscript contains the only original corrections in Monteverdi's own hand, which must have been made after the performance of 1642, and of which the longest is the introductory 'Sinfonia' of the 'Prologo'.[4] Of neither the madrigals nor the church-music has a single original handwritten copy as yet come to light, which means that, in by far the greatest number of the extant works, we are necessarily referred to the first printed editions as the only reliable sources of material. Of these first editions which, in the great majority of instances, (the two printed scores of *Orfeo* dating from 1609 and 1615 respectively, the *Missa* and the *Vespers* of 1610 and the *Selva* of 1641), but not always (the *Scherzi Musicali* of 1607 and 1632, the *Arianna Lamento* of 1623 and the posthumous publications of 1651), were superintended by Monteverdi himself, a few precious copies are preserved in European and American libraries.[5] In default of the missing original handwritten copies made by the composer they constitute the natural basis of every new edition, whether it serve scientific or practical purposes. These first editions exist mostly in the form of individual part-books; entirely so, in the instance of the madrigals and the ecclesiastical works. Only the original edition of *Orfeo* already mentioned comes anywhere near being a full score in the modern sense of the term. In every other instance the part-books had to be collated, i.e. written out in score; a laborious task which E. Vogel duly undertook for the whole of the madrigals, and C. v. Winterfeld for the *Vespers* of 1610. Malipiero's monumental Collected Edition in sixteen volumes is based upon photographic copies of every extant original part-book which, in its turn, constitutes the basis of a legible score for the modern musician, furnished for the most part with the decoding of the early time-signatures, written-out continuo-parts and other simplifications current in *Denkmäler* practice.

The merit of having clarified the situation, of gradually making Claudio Monteverdi's work accessible again and of clearing it from the accumulations of centuries is shared by Italian, French and German scholars.[6] The need was soon felt for new editions of works which had almost entirely disappeared, and among which, up to 1881, only isolated fragments existed in incomplete reprints.[7] It can readily be understood that the generation of scholars of the Richard Wagner epoch started off by showing the keenest interest in the ancestor of the music-drama. The problem of *Orfeo*, 1607, engaged musicologists and practical musicians alike for whole decades. The curiously unfinished state in which this particular operatic work was handed down called immediately for the practical deciphering of the scanty *res facta*. Numerous editions of this *Orfeo*[8] came into being and revealed an increasing, if at the same time unequal, understanding of the problem presented by the opera regarding the interpretation of its actual notation for practical purposes. Monteverdi, more than others, is a composer whose texts need thorough research and interpretation. It can truthfully be said that the original prints and manuscripts of his works are not ambiguous to so great an extent as are those of the majority of his predecessors and many of his contemporaries. He obviously occupies a position between two epochs; anticipating the boldest combinations of harmonic and instrumental sounds, yet often indebted to the scholasticism and the written formulations of the dying Middle Ages. With the exception of the traditional cadential ligature *cum opposita proprietate* in the *Ritorno*, the ligatures ⊏⊐⊏⊐ in the *Incoronazione* and the blackening of the hemiole in the triple-time to be found in *Orfeo* and in the late Venetian operas, and finally, occasional ligatures in the church compositions,[9] Monteverdi writes his music throughout according to modern conceptions of rhythm and phrase lengths. But the old 'prolationes' (time-signatures) occur constantly in all his works. He already writes the Basso Continuo in the progressive style of the High Baroque, but the figuring is sparse to a degree and the practical realization of his continuo parts is consequently rendered extremely difficult. He has in mind a modern, variegated orchestra, but leaves it to posterity to apportion the individual instrumental parts in conformity with the practice of scoring. To put it shortly: in accordance with the conception of the 'Zufallsorchester' of his own epoch he leaves a good half of the work which to-day is termed 'composition' to the taste and the capacity for improvising of whoever may happen to be the conductor or, in other words, the 'producer of sounds'.

Unfortunately, the numerous earlier reprints of Monteverdi's works for the most part evaded the solution of these problems. The Continuo was realized with modern harmonies and the scoring was sometimes even brought into line with Romantic conceptions of orchestral sonority. No appreciable change set in until after 1930, when doubts were raised by a progressive section of musicologists as to the conditions of practical performance revelant to the actual epoch.[10] The way to methodical research into the Monteverdian realm of sound was first cleared by the great Collected Edition in sixteen volumes which G. F. Malipiero published with exemplary persistence from 1926 to 1942. The inestimable importance of this edition consists in its complete handing down of the musical text. Nevertheless, owing to the particular nature of its editorial technique, it can never be used as the basis of practical performances. The realization of the Basso Continuo which is added to this edition is only roughly drafted; the apportioning of the instruments is entirely lacking; in the choral parts the old mensural time-signatures, based on the use of the breve as the unit of notation, have been left unchanged, thus involving considerable visual complications for modern usage. Finally, there is no critical commentary. That Malipiero himself did not consider his edition adequate for practical use is demonstrated by the separate practical editions of *Orfeo*, the *Combattimento* and the

Incoronazione which he undertook and published during the time he was publishing the Collected Edition.[11]

Henceforward, Monteverdi the madrigalist, whose complete works in this category had been available in Vols. I–X of the Collected Edition since 1929, also occupied a central position in musico-historical deliberations. Here, too, where within the very flexible conception of madrigal form the fateful transition from the old motet structure to the expressive solo-cantata was accomplished, methods of practical performance set the most difficult tasks. The impossibility of performing the madrigals, especially those of the later volumes (from *Book V*, 1605 onwards), from the printed editions in which they had been handed down; the necessity for completing the musical ensemble with instrumental parts, and the variegated instrumentation of the Continuo which was only very vaguely sketched, seemed to demonstrate the crying need for editions of these madrigals which would take into consideration the problems of performance at the time of their origin.[12]

The obscurity which still enveloped the productions of Monteverdi the church-musician about twenty years ago has recently been dispelled for the first time by the appearance of the remaining volumes, XIV, XV and XVI of the Collected Edition. The practical edition of the *Vespers* of 1610 prepared by myself in 1933–4 and first used for performance in Zürich[13] in February 1935, was the first attempt to render Monteverdi's sacred music accessible to modern performers. It was based on certain principles regarding performing practice which have subsequently become authoritative—not only for my own practical editions of Monteverdi.

The question now arises: what were the sources which had to be investigated in order to arrive at a historically objective, but at the same time, a truly creative and realistic interpretation of the entire range of sonorities in the *Vespers*; and further, from what hypotheses was the conception of the 'Aufführungspraxis', now authoritative for the new edition, evolved?[14] The sources of information upon 'Aufführungspraxis' during the epoch of Monteverdi are by no means scanty. From the abundance of material, which is still far from being exhausted, we learn first and foremost that we have been fundamentally deceived as to the actual sounds of the music of that period. The part played by the *instrument* as an equal, and sometimes even as a dominating partner of the voice has largely been misunderstood. Madrigals and motets which were taken as evidences of genuine *a cappella* style were frequently performed by instruments only, but chiefly by an equal mixture of voices and instruments. The 'Zufallsorchester' (Schering) dominates the scene; every group of timbres is interchangeable; trombones may replace violas, cornetts substitute violins, and a 'Cappella Fidicinia' (string orchestra) do duty for a chorus of human voices. The sparsely indicated Basso Continuo becomes a powerful body of supporting harmonies, principally by means of the limitless doubling in octaves which was just then becoming a principle of the Early Baroque and which M. Praetorius[15] compressed into a lapidary decree: 'Octavae in omnibus vocibus tolerari possunt; quando una vox cantat, altera sonat.' The melodic lines were broken up into an abundance of elaborate ornamentation by the coloratura of the singing voice and by the decorative passages of the 'ornamenting instruments' (Praetorius). Any combination of timbres was permissible provided it was justified by euphony and by magnificence of tone-colour.

This state of freedom as to creative interpretation holds good in particular for the *res facta* of the motet and the 'sacred concerto', which had become the arena for the boldest experiments in tone-colour. There is one book above all others which is authoritative not only as the most convincing source of information upon the methods of performance of *concertante* music of this epoch in general, but also as a clue to the distribution of timbres in Monteverdi's *Vespers* of 1610 in particular: M. Praetorius's *Syntagma Musicum III*, 1619 (reprinted in 1916 under the editorship of E. Bernoulli), which has already been mentioned several times in these pages. This astounding work devotes its second and third sections entirely to a practical introduction to the realization of the Basso Continuo and to the arranging of originally vocal motet compositions for numerous combinations of instrumental groups. The ideological basis of the *Syntagma* is formed by the treatises of the leading Italian theoreticians of that time: Artusi, Agazzari, Bernardo Strozzi and Viadana. Praetorius's ideals in creative music are represented by G. Gabrieli's splendid work, by madrigals of Marenzio, Gesualdo and Monteverdi, and last but not least, by Monteverdi's *Vespers* of 1610. Two movements of this work, 'Ave maris stella' and 'Dixit Dominus', are reviewed with admiration and classified as stylistic prototypes of the most modern liturgical 'concert style'.[16] In other respects, too, Monteverdi stands in the centre of the theoretical discussion in this book.

His *Scherzi Musicali* of 1607 are lovingly analysed and the madrigals and their problems of metre are repeatedly mentioned. In the whole of the contemporary literature written between 1590 and 1620 there is no theoretical book on music in which Monteverdi's intellectual stature is more convincingly drawn into the centre of discussion than in this *Syntagma III*.

THE AUTHOR'S EDITION OF THE *Vespers*, 1610

The sub-title of the *Vespers* announces that it is 'da concerto': e.g. written in the new *concertante* 'stile nuovo'; further, that it is 'composto sopra canti fermi': e.g. its thematic subject-matter is based on plainchant; and finally, that it is to be performed by 'sex vocibus et sex instrumentis'. Nevertheless, this last statement given in the original is misleading, for on the very first page of the Doxology of the *Vespers* 'Domine ad adiuvandum', Monteverdi already indicates no fewer than twelve different instrumental parts, without counting the Continuo! According to the original instructions, these parts are to be distributed over six staves; an arrangement which is obligatory for most of the Vesper Psalms, but by no means for all of them. The prescription 'Sex instr.' is also to be found on the title-page of the 'great' *Magnificat*, though in this instance it cannot pass for an exhaustive assertion, for the six instrumental parts of the introductory piece are later augmented by numerous wood-wind and brass instruments which are expressly mentioned in the original directions. On the other hand, as soon as the body of instruments is set up as a totality, it always undergoes division into five or six parts, so that the laconic statement is eventually clarified as meaning that Monteverdi requires a six-part division of the instrumental design as such; a prescription which, in its turn, suffices to corroborate the fact that there should be such freedom of arrangement as was formerly conceded as a matter of necessity by the composer to the conductor.

The instrumental division of the Doxology is surprisingly clear in principle. For the two uppermost staves Monteverdi requires two cornetts (Zinken), I and II violini da brazzo; for the two middle staves, I and II violas and one trombone; for the lowest staves, I and II trombones and finally a Basso-continuo instrument which in this instance can easily be recognized as the organ. The expansion of the twelve obligatory parts on to an equal number of staves is, therefore, all that is needed to maintain an appearance of a serviceable score for modern musical practice.

Nevertheless, in the first Psalm, 'Dixit Dominus', the want of clarity in the instrumental arrangement already begins to gain the upper hand. Here, too, is the laconic direction 'sex vocibus et sex instrumentis', but this time, without any more precise description of the instruments. In the purely instrumental ritornelli of this piece, which is composed in six obbligato parts and which, according to a note of Monteverdi's, may be played or omitted 'at will', the distribution of the instruments may not be unduly difficult. But what is to be done with the instruments during the extended choral episodes? At a preliminary glance one might think that the vocal parts were to be sung *a cappella* and to alternate in *concertante* fashion with purely instrumental interludes. But that this is not so, and that here, as also more particularly in the apparently purely choral sections of the Psalms, we are dealing with collective staves for the various parts, is stressed by the following episode from the 'Dixit Dominus'. In the original (Reprint in the Collected Edition, Vol. XIV, p. 143), the 'Cantus' reads:

It requires no further argument to establish that this figuration, with its staccato semiquavers, is typical writing for stringed instruments and is consequently absolutely unsingable. That Monteverdi did not intend the passage to be sung in the notation just given goes without saying in view of the master's infinitely refined sense of tone-colour. The fact that the passage is accompanied by words is no proof of its 'vocality', as M. Praetorius has already shown us when he wrote:[17] '. . . that instead of the concertat part da (Voce) which is written, the instruments can be used as a ritornello. . . .' What is necessary is to conceive the analysis of these 'synthetic' voices into musical timbres in such a manner as to realize that the accessory strings were intended to play the passage in the original notation, while the chorus performed their part in the following logical reduction. (Cf. the corresponding passage on the same motive, Reprint, p. 140.)

In one of the succeeding pieces, 'Audi Coelum', the continuo
part calls for a perfectly free arrangement of details for supplying
colour, simply in order to ensure the necessary counterpoise to the
long *sostenuto* notes throughout the vocal part.   The interchange-
ability between a vocal and an instrumental part recognized at that
period straightway permitted transformation of the vocal echo
part of the opening into a gamba part in the reprint.   In accordance
with the great use made of coloratura by the original solo vocal
parts, the parts for the gamba and organ had to be kept in this
particular style.   The following example, which places the opening
bars of the piece in the original side by side with the reading of the
practical edition, may give an idea of the problems of supplementing
the old musical text which confront the modern interpreter endowed
with a sense of responsibility.[18]

Original*

*Some bar-lines are missing in the original.

Practical edition of 1934 (publ. 1949).
Sopr. Solo

Among the other pieces, the famous 'Sonata sopra Sancta Maria a 8', with its extravagant original instrumentation, is by far the most remarkable. The piece requires two cornetts (Zinken), three trombones, violins, violas and continuo instruments, the apportioning of which leaves much to be decided. For instance, the sixth stave (from the top) is marked 'Trombone overo Viola da brazzo', which proves how flexibly Monteverdi insisted on treating the distribution of timbres in practical performance. Nevertheless, the apportioning of instruments in the hymn 'Ave maris stella a 8' turns out to be a particularly delicate matter. In this instance, the original entirely avoids giving any indication as to the instruments required. Indeed, the very word 'instrumenta' is missing from the title of the piece. Yet the regularly recurrent ritornelli without any words, written in typically instrumental triple time and kept in five parts in contrast to the four-part semi-chorus, reveal convincingly enough that in this case we are dealing with purely instrumental interludes such as we have already become familiar with in Monteverdi's 'balletto' *Della Bellezza*.[19] That Monteverdi had in mind obbligato instrumental collaboration, not only in the ritornelli but also in the apparently purely vocal parts, is effectively testified by M. Praetorius. In his *Syntagma III*, when giving the definition of the term *Ritornello*,[20] he seizes the opportunity of going exhaustively into the subject of the 'Ave maris stella'. He frequently emphasizes the obligatory use of instruments and also mentions that in the concluding portion of the hymn 'Sit laus', which combines the forces of the two semi-choruses, accessory instruments are to join in, concerning which intention there is not a single word to be found in the original.

From the foregoing, the uselessness of the score published in Vol. XIV of the Collected Edition for the purposes of practical performance may be inferred. In contradistinction to the presentation of Romantic music, the notation of which is the very embodiment of unrestrained and unique subjectivity, a rigidly literal interpretation of the work in question would consititute a crime against the spirit of Monteverdi's style. Anyone who has become aware of the fragmentary character of the original notation is in duty bound to supplement the written copy (i.e. to make it usable) in the spirit of the original style which characterizes Monteverdi and his period. For this purpose it is necessary to reconstruct the whole musical apparatus of the *Vespers* in accordance with the conventions of style current in those days, the customary ornaments and embellishments and the usual acoustical combinations of that period of eager experimenting in sound. Only upon a basis of this kind which is equally reliable in point of both history and style, can the task of practical arrangement of the score be undertaken with any artistic certainty. The results of the research methods which have been sketched only in their main outlines will help to conjure up an approximate representation of the realities of sound of the *Vespers*, 1610, whose traditional aspect of notation will then be revealed to us as a meagre abbreviation of its elementary acoustic indications.

THE AUTHOR'S PRACTICAL REVISIONS OF
Orfeo (1607) AND THE *Incoronazione di Poppea* (1642)

The results of my revision of the *Vespers* which have been summarized in the foregoing section have also had a determining influence upon subsequent practical editions of *Orfeo* and the *Incoronazione*.[21] A detailed account of the outcome of my researches in this connexion does not fall within the scope of the present volume. I have elsewhere published an exact account of the conclusions of my editorial activities relating to these two greatest examples of Monteverdi's powers as a composer of music-dramas.[22] Only a few points of general interest which were not touched upon in the preceding section will now be briefly indicated.

The realization of the Monteverdian Basso Continuo has at all times been a rock upon which many editors have foundered. Wherein does the fundamental difficulty of this problem consist? Monteverdi's Continuo basses are figured only in rare instances. If they are provided with any indication of this kind, whether it be a number, a sharp or a flat, it is generally susceptible of several interpretations owing to the peculiar transitional position of the Accidental in that period. From the instructions on practical performance of Basso Continuo arrangements which have been transmitted to us by M. Praetorius, Agazzari, Viadana and others, and from the forewords to the first operas by Peri, Caccini and da Gagliano,[23] it may be gathered that the 'realized' Basso Continuo was performed by a complete orchestra of 'Fundamentinstrumenten'. The scantily figured bass had to crystallize into this orchestra so that it might form a substructure capable of supporting the protracted recitative. For this special instrumentation of the 'Continuo orchestra' the indications given in *Orfeo* are few, but all

First page of the printed Score of Monteverdi's opera
La Favola d'Orfeo, 1607 (publ. 1609)

[*facing page 160*

Piazza di San Marco, Venice (17th cent.)

facing page 161]

the more enlightening. At dramatic climaxes the original suddenly gives very exact directions as to the instrumental accompaniment of the continuo part which has remained for long stretches without any specification whatsoever. For instance, in the Facsimile edition (A. Sandberger, p. 36), at the entry of the messenger of ill-tidings in Act II, we find 'Un organo di legno ed un Chitarrone'. Five bars later, the shepherd replies to the sounds of 'un clavicembalo, Chitarrone et Viola da braccio'. From these statements alone it is quite clear what great dramaturgic significance Monteverdi attached to the colourful elaboration of the continuo part. The principal misunderstandings of these points by all editors of *Orfeo* up to the present time are to be seen at their most concentrated in the edition by G. F. Malipiero,[24] which includes a complete arrangement of the continuo in the form of a piano-score without any more precise directions as to the instrumentation. Malipiero here makes the fundamental mistake of converting the pedal-point-like continuo basses into notes of longer duration without taking into account that the writing of notes of lesser duration (at the same pitch) is obviously an indication that the chords are to be struck repeatedly.[25] One example will suffice: the passage 'Poichè non ho più speme' which in the original (Facs. Ed., Sandberger, p. 89) is written by Monteverdi as:

is given by Malipiero (loc. cit. p. 138) as:

In the first place, the use of alternate angular and curved slurs (or ties) which is remarkable throughout *Orfeo* shows that here it is not a matter of simple contraction. Rather should it be inferred that the slurring merely indicates the harmonic similarity of the chords actually sounding, but that in the case of the small curved slurs, the chords are to be struck repeatedly. Another mistake has crept into Malipiero's edition concerning the principle of interpreting the accidentals. Next to the ♭ (which may indicate a tendency towards flattening as well as towards sharpening) Monteverdi uses the sign xx (lesser sharpening) and ✖ (greater

M

sharpening) according to the number of semitones the succeeding (or even the preceding) note is to be sharpened. Of course these signs operate retrospectively. Indeed, they are often intended as a warning against undertaking any superfluous flattening.[26] Nevertheless, the fact that accurately figured continuo basses are also submitted to patently incorrect interpretation is clearly shown by a particularly glaring example. The passage in the original (loc. cit., p. 36)

is interpreted by O. Respighi[27] as the chord of C sharp minor, although every editor of *Orfeo* should know that at the period in question a **xx** against the bass-note denotes the first inversion, even when it is not added in writing.[28]

The rhythmic constitution of *Orfeo* and the interpretation of its frequently intricate-looking notation have for long been the subject of research. One of the most important functions of the conscientious editor is to reveal the rhythm of triple-time which often masquerades as $\frac{4}{4}$ in this score.[29] The most elementary rules of declamation prove that the well-known 'leitmotive' 'Ahi caso acerbo' (Act II) when it makes its choral entry should not be written as:

(Malipiero, 1930)

but as:

(Redlich, 1936)

Ahi   ca - so a-cer - bo, Ahi __ fat' em - pio e cru-de - le

Similarly, the rules of accentuation in natural declamation must set the standard for the notation of extensive sections of recitative. For Monteverdi, the bar-line had not yet acquired the architectonic significance of later epochs. The signature C, which is placed even before passages wherein the beats are markedly divisible into threes, may probably be explained as a psychological relic of the hesitation felt in earlier periods for noting down triple time.

One final word on textual criticism and its practical use as exemplified in my revision of the *Incoronazione*. The quite incredible carelessness in the writing of the Venetian manuscript[30] (made by several copyists) can be seen from the exact enumeration of the many problems which come to light in it and which are included in H. Goldschmidt's critical commentary.[31]

The indication of clefs in the Venetian manuscript, in particular, causes the modern interpreter much anxious thought.[32]   For instance, Goldschmidt draws attention to the remarkable fact that Ottone's part in Acts I and II is written in the mezzo-soprano clef, whereas in Act III it is in the alto clef.[33] This circumstance has involved modern editors in disagreement as to the effective register of the part. T. Wiel designates it as 'mezzo-soprano'; H. Kretzsch-mar[34] conceives it as counter-tenor, while H. Goldschmidt, in view of the explicit repeated occurence of the principal octave, C^1-C^2, would prefer to have it treated plainly as an alto part. Against this conception there is, of course, the fact that even definitely female characters were still often sung by men (accordingly counter-tenors) in Venice towards 1640. While Malipiero's edition (Collected Edition, Vol. XIII) scrupulously records these alternations in the vocal clefs, the alternations between the bass and tenor clefs in the *continuo* part are unfortunately omitted.   Consequently, the only authentic indications of the variation in instrumental tone-colour in this register are lacking:[35] a defect which can now be rectified in dependable manner from the facsimile reprint of the Venetian manuscript (Benvenuti). The appearance of the tenor clef in the continuo makes it absolutely certain that the bass instruments sounding an octave lower (contrabasses, chitarroni and bass gambas) are to remain silent and that the general orchestral environment is to be directed 'upwards'.[36]

The solution of the *orchestral* problems in *Orfeo* often proceeds from hypotheses similar to those in the *Vespers*. Lack of space, alone, prevents my treating of these solutions here. The reader who is interested in them may be referred once again to the special studies already cited much earlier.

In contrast to the methods exemplified in my own editions of Monteverdi from 1933 onwards, here explained in rough outline, there are, on the one hand, unrestrainedly Romantic revaluations of

Monteverdi's conceptions of sound, such as the new interpretation of *Orfeo* by O. Respighi and G. Benvenuti, 1934–5,[37] as well as Ernst Křenek's version of the *Incoronazione*, Vienna, 1937, the stylistic hypotheses of which have been expounded at some length by the editor himself.[38] The revision of the *Vespers*, 1610 which Paul Collaer[39] has recently undertaken, appears, on the other hand, to be actuated by an intransigent 'Musealer Klangmaterialismus'.* Far more convincing results had indubitably already been attained over ten years ago by Nadia Boulanger, whose gramophone recordings of Monteverdi (H.M.V.) have done much for the wider diffusion of his music. The fact that Nadia Boulanger's revisions are not as yet available in print makes it difficult to express any final opinion as to the scientific principles upon which they are based. The same applies to the revisions of Monteverdi, still substantially in manuscript, by J. A. Westrup,[40] to whom the honour of having rediscovered Monteverdi for the English musical public should undoubtedly be accorded.

* See Glossary: 'Musealer Klangmaterialismus'.

NOTES'

The page numbers shown in brackets below and at the heads of the forthcoming pages indicate the text-pages to which the endnotes apply.

PART I. THE STAGES OF MONTEVERDI'S CAREER

(pp. 1-9)

CHAPTER I

GENERAL SURVEY

[1] Cf. G. F. Malipiero (1930), op. cit., p. 127 ff.
[2] Preserved for the most part in the City Archives at Mantua and the Library of the Church of S. Marco, Venice. Reprinted in books on Monteverdi by E. Vogel, L. Schneider, G. F. Malipiero and D. de Paoli.
[3] Cf. Bibliography.
[4] Cf. Calendar, in Appendix.

CHAPTER II

YEARS OF APPRENTICESHIP IN CREMONA 1567-90

[1] Cf. D. de Paoli, op. cit.
[2] Two of his letters are extant, both dating from 1608, i.e. when his son Claudio was already a widower.
[3] He was dismissed from service at the Mantuan court at the same time as Claudio, 31 July 1612.
[4] Reprinted in fascimile in *Musica I* (Sanzoni), Florence, 1943.
[5] Facsimiles included by L. Schneider, and G. F. Malipiero, op. cit.
[6] In this connexion cf. the various forms of Palestrina's names: Pierluigi da Palestrina, Praenestinus, Johannes Praenestinus, Giovanni da Penestrina, Pallestrina, Palestina, and finally, even del Pelestino. All these variants are now by common consent reduced to Palestrina.
[7] Cf. Gaetano Cesari and Guido Pannain in *La Musica in Cremona nella seconda metà del sec. XVI*, Milan, 1939. (*Ist. e Monum.*, Vol. VI.)
[8] Cf. E. Dohrn, op. cit.
[9] Cf. *Ist. e Monum. della Musica Ital.*, Vol. VI (1939), which includes a large selection of the madrigals and church compositions.
[10] Not until 1897 (*Kirchenmusikalisches Jahrbuch*) did F. X. Haberl rectify the misconception of several centuries.
[11] Cf. E. Dohrn, op. cit., p. 19.

CHAPTER III

YEARS OF SERVICE AT MANTUA

[1] According to a letter dated 23 September 1594 from the Prefect of Police, G. Cossa.

[2] Cf. Monteverdi's letter of 28 December 1610.

[3] The first performance of this *Dafne* did not take place until 1597.

[4] Cf. Giulio Cesare Monteverdi's *Dichiarazione* (*Scherzi Musicali*, 1607).

[5] 'Anima mia perdona' and 'Che se tu se'il cor mio' (*IV Bk. of Madrigals*, 1603), 'Cruda Amarilli' and 'O Mirtillo' (*V Bk.*, 1605). Artusi makes a special point (cf. *Imperfettioni I*, 1600, p. 40a) of attacking the clusters of dissonances figuring in 'Anima mia perdona' and 'Che se tu se'il cor mio'. He quotes especially the concluding bars of each item as (anonymous) examples of improper use of dissonances, but slyly omits the *words* in both cases, giving his quotations as if they were taken from instrumental compositions. Yet these (omitted) highly emotional words, from Guarini's *Pastor fido*, coming at the end of a stanza and abounding in passionate and exclamatory phrases are no doubt the psychological key to the choice of Monteverdi's characteristic harmonies. Here are Artusi's two quotations:

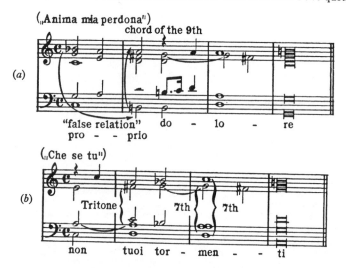

That the false relation and unprepared chord of the Ninth in (a) and the three chords of the Dominant Seventh plus the Tritone within the space of two bars in (b) must have been as startling in 1600 as Wagner's *Tristan* chromaticisms in 1859 may readily be admitted. It might be added that in this first part of Artusi's polemical essay (which is presented throughout as the dialogue of two lovers of Music, the name of one of whom, Antonio Goretti from Ferrara, is that of a real person, a musical amateur well known to Monteverdi) the bold use of 'Musica ficta' (Accidentals) by the modern section of Italian composers (especially A. Gabrieli and Cypriano de Rore) arouses Artusi's ire so strongly that he finally vents his indignation in the dictum (*Imperf. I*, p. 37) 'Il componere d'hoggi e una mescolanza' (meaning a mixture of diatonic, chromatic and enharmonic elements).

In the same volume (*Imperf. II, Ragg. II*, p. 46 et passim) Artusi heaps abuse upon two madrigals in *M.B.V.* (1605) which he again dishonestly mentions as 'nuovi Madrigali' (without indicating their composer's name) and quotes without their text. Both madrigals—'Cruda Amarilli' as well as 'O Mirtillo'—are again taken from Guarini's *Pastor fido*. The imaginative treatment of unprepared dissonances in the former in particular comes in for severe castigation and is labelled 'stile da barbaro' (barbaric style), the passage 'ahi lasso' and the subsequent passage on the significant word 'amaramente' (bitterly) being quoted without their emotional explanatory text. The following passage is Artusi's especial *bête noire*. It is here quoted in Artusi's manner (without the words 'amaramente insegni'):

(„Cruda Amarilli")

free 7th   Dissonance

The beginning of 'O Mirtillo' is termed by Artusi an 'impertinenza d'un principio' because this madrigal opens with a cadence tending towards F major via the subdominant, whereas the composition ends with a cadence leading to the final chord of D major. For the remaining items of Monteverdi's subjected to Artusi's pedantic criticism cf. notes 7 and 11.

[6] Cf. E. Vogel, op. cit.

[7] 'Era l'anima mia' and 'Ma se con la pietà' (*V Bk. of Madrigals*, 1605). Cf. H. F. Redlich, op. cit., p. 110 ff. In his *Imperfettioni II* (1603, p. 25 et passim) Artusi returns to his attack on Monteverdi's (still unpublished) progressive madrigals. This time, it is the turn of 'Era l'anima mia' and 'Ma se con la pietà' to be heavily censured and to be compared with 'Giustiniane alla Venetiana' (little Venetian street-songs). Both madrigals abound in bold suspensions, chordal combinations, imaginative chromaticisms and exclamatory intervals, especially those of the falling fourth so eminently characteristic of Monteverdi's new 'affettuoso' style, now in process of fermentation.

[8] Cf. the letters of 22 October 1633 and 2 February 1634.

[9] Further details in Part II, The Works.

[10] 'O Rosetta', 'Damigella', 'Clori Amorosa'.

[11] Cf. H. F. Redlich, op. cit., pp. 123, 128. The three items from Monteverdi's *Scherzi Musicali*, (publ. in 1607 by his brother Giulio Cesare) are attacked in Artusi's *Discorso secondo musicale di A. Braccini da Todi per la Dichiarazione*, etc. (1608), the continuation of *Discorso I* published in 1606 as a reply to Monteverdi's polemical preface to his *M.B.V.*, 1605. In this latter instance Artusi declares that Monteverdi seems to have no clear conception of rhythm and metre, as his time-signatures appear to be faulty. He specially attacks the signature C which, according to his reasoning, if applicable to 'O Rosetta' and 'Damigella', cannot possibly fit 'Clori Amorosa'. But here, Artusi is obviously mystified by Monteverdi's subtle art of cross-bar rhythm and by the fact that the triple bar rhythm is camouflaged by syncopation. Only a pedant insistent upon the obvious and insensitive to disguised rhythms could declare the composer of these three delightful 'balletti' to be deficient in the understanding of rhythm. A quotation of the first bar of each item will make it quite clear that the rhythm is in triple time in each case, but that it is simply masked by 'black' notes and Hemiolia notation:

„Damigella tutta bella"

„O Rosetta"

„Clori Amorosa"

¹² Cf. Letter of 22 October 1633.

¹³ On Monteverdi's erroneously expressed assumption in his letter of 28 November 1601 that B. Pallavicino had died, see Chapter IX, note 21.

¹⁴ 'Maestro de la Camera et de la Chiesa sopra la Musica', runs the title according to Monteverdi's own definition. (Cf. his letter of 28 November 1601.)

¹⁵ Cf. D. de Paoli, op. cit., p. 80; also E. Vogel, *Bibliothek der gedruckten Vokalmusik Italiens*, 1891. G. F. Malipiero (op. cit.) inexplicably omits this preface from his collection of documents.

¹⁶ Cf. Claudia's only extant petitionary letter of 16 November 1606 (E. Vogel and D. de Paoli, loc. cit.) in which she refers to her family's financial insecurity in the following moving words: '. . . our dues to the Customs are paid by Viadana, which continuing favour is of the utmost consequence in view of the cold weather which has set in. Longstanding serious illness was the cause of my spending money that I could not really afford. . . .'

¹⁷ Cf. the correspondence on this subject between the two brothers, D. de Paoli, p. 106 ff.

¹⁸ During Claudio's summer residence in Cremona, which was saddened by the deterioration in his wife's health, Giulio Cesare published the *Scherzi Musicali* in Venice at his brother's behest, together with the *Dichiarazione*. The work, the preface to which is dated 21 July 1607, is dedicated to Francesco Gonzaga.

¹⁹ Cf. more detailed information on this point in Part II.

²⁰ Cf. D. de Paoli, op. cit., p. 124.

²¹ Cf. his bitter remark that the Duke had paid Gagliano 200 scudi 'for nothing', whereas he (Monteverdi) had gone unrewarded 'for something'. (Letter of 2 December 1608.)

²² Letter of 1 May 1627.

²³ Ferdinando Gonzaga's letter of 2 February 1608.

²⁴ He was Monteverdi's collaborator in the sacred opera *Maddalena*.

²⁵ Cf. A. Solerti, *Le origini del Melodramma* (1903), pp. 139, 182, 213 ff.

²⁶ Ademollo's statement that Peri composed the recitatives in *Arianna* was convincingly repudiated by D. de Paoli, op. cit., p. 143 ff.

²⁷ Letters dated 8 and 27 November 1608. (Cf. E. Vogel, op. cit.)

²⁸ Dated 2 December 1608.

²⁹ Monteverdi's dedicatory preface to Francesco Gonzaga is dated from Mantua (22 August). The extant letters of this period prove, however, that he actually remained in Cremona until after 10 September that year.

³⁰ Cf. the letter of 16 July 1610 from the singer, Casola, to Ferdinando Gonzaga, E. Vogel, op. cit., p. 365.

³¹ The preface to the printed edition of the Missa is dated September 1610.

Could the work actually have been in print when Monteverdi travelled to Rome? A letter of Francesco Gonzaga's dated 14 September that year gives the first tidings of the plans for the printed edition, the exact dating of which cannot at the moment be ascertained.

[32] Letter of 6 November 1615.

CHAPTER IV

MAESTRO DI CAPPELLA OF SAN MARCO

[1] Cf. Part II.

[2] Cf. de Paoli, op. cit., p. 188.

[3] de Paoli, op. cit., p. 192 ff.

[4] When Monteverdi entered upon his duties, the staff under his leadership comprised a deputy maestro di cappella, two organists, thirty or more singers, twenty or more instrumentalists (strings and wind). cf. de Paoli, loc. cit., p. 199 ff. The deputy maestri di cappella who held appointments under him were: Marc. A. Negri (until 1620), Alessandro Grandi (until 1627) and G. Rovetta (after 1627). The last-named became principal maestro di cappella after Monteverdi's death in 1643, was confirmed in his office in 1649 and died in 1668. Grandi and Rovetta, both pupils and admirers of the master, were, together with the Siennese, Claudio Saracini, notable champions of the tendencies in style he inaugurated.

[5] See the letter of 9 January 1620.

[6] Cf. A. Banchieri, *Lettere armoniche*, 1628; also G. F. Malipiero, op. cit., p. 10 ff.

[7] Cf. G. F. Malipiero, op. cit., p. 55.

[8] The young consort of Maria Gonzaga, daughter of Francesco IV.

[9] By the decree of 6 June 1628.

[10] Cf. Part II.

[11] Cf. letter of 24 February 1630.

[12] Cf. de Paoli, op. cit., p. 302 ff.

[13] Possibly this opera was also performed in Vienna where the Empress Eleonora Gonzaga was influential as Monteverdi's most powerful advocate. This would also explain the existence of the only extant manuscript score preserved in the copy in the Vienna State Library. Cf. also D. de Paoli, loc. cit., pp. 284 ff. and 318 ff. on this subject.

[14] Cf. Bibliography.

[15] Cf. G. Benvenuti's preface to his facsimile edition of the Venetian Manuscript, Milan, 1938.

[16] Cf. G. F. Malipiero, op. cit., p. 50 ff.

CHAPTER V

THE MAN AND THE ARTIST

[1] Cf. the chapter on Monteverdi in H. J. Moser's *Heinrich Schütz*, 1936.

[2] Cf. J. M. Müller-Blattau, *Die Kompositionslehre H. Schützens*, Leipzig, 1926.

[3] Cf. the portrait of Monteverdi in Marinoni's *Fiori Poetici*, 1644 (cf. Plate I), and the oil-painting of Schütz in the Catalogue-Room of the University Library at Leipzig.

[4] Cf. H. F. Redlich, op. cit., p. 220.

[5] Cf. letter of 2 February 1634.
[6] Cf. letters of the year 1627 (on *La Finta Pazza Licori*).
[7] Letter of 1 May 1627.
[8] Cf. Monteverdi's malicious letter of 28 November 1601.

CHAPTER VI

MUSIC AND SOCIETY IN MONTEVERDI'S LIFETIME

[1] He wrote—among others—the libretti to four celebrated Roman operas of the time: *S. Alessio*, music by S. Landi, 1634, *Chi soffre, speri*, music by V. Mazzocchi, and M. Marazzoli, 1639, *Il Palazzo incantato*, music by L. Rossi, 1642 and *Erminia sul Giordano*, music by Michelangelo Rossi, 1633, the last two after two subjects taken from Ariosto's *Orlando furioso* and T. Tasso's *Gerusalemme liberata*.

[2] The castrato Gualberto Magli from Florence was the first of his kind to create an operatic part. He sang the title role in Monteverdi's *Orfeo*, 20 February 1607. Cf. F. Haböck, *Die Kastraten und ihre Gesangskunst*, Stuttgart, 1926, page 228 et passim.

[3] Cf. Frescobaldi's later keyboard music and John Bull's Antwerp MS. of 1629.

[4] Cf. the printed edition of *Orfeo*, Venice, 1609. See also the similarly difficult coloratura passages in the Psalm 'Duo Seraphim' in Monteverdi's *Vespers*, 1610.

[5] So much so, that as late as 1671 Monteverdi's German 'opposite number', Heinrich Schütz (1585–1672) asked his pupil Chr. Bernhard to compose a motet 'in Palestrina's style' for his exequies.

[6] As early as in 1607 Franscesco Gonzaga praises the castrato Gualberto Magli for having memorized the whole part of Monteverdi's *Orfeo* and for having acted and sung it by heart with so much feeling (Cf. the letter to his brother, dated 23 February of that year.).

[7] Cf. O. Benevoli's gargantuan Mass in 48 parts for the consecration of Salzburg Cathedral, 1628.

PART II. THE WORKS

CHAPTER VII

MUSIC IN ITALY AT THE TIME OF MONTEVERDI'S ADVENT

[1] The famous MS. bearing his name (Florence, Cod. palat. 87) represents the most important source for the knowledge of the Italian 'Ars Nova'. Cf. J. Wolf, *Geschichte der Mensural-Notation*, Vol. I (1904), p. 228 et passim.

[2] Cf. H. F. Redlich, op. cit., p. 15 et passim.

[3] Cf. his *Symphoniae Sacrae* I–II, of 1597 and 1615 and his well-known *Sonata* 'Pian e Forte'.

CHAPTER VIII

PRINCIPLES

[1] Ist. e Monum. Vol. I, 1931.
[2] Cf. Pt. I, Chap. II ('Years of Apprenticeship in Cremona').
[3] Cf. H. F. Redlich, op. cit., Pt. III, chap. b/3.
[4] Cf. Monteverdi's preface to the *V Book of Madrigals*, 1605 and his brother's statements in the *Dichiarazione* to the *Scherzi Musicali* of 1607. (G. F. Malipiero, 1930, loc. cit.)
[5] Cf. Monteverdi's preface to the *VIII Book of Madrigals* (Malipiero, ibid., p. 90), where he writes, among other things, ' . . . diedi di piglio al divin Tasso, come poeta che esprime con ogni proprietà et naturalezza con la sua oratione quelle passioni, che tende a voler descrivere et ritrovai la descrittione, che fa del combattimento di Tancredi con Clorinda, per haver io le due passioni contrarie da mettere in canto Guerra cioè preghiera et morte . . .'
[6] There are no fewer than twelve settings of poems by Tasso in the *I, II, III, Books of Madrigals* (1587–92).
[7] *Nigra sum, Pulchra es, Audi coelum, 1st Magnificat.*
[8] *Combattimento, Lamento della Ninfa (VIII Book of Madrigals) Lettera amorosa (VII Book of Madrigals).*
[9] Tremolo and Pizzicato—effects in the *Combattimento*.
[10] Cf. (Pt. I. Chapter V, 'The Man and the Artist').

CHAPTER IX

THE LAST MADRIGALIST

[1] In my dissertation, *Das Problem des Stilwandels in Monteverdi's Madrigalwerk* (published as *Cl. Monteverdi, Vol. I, Das Madrigalwerk*). I would draw special attention to the synopsis in Chap. I/b, *Spezielle Problematik und zeitgeschichtliche Stellung des Monteverdischen Madrigals*. In the principal section of this publication, Pt. II *Das Madrigalwerk*, every individual Madrigal is submitted to thorough analysis of its form.
[2] Principally in the introduction dealing with the evolution of style, p. 9 ff, but also in Pt. III/a, *Vorgänger und Zeitgenossen in Monteverdis Denkwelt*, p. 220 ff.
[3] In the section *Dichter und Dichtungen*, p. 266 ff. and *Das Madrigal-Moment in Oper und Kirchenmusik*, p. 269 ff.
[4] *III and V Books of Madrigals* to the Duke, Vincenzo I Gonzaga; the *Scherzi Musicali*, 1607 to the subsequent Duke, Francesco IV Gonzaga; *VII Book of Madrigals* to Caterina di Medici, consort of Ferdinando I Gonzaga; *VII Book of Madrigals* to the Emperor Ferdinand III, consort of Eleonora Gonzaga.
[5] In the momentous *Pronunciamento* of the preface to the *V Book of Madrigals*, 1605 (with the supplementary *Dichiarazione* drawn up by his brother); and finally in the preface to the *VIII Book of Madrigals*, 1638 wherein his aesthetic reasoning is based on Plato and the 'stile concitato' is announced for the first time.
[6] Cf. H. F. Redlich, op. cit., p. 17 ff. et passim.
[7] With the exception of the 'Sacred Madrigals' which will be reviewed in Pt. II Chap. XII, 'The Church Musician'.
[8] As in 'Non così', and in the ballet 'Della Bellezza' (possibly by his brother),

a historically important prototype of the later Baroque dance suite with rudimentary dance types of the Pavane-Galliard, Allemande and Tripla.

[9] The *Dichiarazione* explains each separate point of the programme in the preface to the *V Book of Madrigals*, which itself concludes with the terse sentence, '. . . Il moderno compositore fabrica sopra li fondamenti della verità . . .'

[10] Cf. H. F. Redlich, op. cit., p. 43.

[11] 'Ardo sì' with 'risposta' and 'contrarisposta'.

[12] Cf. Th. Kroyer, *Dialog und Echo i.d. alten Chormusik*, in *Peters Jahrbuch*, 1916.

[13] Cf. the poetically objectifying coda in 'E dicea l'una sospirando' in the *Second Book of Madrigals*.

[14] Vattene pur crudel, Poi ch'ella, Là tra l'sangue.

[15] Stracciami pur, O primavera, Perfidissimo volto.

[16] Cf. Pt. I, Chap. III (Years of service in Mantua).

[17] Cf. also E. Vogel, *V.J.M.* III, 1887, pp. 331 ff.

[18] Cf. Leichtentritt SIMG XI, 1910, also Prunières in the new edition of his book on Monteverdi, 1926, where he writes on p. 57 as follows: 'Le Madrigal "O Mirtillo" a été certainement conçu par M. en vue de l'exécution par une voix seule'. Prunières adds the beginning of the piece in musical notation as it is given here.

[19] That Monteverdi did not wish these pieces—which had not as yet assumed the external features of monody—to be separated from the functions of the early Basso Continuo is implicit in the sub-title of the *Fifth Book of Madrigals*, which runs:—'Il quinto libro . . . col basso continuo per il Clavicembalo, Chitarrone, od altri simile istrumento; fatto particolarmente per li sei ultimi (the declared monodies) et per li altri (the polyphonic pieces) a beneplacito'. This observation by the composer throws a retrospective spotlight upon the performing possibilities of many of the pseudo-polyphonic numbers of the *Third* and *Fifth Books of Madrigals*.

[20] Cf. the quotation on p. 8 of Malipiero's book on Monteverdi, Milan, 1930, which is as follows: 'Essendo alcune parti in Dissonanza, e l'altre devono accordare fra di loro, se non fosse per esprimere un affetto di gran durezza, come fece Claudio Monteverdi nel Madrigale "O Mirtillo" sotto le parole "crudelissima Amarilli"'.

[21] B. Pallavicino certainly did not die in 1601 (as Cl. Monteverdi wrongly assumed in his letter of 28 November 1601). Indeed, he entered the order of monks of Calmaldoli and continued to publish numerous volumes of madrigals as well as of sacred music until after 1612, many of these works being dedicated to the House of Gonzaga. Cf. E. Vogel, *Bibl. d. gedr. welt. Vokalmusik Italiens*, Vol. II, p. 49 ff.: Eitner's *Q. L.*; Grove's Dictionary, 1927, and lastly, Pt. I, Chap. III, 'Years of service in Mantua'.

[22] Cf. H. F. Redlich, op. cit., p. 10, note 146. The reprint of 1615 (Antwerp, Phalesius), obviously unauthorized by Monteverdi, includes an additional Basso Continuo part, which is, however, in turn omitted from the Venetian reprint of 1620. Cf. D. de Paoli, op. cit., p. 55 ff.

[23] Cf. Note 19.

[24] Cf. H. F. Redlich, op. cit., p. 65 (note).

[25] *Il Primo Libro dei Madrigali*, Venezia 1611 (Collected Edition, Vol. IX).

[26] On the swift decline in the cultivation of the madrigal in the first third of the seventeenth century, cf. Pietro della Valle, G. B. Doni and other contemporary critics. See also H. F. Redlich, op. cit., p. 10, note 3 ff.

[27] Cf. the letter of 26 July 1610 from the singer, Casola, printed as Document 8 by E. Vogel, op. cit.

[28] Cf. H. F. Redlich, op. cit., p. 134 ff., 145 ff. In the later, new editions of the *V and VI Books of Madrigals* which were supervised by Monteverdi himself (the

VI was newly issued in 1615, 1620 and 1639), a supplementary Basso Continuo part was added, even to the definitely *a cappella* items. Cf. H. F. Redlich, op. cit., p. 146, note.

[29] On A. Coppini's sacred 'parodies' of Monteverdi's secular madrigals, cf. H. F. Redlich, op. cit., p. 32 ff.

[30] For further particulars of the 'Stile concitato', cf. Pt. II, Chap. XI, 'The first opera composer'.

[31] Cf. Pt. I, Chap. IV, 'Maestro di Cappella of San Marco'.

[32] Cf. Pt. II, Chap. XI, 'The first opera composer'.

[33] Cf. H. F. Redlich, op. cit., pp. 166–68. Here should be mentioned a passage (not quoted there) from G. B. Doni's 1594–1647 *Trattato della Musica scenica* (reprinted in part in A. Solerti's *Origini*, op. cit., p. 218 ff.), in which the style of these pieces and its limitations are critically examined with the corollary that they are 'mezza pesce e mezza carne' ('neither fish nor flesh').

[34] On the problems of practical revision of this piece, cf. H. F. Redlich, op. cit., p. 168 ff. and Pt. IV, of the present volume.

[35] In his contemporary theoretical treatise *Syntagma Musicum III*, 1619. Cf. H. F. Redlich, op. cit., p. 168 ff.

[36] Op. cit., p. 869.

[37] E. Schmitz, *Zur Geschichte des ital. Continuo Madrigals im 17. Jahrhundert.* S.M.G. XI, 511 ff.

[38] The distinguishing feature of the theme is once again the famous *ostinato* fourth exemplified in 'Tempro'.

[39] Cf. R. Haas, *Musik des Barocks*, pp. 197 ff.

[40] Cf. Pt. II, Chap. XI, 'The first opera composer'.

[41] The 'martial' chamber-duet 'Armato il cor', which was first published in 1632, but which turns up here, as also later in the posthumous publication of the *Madrigali e Canzonette* of 1651 (reprinted in Malipiero's Collected Edition, 1926–42, Vol. IX), exerted a most profound effect upon H. Schütz, as did also the ciacona 'Zefiro torna' included in the publication of 1651. On Schütz's recreative paraphrasing of both these pieces in Pt. II of his *Symphoniae Sacrae* of 1647, cf. H. F. Redlich, op. cit., p. 213, note.

[42] Cf. H. F. Redlich, op. cit., p. 197 d.

[43] Cf. Pt. II, 'The first opera composer'.

[44] Cf. Redlich, op. cit., p. 208 ff.

[45] Cf. the Variations on the 'Romanesca' Bass in *VII Book* ('Ohimé dov'è il mio ben').

[46] See note 41.

[47] 'Perchè se m'odiavi' and 'Su su, Pastorelli vezzosi', printed in monodic form in A. Vincenti's Collection of 1634, and first published in reprint by D. de Paoli, op. cit., (1945).

[48] Cf. H. F. Redlich, op. cit., p. 218 ff.

CHAPTER X

THE POETS OF MONTEVERDI'S MADRIGALS

[1] Cf. *Lyra Barberina* (1763). *Tratt. di Mus. scen.* App. p. 62 et passim.

[2] Cf. R. Schwartz, D.T.B. V/2, p. xxi et passim, D.T.B. XI/1, Intr. p. xi et passim. See also G. Cesari, *Die Entstehung des Madrigals*, Cremona, 1908, p. 41 et passim.

[3] Cf. A. Einstein, *The Italian Madrigal*, 3 vols. Princeton, U.S.A., Oxford University Press, London, 1949; also the same writer's edition of Marenzio's 5-pt. Madrigals (Books I–III), Leipzig, 1929; his *Dante im Madrigal*, A. F. MW. III/4, 1921; his *Ph. da Monte als Madrigalkomponist*, IGM, Congr. report, 1930 and finally his chapter in G. Adler's *Handbuch der Musikgeschichte*, 1930, p. 361 et passim. Cf. also H. F. Redlich, op. cit., p. 268 et passim, where more books on this subject are enumerated.

[4] Cf. E. Dohrn, *Ingegneri als Madrigalkomponist*, Hanover, 1936, p. 50 et passim.

[5] *Inedito*, Nr. 2, Rome, 1944.

CHAPTER XI

THE FIRST OPERA COMPOSER

[1] As early as 1590 two musical pastoral-plays by E. de Cavalieri (*Il Satiro* and *La disperazione di Fileno*) were performed, the music of which has been lost.

[2] For further details relating to the circumstances of the remarkable first performance see Pt. I. The bibliography will be found in Pt. IV and the question of the practical revision of this opera will be treated more fully in Pt. IV.

[3] Cf. D. de Paoli, op. cit., p. 111 ff.

[4] The list of the orchestra in the 'Intermedium' *Psiche ed Amore* (1565) by Striggio sen. and Corteccia comprises forty-four different instruments.

[5] Foremost Beaujoyeulx' *Ballet comique de la Royne*, Versailles, 1581.

[6] O. Vecchi's *Il Amfiparnasso*, printed in 1597.

[7] E. de Cavalieri's *Rappresentazione di anima e di corpo*, first performed in Rome, 1600.

[8] Cf. Vincenzo Galilei's theoretical and practical efforts: the *Dialogo* of 1591 and the monodic composition of the Ugolino stanzas from Dante's *Divina Commedia*. (Cf. Count Bardi's letter of 1634 to G. B. Doni, printed in A. Solerti, op. cit., p. 143 ff.)

[9] The first three pioneer works of the new species 'dramma per musica' which run on the same lines as Monteverdi's own later productions are given here in chronological order: 1597, *Dafne* (Peri-Corsi), 1600, *Euridice* (Peri), 1602, *Euridice* (Caccini). The last two produce the effect of being lyrically hesitant preliminary studies to the differently conceived treatment of the same material in Monteverdi's *Favola d'Orfeo*.

[10] For instance, Poliziano's Mantuan *Orfeo* as early as 1471.

[11] Guarini's *Pastor Fido* and Tasso's *Aminta*.

[12] Cf. M. Schneider, *Die Anfänge des Basso Continuo*, Berlin, 1918.

[13] Cf. E. de Cavalieri's preface (Reprint in A. Solerti, op. cit., p. 9 ff.).

[14] Cf. Peri's preface to his *Euridice* (Reprint in A. Solerti, op. cit., p. 43 ff.).

[15] Cf. R. Haas, *Aufführungspraxis*. Potsdam 1931, p. 118 ff.

[16] Cf. the great aria *Possente spirto* (Act III) and Orfeo's two songs with several verses: 'Ecco pur' and 'Vi ricorda, o boschi ombrosi' (Act II).

[17] Cf. Ambros-Leichtentritt, *Geschichte der Musik*, Vol. IV, p. 561 ff. See also A. Heuss, *Instrumentalstücke des Orfeo*, SIMG, Vol. IV.

[18] Thus, the much-debated syncopated passage in the ritornello of the song 'Vi ricorda' (Act II) unmistakably demonstrates the influence of contemporary French rhythm which was later also to obtrude itself perceptibly in the 'alla francese' pieces in the *VII Book of Madrigals*. Cf. H. F. Redlich, op. cit., p. 127 ff.

[19] Cf. Pt. I, Chap. III, 'Years of service at Mantua'.

[20] Letter of 9 December 1616. Cf. G. F. Malipiero, op. cit., p. 166 ff.

²¹ Cf. also Monteverdi's preface to the *VIII Book of Madrigals*, 1638.

²² For the bibliography to *Arianna*, cf. Appendix.

²³ Letter of 20 March 1620.

²⁴ Cf. A. Solerti, op. cit., p. 82 ff.

²⁵ Cf. A. Solerti, op. cit., p. 213 ff., 131 ff. For Follino, cf. D. de Paoli, op. cit., p. 159 ff.

²⁶ Dido's *Lament* in Purcell's *Dido and Aeneas, c.* 1689 may be mentioned as one of the last and most beautiful of these successors of Monteverdi's *Lamento*.

²⁷ Letter of 20 March 1620 to A. Striggio. See also the letter of 22 October 1633, in which Monteverdi affirms that *Plato* was his chief instructor in the natural method of portraying the emotions when he was working at *Ariadne's Lament*.

²⁸ Cf. H. F. Redlich, op. cit., p. 140 ff.

²⁹ Further details in the bibliography to *Arianna* in Pt. II, Chap. XII ('The Church Musician'). Cf. also H. F. Redlich, p. 134 ff.

³⁰ Reprint in Vol. XV/2 of the Collected Edition (Malipiero). The continuo bass of the sacred *Kontrafaktur* repeatedly shows a different reading from the other copies. Further details in Pt. II, Chap. XII ('The Church Musician').

³¹ Cf. F. Torrefranca, *Inedito*, no. 2, Rome, 1944, which includes a complete reprint of this rediscovery. In this same copy-book of Fuci's, the third copy of the *Arianna-Lamento*, previously mentioned, may also be found. A *Lamento di Apollo* (Text by A. Striggio jun.) of 1619 is one of the many lost works belonging to Monteverdi's Venetian period.

³² Cf. D. de Paoli, op. cit., p. 145.

³³ According to H. Prunières, op. cit., it is the only Ballet 'a la francese' which has been preserved intact.

³⁴ The work ends with a short vocal ballet *Della Bellezza*.

³⁵ 'Vi ricorda, o boschi ombrosi', cf. also G. F. Malipiero, op. cit., p. 39.

³⁶ For further information as to the authors of the libretti of these operas, see Bibliography.

³⁷ *Melissa e Bradamante*, *Didone*, *Gli Argonauti* and *Adone*, 1639, the last-named possibly by F. Manelli. On this point, cf. A. Loewenberg, *Annals of Opera*, Cambridge, 1943.

³⁸ Information on this first *Ulisse* opera of Monteverdi's in G. Giordani's *Intorno al Gran Teatro del Comune ed altri minori in Bologna*, Bologna, 1855, the source of which is a little-known pamphlet: *Le glorie della Musica e della Poesia rappresentandosi in Bologna la Delia e l'Ulisse nel teatro degli illustrissimi Guastavillari*, Bologna, 1630 (4to). This title (also mentioned by de Paoli, op. cit., p. 284), does not, however, include any kind of indication of the fact that the music for these texts was the work of Monteverdi or Manelli. The relevant paragraph must therefore be regarded as a totally unfounded assumption of Giordani's. Cf. also Kretzschmar, *Geschichte der Oper*, 1919, op. cit.

³⁹ Cf. Monteverdi's letters of 21 and 24 November 1615 to A. Striggio.

⁴⁰ I have so far been unable to identify either the librettist or the probable instigator of this musically enchanting little work, which recalls the *Ballo dell' Ingrate*, and of which the instrumental movements are influenced by French models.

⁴¹ See letter of 21 November 1615.

⁴² On Monteverdi's relationship to Tasso cf. Pt. I, Chap. V ('The Man and the Artist') and Pt. II, Chap. IX ('The last madrigalist').

⁴³ Cf. Monteverdi's preface to the *VIII Book of Madrigals*.

⁴⁴ 'Qui si lascia l'arco, e si strappano le corde con duoi diti', runs the remarkable direction for actual performance in the original.

⁴⁵ Cf. Monteverdi's preface to the *VIII Book of Madrigals*. In 1627 Monteverdi returned once again to Tasso's inexhaustible epic in his opera *Armida*, now lost.

[46] Cf. letter of 9 January 1620.

[47] After 1638 Manelli was installed as a bass singer at the church of San Marco, and was consequently a close collaborator of Monteverdi's, with whom his name was repeatedly connected as a composer of opera. Cf. A. Loewenberg, op. cit., D. de Paoli, op. cit.

[48] Cf. C. Sachs, *Barockmusik*, 1919.

[49] The music (now lost) was ascribed to Monteverdi by G. C. Bonlini in his *Le Glorie della Poesia e della Musica*, Venice, 1730. On the other hand, the (extant) libretto contains a dedication to A. Grimani signed by F. Manelli. Monteverdi is not mentioned therein. G. Radiciotti (in *L'Arte musicale in Tivoli*, 1921) regards Manelli as the composer. Cf. also O. Sonneck, *Catalogue of Opera Librettos before 1800*, Library of Congress, 1913–14, and A. Loewenberg, op. cit.

[50] On this occasion Rinuccini's text was newly published by Bariletti, Venice, 1640. In Bariletti's dedicatory preface, Monteverdi's name is written as 'Signor Claudio Monte Verdi', fresh evidence against the spelling of his name as 'Monteverde' still prevalent to-day. The reprint also includes an enthusiastic sonnet from the pen of the versatile B. Ferrari. In the preface and the sonnet Monteverdi is described as 'celebratissimo Apollo del secolo, e prima intelligenza del cielo harmonico', and as 'oracolo della Musica'.

[51] The music is lost, whereas the libretto is preserved in hand-writing. Cf. O. Sonneck, op. cit., p. 805.

[52] The music is lost, but a complete scenario has been preserved from Morandi's libretto. Cf. A. Solerti in *Riv. Mus. Ital.*, fasc. 1, 1904.

[53] No. 18763, Sec. II. For further bibliographical details, cf. Appendix.

[54] Cf. W. Ambros (Leichtentritt), *Geschichte der Musik*, Vol. IV, p. 591 ff.

[55] *Vierteljahrschrift für Musikwissenschaft*, III, 1887.

[56] *Studien zu Gesch. d. ital. Oper im 17. Jahrhundert*, Vol. 2, 1901–4, and *SIMG* IV and IX.

[57] *DTOE*, 1922 (ed. R. Haas) and Vol. XII of the Coll. Ed. (Malipiero) 1930. Further bibliographical details in Pt. IV.

[58] *La Delia e l'Ulisse*, performed in the Teatro Guastavillari at Bologna, 1630, cf. note 38; also D. de Paoli, op. cit., pp. 284 and 318; G. Pannain (*Ist. e Monum.* Vol. VI, 1939, Introduction).

[59] Cf. G. Pannain, op. cit.

[60] Coll. Ed. Vol. XII, Introduction.

[61] L. Schneider and D. de Paoli, op. cit., give complete tables of the contents of the opera.

[62] See further below in the discussion of the music to the *Incoronazione*.

[63] *Il Ritorno di Ulisse in Patria, trascrizione e riduzione per le scene moderne di Luigi Dallapiccola* (Milan, 1942).

[64] Cf. the essay on this subject in 'Musica' (Sanzoni) II, 1943.

[65] Gazzettino, Venice, 17 May 1942.

[66] No. 439 *IT. CL.* 4 of a collection made by G. Contarini of about 124 indeterminable seventeenth- and eighteenth-century opera scores from the estate of Marco Contarini, the Procurator of San Marco. Cf. T Wiel, *I codici Contariniani del secolo XVII*, Venice, 1888; also H. Goldschmidt, *Studien etc.*, Vol. II, 1904.

[67] Complete reprint of this in Goldschmidt, op. cit., pp. 33 ff.

[68] Cf. L. N. Galvani, *I teatri musicali del Venezia nel sec. XVII*, 1878, p. 31.

[69] L. Schneider, (op. cit.) thinks it possible that this 'argomento', which is inaccurate in its contents, emanates from the publisher Giuliani rather than from Busenello.

[70] Reprints of this in H. Goldschmidt, op. cit., Vol. II (incomplete), and in the Coll. Ed. (Malipiero) Vol. XIII (complete).

[71] MS. copy in the Library of the R. Conservatorio S. Pietro da Maiella, Naples.

[72] All the sections of the score which were newly added to the Naples MS. were first printed in the Supplement to Vol. XIII of Coll. Ed. The opera, which was revived at SS. Giovanni e Paolo during Carnival 1646, was given a later performance by the *Febi Armonici* company in Naples in 1651. A. Loewenberg (op. cit.) considers this as possibly the first performance in Naples of any opera whatsoever! Malipiero (cf. preface to Vol. XIII) assumes that the Naples MS. was originally prepared for the first performance there. These new portions of the score, prepared eight years after Monteverdi's death, cannot therefore be authentic. They may possibly be traced to the second Venetian performance of the work in 1646, which may have taken account of indications given by the composer *after* the original performance. (See his revisions of the Venetian MS.) A facsimile of the Venetian MS., in which Monteverdi's subsequent revisions may clearly be distinguished from the handwriting of three different copyists, was published by G. Benvenuti, Milan, 1938. He further proves the inauthenticity of the Naples additions in an earlier article (*Riv. Mus. Ital.* 1937, No. 2).

[73] With this work Busenello inaugurated the series of operatic subjects based on historical facts which, at an epoch when preference was given to Greek and Roman mythology, still gave an impression of rarity.

[74] Busenello was considered one of the best qualified literary amateurs in Venice. In his hours of leisure he wrote the five libretti, of which four were composed by Cavalli and the fifth was the *Incoronazione*, and all of which were published together in one volume in 1656 as *Ore Ociose*. They comprise: *Gli amori di Apollo e di Dafne*, *La Didone*, *La prosperità di Giulio Cesare* (historical subject), *La Statira* and *L'Incoronazione* (historical subject). Cf. H. Kretzschmar *V. f. MW*, VIII, 1892.

[75] *V. f. MW.*, Vol. X, 1894.

[76] Kretzschmar, for instance, (in *Beiträge zur Gesch. d. venez. Oper, Peters Jahrb.*, 1907) is able to give information upon the pecuniary difficulties of this very theatre.

[77] For further information on this point, cf. H. F. Redlich, *Monteverdis 'Incoronazione di Poppea', Schweiz. Musikzeitung*, No. 23, 1927, p. 621 ff.

[78] This choral ending of Busenello's, included in the Naples MS., is composed for four-part choir and orchestra in Cavalli's magnificent style, an elaboration which was certainly not in keeping with Monteverdi's intentions.

[79] First and foremost, by H. Kretzschmar, H. Goldschmidt, E. Wellesz, (*St. z. MW. I*) and R. Haas, *Musik des Barocks*, 1929, and *Beiheft IX* of *DTOE* 1922).

[80] Cf. H. Goldschmidt, op. cit., Vol. II, p. 12 ff.

[81] In the introduction to the Facsimile-Reprint of the Venetian MS., Milan, 1938, as also in the *Riv. Mus. Ital.* 1937, No. 2.

[82] Details of musical criticism of the text of the *Incoronazione* MSS. are surveyed in the following publications: H. F. Redlich, *Notationsprobleme in Cl. Monteverdis 'Incoronazione di Poppea', Acta Musicologica*, Vol. X, Fasc. III, 1938, Copenhagen; also in the same author's article, *Schweiz. Musikztg.*, No. 23, 1937 and lastly, D. de Paoli, op. cit.

CHAPTER XII

THE CHURCH MUSICIAN

[1] The comparative length of this chapter may be justified by the facts that, at the present day, Monteverdi's collected church compositions are available in the reprints of the Complete Edition (ed. Malipiero) and that more accurate

N

analyses and more reliable appreciation are consequently possible for the first time. The works dealt with here have received only very slight, if any, attention in earlier biographies of Monteverdi and even in specialist studies of church music.

[2] Cf. *Dichiarazione*, 1607 (Reprint by Malipiero, loc. cit., p. 78): 'cioè che considera l'armonia non comandata, ma comandante, e non serva ma signora del oratione . . .'

[3] Cf. E. E. Lowinsky, *Secret Chromatic Art in the Netherlands Motet*, Columbia Univ. U.S.A., 1945.

[4] Cf. *Dichiarazione*, 1607, loc. cit., '. . . seconda Prattica . . . sia quella che versa intorno alla perfettione della melodia, cioè che considera l'armonia comandata, e non comandante, e per signora dell'armonia pone l'oratione . . .'

[5] Letter of 22 October 1633.

[6] Preface to the *V Book of Madrigals*, 1605.

[7] Preface to the *VIII Book of Madrigals*, 1638.

[8] D. de Paoli, op. cit., p. 185 ff.

[9] *Esemplare o sia Saggio fondamentale di contrappunto*, 1774–75, 2 Vols. Vol. II, p. 242 ff.

[10] Cf. Mozart's Salzburg Masses.

[11] Thus, as early as 1611 M. Praetorius printed in his *Hymnodia Sionia* a 'Confiteor a 5 a la francese' which Monteverdi himself had not published until 1641 in the *Selva*. The piece *must* therefore have originated before 1611, i.e. during the time he was working on the *Vespers* in 1610. (Cf. Leichtentritt op. cit.)

[12] The extant bass part was published in facsimile reprint as a supplement to Vol. XVI of the Coll. Ed.

[13] The *Madr. Spir.* comprise twenty-one items, the *Cant. Sacrae*, twenty-three and the *Canzonette*, twenty-one, all of which are of short duration and small proportions.

[14] Cf. the preface to the *Madrigali Spirituali*, dated 31 July 1583, (printed in the Supplement to Vol. XVI of the Coll. Ed.).

[15] For the Bibliography, see Appendix.

[16] During this year Peri was commissioned to compose the music to Rinuccini's *Dafne* libretto. The opera itself was not given its first performance until 1597. Cf. O. Sonneck, *Dafne, the first opera*, *SIMG*, Vol. XV, 1913–14.

[17] Cf. *Ist. e Mon. della Mus. Ital.*, Vol. VI, 1939.

[18] Nevertheless, see Monteverdi's letter of 1601, published Malipiero, op. cit., p. 34 ff., wherein he speaks of Masses and Motets which must have originated before this year.

[19] Cf. Pt. I, Chap. II ('Years of Apprenticeship in Cremona').

[20] P. Wagner, *Geschichte der Messe, I*, 1913, p. 415.

[21] C. v. Winterfeld, *Gabrieli und sein Zeitalter*, Vol. II, p. 58 ff. (1834).

[22] Letter of 5 October 1887 to Arrigo Boito. (Cf. G. Verdi, *Ausgewählte Briefe*, ed. Franz Werfel, 1926, p. 331.)

[23] A fourth Mass, written for the celebration of the ending of the plague in Venice and, according to contemporary reports, conceived in the pompous style of the 'Seconda Prattica', has been lost.

[24] Here, for the sake of clarity, designated as A, B, and C.

[25] Details as to Bibliography in Pt. IV.

[26] *Crucifixus* and *Resurrexit*, the expressive sections of the *Credo*, in which Monteverdi regarded modernist treatment of the material as permissible, not to say more appropriate.

[27] In the foreword to Tirabassi's reprint of the Mass (Brussels, 1914).

[28] Cf. Vol. XV, Coll. Ed. (Malipiero).

[29] Syllabic declamation had already been a characteristic of M. A. Ingegneri's Masses. Cf. G. Pannain, op. cit. and P. Wagner, op. cit.

30 'Il qual Crucifixus servirà per variatione della Messa a 4 pigliando questo in loco di quello notato tra li due segni' (Coll. Ed., Vol. XV/1, p. 187.).

31 Cf. M. Praetorius' *Syntagma Musicum*, III, 1619 (Reprint by E. Bernoulli, 1916), p. 121 ff., Chapter VII, the original title of which runs: 'Welcher Gestalt ein jedes Concert und Mutet mit wenig oder vielen Choren in der Eil und ohne sonderbare Mühe mit allerley Instrumenten und Menschenstimmen angeordnet und distribuiert werden könne'.

32 For instance, in the preface to his *Auferstehungshistorie* of 1623.

33 Coll. Ed. Vol. XV, 1, p. 117.

34 The original title of the Publication of 1610 runs: 'Sanctissimi Virgini Missa senis vocibus ad ecclesiarum coros ac Vesperae pluribus decantandae cum nonnullis sacris concentibus, ad sacella sive Principum Cubicula accomodata. Opera a Cl. Monteverdi nuper effecta . . . 1610'.

35 That G. Gabrieli's and Monteverdi's lists of orchestral instruments were entirely in keeping with practical conditions in Venice at that time may be seen from the contemporary orchestral list at San Marco which comprised 8 violins, 11 small viols, 2 tenor viols, 3 large viols, 2 cornetts, 1 bassoon, 3 trombones and 4 theorboes. Cf. R. Haas, *Aufführungspraxis*, Potsdam, 1932, p. 167 ff.

36 Today, the Vespers are liturgically combined with the Mass only on Holy Saturday, whereas in the seventeenth century this liturgical association was more frequent, as may be seen, for instance, from the *Chorordnung* of Augsburg Cathedral, 1616 (Cf. O. Ursprung, *Katholische Kirchenmusik*, Potsdam, 1931. p. 194 ff.).

37 On the obligatory combination of Vespers and Magnificat in the Middle Ages, particularly on the suitable polyphonic execution of the latter on festivals during Advent-and Easter-weeks, cf. M. Seiffert's exposition of the problem of Pachelbel's *Magnificat Fugues* in *DTB*, II, 1, p. xxi ff. The passage is of particular interest as it deals with the function of the Magnificat in the Roman as well as in the Lutheran rite.

38 Cf. Pt. IV (The problems of editing and performance).

39 For further information see H. F. Redlich, *Cl. Monteverdi, Schweiz. Musikztg.* No. 19–20, 1934.

40 Reprint in *Bärenreiter* Edition, Cassel, 1941 (ed. by K. Matthaei).

41 Cf. the account of M. Praetorius' earlier printing of this piece, Ch. XII, Note 11.

42 Cf. H. F. Redlich, op. cit., p. 178 ff.

43 Cf. H. F. Redlich, *Monteverdi's Religious Music, Music and Letters*, October 1946.

44 Cf. H. F. Redlich, *Monteverdi's Religious Music, Music and Letters*, October 1946.

45 Cf. H. Schütz, *Dialogo per la Pascua* (Coll. Ed. Vol. XIV).

46 The reprint in duplicate of the composition (pp. 227 and 510) in the same volume (XVI) of the Coll. Ed. without any kind of editorial reference to the complete identity of the two versions is hardly justifiable.

47 On the last-named piece, cf. H. F. Redlich, *Music and Letters*, October 1946, op. cit.

48 The three items mentioned had already been published in a reprint in 1935 by A. Adrio, who submitted them to careful analysis in his excellent study *Die Anfänge des Geistlichen Konzerts*, 1935. Another commendable specialist study on the same subject is Bettina Lupo's essay *Sacre Monodie Monteverdiane (Musica,* Sanzoni, II, Florence, 1943).

49 Cf. H. F. Redlich, op. cit., p. 32 ff.

50 Cf. Coll. Ed., Vol. XV/2, p. 762, at the passage 'heu iam' (*see overleaf*).

CHAPTER XIII

THE MUSICAL INVENTOR

[1] Cf. the preface to the *V Book of Madrigals*.

[2] Climaxes: Orfeo's aria in the underworld, 'Possente spirto', with harp, violins, oboes and string ensemble; the 'Sonata sopra Sancta Maria' of the *Vespers*, 1610, in which a group of brass instruments after the manner of G. Gabrieli together with a string orchestra weave a pre-symphonic fabric around

the choral intonation of a motive from Plainchant. The final section of the
'Sonata' itself may be described as an anticipation of the symphonic recapitulation.
³ Cf. Monteverdi's preface to the *VIII Book of Madrigals*, 1638.
⁴ Cf. J. M. Müller-Blattau, *Die Kompositionslehre Heinrich Schützens in der
Fassung seines Schülers Ch. Bernhard*, Leipzig, 1926, p. 90 ff.
⁵ As it appears at its most distinctive in Guédron's *Airs de Cour*.
⁶ Most of all in the *Incoronazione*. Cf. also Pt. II, Chap. XI ('The first opera
composer').
⁷ Cf. H. F. Redlich, op. cit., p. 270.
⁸ Cf. the Facsimile Edition of the *Incoronazione*, Milan, 1938.
⁹ E. de Cavalieri's *Rappresentazione di corpo e di anima*, 1600, combining gesture
and operatic costume with the musical structure of an oratorio, is probably the
only predecessor which comes into consideration.

PART III

MONTEVERDI IN THE EYES OF POSTERITY

¹ New editions of the *I–VI Books of Madrigals* followed one another in rapid
succession until 1620. After that date there were no new editions of *Books I–V*,
and the few new editions of *Books VI–VII* were spread over a long period from
1621 to 1643. The *VIII Book of Madrigals* was not reissued during Monteverdi's
lifetime, nor subsequently, despite its experimental character and the revolutionary
novelty of its contents. Cf. E. Vogel, *Bibliothek der gedruckten weltlichen Vokalmusik Italiens*, 2 Vols., 1892.
² Cf. the treatises by G. B. Doni, Pietro della Valle, etc. Further details in
H. F. Redlich, op. cit., p. 28 ff., and in A. Solerti, *Origini del Melodramma*, 1903.
³ M. Praetorius, *Polyhymnia*, 1611, *Syntagma III*, 1619, S. Schein, *Opella
Nova*, 1618, 1626, H. Schütz, *Symphoniae Sacrae I*, 1629, and the collective
publications of Donfried, 1621 and Calvus, 1620.
⁴ Only some of the operas inspired by Cardinal Rospigliosi, later Pope Clement
IX, will be mentioned here: *Che soffre, speri*, 1639 by Mazzocchi-Marazzoli, and
S. Landi's *San Alessio*, 1634, to which he also contributed the librettos.
⁵ A. Profius, *Geistliche Concerte und Harmonien*, 1641–46.
⁶ Cf. H. F. Redlich, op. cit., p. 213 ff., 215 ff.
⁷ Cf. Chapter XIII, Note 4.
⁸ Cf. J. M. Müller-Blattau's *Einleitung*, op. cit., p. 3 ff.
⁹ *Laconismo delle alte qualità di Claudio Monte Verde* . . . , Reprint in Malipiero,
op. cit., p. 50 ff.
¹⁰ Reproduced in *Lyra Barberina*, 1763. Cf. also H. F. Redlich, op. cit., p.
153 ff.
¹¹ In his *Zang Bloemzel*, 1642. Cf. H. F. Redlich, op. cit., p. 33 ff.
¹² In his fundamental treatise on counterpoint, *Esemplare o sia Saggio fondamentale*, 1774, in which, among other works, two madrigals and the *Agnus Dei*
from the Mass *In illo tempore* are reproduced in full. Cf. H. F. Redlich, op. cit.,
pp. 34, 69 ff., 104 ff.
¹³ Edited by R. Eitner in Vol. X of the *Publ. für Musikforschung*, 1881.
¹⁴ *V.f. MW.*, 1887, and *Bibliothek der gedruckten weltlichen Vokalmusik Italiens*,
1892, 2 Vols. (With supplement by A. Einstein in the American journal *Notes*,
1945–46.)
¹⁵ For details, see Bibliography.

16 For details, see Bibliography.

17 Bibliographical details of the ten practical editions since 1905 in the Appendix.

18 Cf. op. cit., of this book.

19 For details see op. cit. of this book.

20 See Bibliography.

21 Reprinted selections edited by A Mendelssohn, L. Landshoff; analytical studies by H. Leichtentritt, 1908, E. Schmitz, 1910. See also Bibliography.

22 Frankfort Dissertation, 1931, published as a book, Berlin, 1932.

23 C. v. Winterfeld in his *Gabrieli*, 1834. He scored the *Vespers* of 1610 as Vol. 58 of his Collection of Manuscripts. Cf. also Ambros-Leichtentritt, *Geschichte der Musik*, Vol. IV (new edition), 1909, and H. Leichtentritt's *Geschichte der Motette*, 1908.

24 For bibliographical details, see Appendix.

25 The last-named in a new edition with a critical commentary reprinted yet again in *Ist. e Monum. della Mus. Ital.*, Vol. VI, 1939.

26 Vol. XIV of the Coll. Ed.

27 1935, cities in Switzerland (the Häusermann Privatchor, conducted by H. Dubs); 1937, New York (Schola Cantorum, Hugh Ross); 1942–45, Radio Beromünster, Switzerland (conductor, H. Scherchen); 1946–47, London, Morley College and B.B.C. (conductor, Walter Goehr).

28 Cf. K. Matthaei's preface to his edition, *Bärenreiter* Edition, 1941.

29 Pt. IV ('The problems of edition and performance') will include a discussion of this antithesis and its significance for the perception of the realities of Monteverdi's style.

30 Malipiero's book is of special importance as the first collection of all Monteverdi's extant letters, personal documents, etc. It also includes the majority of the original prefaces, as well as extracts from polemical treatises, eulogies and obituary notices relating to Monteverdi. It is unfortunately deficient in scholarly completeness.

31 S. Landi, *La Morte d'Orfeo*, 1619, L. Rossi, *Orfeo* (Paris, 1647), H. Schütz, *Orpheus* Ballet (Dresden, 1638, lost).

32 Two of which—*Orpheus* and *Armida*—were composed on subjects once chosen by Monteverdi himself.

33 Cf. Wagner's essay, *Oper und Drama*, 1851.

34 Cf. Monteverdi's rejection of Busenello's pompous finale for *L'Incoronazione* and the significant substitution of the final love duet, with words by the composer himself.

35 *Orpheus* (in three versions: Mannheim, 1925, Munich, 1931 and Dresden, 1940), *Klage der Ariadne* (1940), *Tanz der Sproeden* (1940).

PART IV

THE PROBLEMS OF EDITING AND PERFORMANCE

1 op. cit., p. 174.

2 Cf. D. de Paoli, op. cit., p. 328. Passages in this book are supplemented by Prof. de Paoli's correspondence with the present writer. Cf. also G. Benvenuti's preface to the Facsimile Edition of the *Incoronazione*, 1938.

3 (*a*) MS. in the Bibl. Naz. Florence: MSS., Cl. XIX, No. 114; (*b*) Transcript by the copyist F. M. Fuci in his *Grilanda*, discovered by F. Torrefranca, *Inedito*, *II*, 1944, Rome.

4 Cf. Plate V.

[5] The majority of the original editions are in the library of the Liceo Musicale, Bologna. The places where these extant copies are to be found may be ascertained from R. Eitner's *Quellenlexikon* and E. Vogel's *Bibl. der gedr. welt. Vokalmusik Italiens*, 1892.

[6] R. Eitner, E. Vogel, T. Wiel, H. Goldschmidt, R. Haas, H. Prunières, Cl. Tessier and others. See also Plate VII.

[7] Cf. Pt. III.

[8] Cf. Bibliography.

[9] The problems of notation are discussed in my article *Notationsprobleme in Cl. Monteverdis Incoronazione, Acta Mus. X*, Fasc. III, 1938, Copenhagen.

[10] R. Haas, *Aufführungspraxis*, Potsdam, 1931 and A. Schering, *Aufführungspraxis alter Musik*, Berlin, 1931.

[11] *Orfeo*, London, 1923, *Combattimento*, London, 1931, *Incoronazione*, Italy, 1937 (MS).

[12] Thus, as early as 1933 the Häusermann Privatchor, Zürich, gave a performance of several madrigals from the *Seventh* and *Ninth Books of Madrigals* in a new edition prepared by myself. On this occassion a group of variegated accompanying instruments, with harpsichords, gambas, viols, and guitars, formed part of the obbligato ensemble. Since then, these new versions of the madrigals have repeatedly been performed in U.S.A. and England.

[13] Cf. Part III.

[14] See the detailed treatment of this complicated subject in my series of articles *Claudio Monteverdi*, in *Schw. Mztg*. No. 19–20, 1934.

[15] *Syntagma III*, Kap. XIII, p. 72 (New edition by Bernoulli, 1916).

[16] *Syntagma III*, p. 84 ff.

[17] Ibid. p. 155 ff.

[18] For instance, in the introduction to his new edition of Praetorius' *Syntagma III*, Ed. Bernoulli informs us as to the extent of the improvisatory colouring of all the parts customary at that period. On page xxv he writes: ' . . . That, in respect of this diminution, or colouring, e.g. the sub-division of the rhythmic value of a note into several shorter notes through paraphrasing the principal note, it was *not only* the part entrusted with the melody which came into question, is proved by the indications in the Basso continuo part of No. XIV (of the *Polyhymnia Panegyrica*) . . . .' At the end of Cantus I in the very first item of the *Pol. Pan.*, for instance, the following alternatives are printed one below the other:

(Res facta)

[19] *Scherzi Musicali*, 1607, Coll. Ed. Vol. X.

[20] Ibid. p. 83 ff.

[21] My practical edition of *Orfeo* was first performed in February 1936 in Zürich by the Häusermann Privatchor, conductor H. Dubs. The practical edition of the *Incoronazione*, which was begun at the same time for use in Switzerland, was ready in 1937 for performance. The first performance in Switzerland,

which had been arranged for 1939, was necessarily cancelled owing to the outbreak of the Second World War. This version, portions of which had already been given concert-performance in London in 1945, was first performed in its entirety in London on 17 May 1948 by the Morley College Society and the B.B.C., conducted by Walter Goehr.

[22] Cf. H. F. Redlich, *Zur Bearbeitung von Monteverdis 'Orfeo', Schweiz. Musikztg.* Heft 2/3, 1936. By the same author, *Monteverdis 'L'Incoronazione di Poppea', Schweiz. Musikztg.* No. 23, 1937.

[23] Cf. A. Solerti, *Gli albori dei melodramma*, 1903.

[24] Coll. Ed., Vol. XI. This edition contains a great many obvious misprints which, if accurately compared with the facsimile prints, are seen to be quite unambiguous, and which have to some extent been uncritically adopted by other editors.

[25] This erroneous conception has already been censured by A. Sandberger, op. cit., p. 6.

[26] Cf. H. F. Redlich, op. cit., p. 141 on the chromaticism of the *Arianna Lamento.* Also, J. Wolf, *Handbuch der Notationskunde*, 1913, Vol. II, p. 461.

[27] *'Orfeo'—Realizzazione orchestrale*, Milan, 1935, p. 62.

[28] Cf. H. Riemann, *Geschichte der Musiktheorie*, 1918, p. 144 ff.

[29] Cf. R. Haas, *Aufführungspraxis*, 1931, p. 154 ff.

[30] That this hasty writing, which often degenerates into the merest sketch, is a distinguishing mark of all the scores of the Contarini Collection in the Library of San Marco has already been established by E. Wellesz (*St. z. MW*, I, 1913). Cf. also G. Benvenuti's frequently quoted studies to the *Incoronazione*, 1937–38.

[31] *Studien*, II, p. 57 ff.

[32] Cf. R. Haas, *Beiheft IX der DTOE*, p. 5; also H. F. Redlich, *Notationsprobleme zu Monteverdis 'Incoronazione'*, *Acta. Mus.* Vol. X, Fasc. III.

[33] Cf. Coll. Ed., Vol. XIII, pp. 12 and 209.

[34] V. f. MW., Vol. X, 1894.

[35] Cf. *DTOE*, Vol. XXIX (*Ritorno*) Rev. Ber., p. 128, and *Beiheft IX*, p. 36, where the tenor clef which frequently appears on the stave of the continuo part in the *Ritorno* is explicitly appraised by R. Haas as 'the pivotal point of the instrumentation' and is consequently clearly reproduced every time it occurs.

[36] R. Haas, too, interprets this change of clef in the same manner in his practical edition of the *Ritorno*, op cit.

[37] I have not as yet had access to either the gramophone records or the manuscript of the revision which G. Benvenuti made to his version of *Orfeo* with D. de Paoli's assistance in 1938.

[38] E. Křenek, *Meine Textarbeitung von Monteverdis Poppea, Anbruch XVIII,* Heft 4–5, 1936. The same author also in *Schweiz. Musikztg.*, No. 20, 1936.

[39] Brussels, 1946. Cf. also Paul Collaer's article, *L'orchestre de C. Monteverdi* in *Musica*, Sanzoni II, Florence, 1943.

[40] *Orfeo*, Oxford, 1925; *Incoronazione*, Oxford, 1927.

APPENDIXES

BIBLIOGRAPHICAL TABLE OF THE WORKS

I. The Madrigals

Original Title	Date of the Preface (First edition or first performance)	First Editions	Reprint
Canzonette a 3 voci	1584	1584	Coll. Ed. vol. X and Ist. e Mon. Vol. VI (ed. G. Pannain), 1939
Il I° libro dei Madrigali	1587	1587 (1607, 1621)	Coll. Ed. vol. I
Il II° libro dei Madrigali	1590	1590 (1607, 1609, 1621)	Coll. Ed. vol. II
Il III° libro dei Madrigali	1592	1592 (1594, 1600, 1604, 1607, 1611, 1615, 1621)	Coll. Ed. vol. III
Il IV° libro dei Madrigali	1603	1603 (1605, 1607, 1611, 1615, 1622, 1644)	Coll. Ed. vol. IV
Il V° libro dei Madrigali	1605	1605 (1606, 1608, 1610, 1611, 1613, 1615, 1620)	Coll. Ed. vol. V
Scherzi Musicali a 3 voci	1607	1607 (1609, 1615, 1628)	Coll. Ed. vol. X
Il VI° libro dei Madrigali	1614	1614 (1615, 1620, 1639)	Coll. Ed. vol. VI
Il VII° libro dei Madrigali 'Concerto'	1619	1619 (1622, 1623, 1628, 1641)	Coll. Ed. vol. VII
Scherzi Musicali cioè Arie e Madrigali in stile recitativo	1632	1632	Coll. Ed. vol. X
Il VIII° libro dei Madrigali 'Madrigali Guerrieri ed Amorosi'	1638	1638	Coll. Ed. vol. VIII, 1–2
Madrigali e Canzonette	1651 (ed. All. Vincenti)	1651	Coll. Ed. vol. IX

II. *Works for the Stage*

Title (librettist)	Date, etc.	First Editions	Reprints	Performing Editions
La Favola d'Orfeo (A. Striggio jun.)	24 February 1607	1609 (1615) (Libretto 1607)	1881 (Eitner) / 1923 (Malipiero) / Coll. Ed. vol. XI (Malipiero) / 1927 (Sandberger Facsimile Ed. of the edition of 1609)	1905 (V. d'Indy) / 1909 (G. Orefice) / 1925 (J. Westrup, MS.) / 1929 (C. Orff) / 1934 (O. Respighi) / 1934 (1938) (G. Benvenuti) / 1936 (H. F. Redlich, MS.)
L'Arianna (Rinuccini)	28 May 1608 (1623)	Music lost (except 'Lamento', q.v.) Libretto extant (publ. Mantua, 1608)		
Il ballo dell'Ingrate (Rinuccini)	4 June 1608	1638 (VIII M.B.)	Torchi in 'L'Arte musicale in Italia', Vol. VI / Coll. Ed. vol. VIII/2	'Tanz der Spröden' (Carl Orff), 1924 / Edition by A. Toni (1932), by E. J. Dent (1945, MS.)
Prologue to 'L'Idropica' (Guarini, Chiabrera)	2 June 1608 Mantua	Music and Text lost		
Tirsi e Clori (A. Striggio jun.)	April 1616 Mantua	1619 (VII M.B.)	Coll. Ed. vol. VII	
La Maddalena (G. B. Andreini)	1617	Music and Text lost (except Fragment, q. v.)		
La Favola di Peleo e di Tetide	1617 Mantua	Music and Text lost		
Andromeda (E. Marigliani)	1617 Mantua			
Il Combattimento di Tancredi e Clorinda (T. Tasso)	1624 Venice	1638 (VIII M.B.)	Torchi, Vol. VI / Coll. Ed. vol. VIII/1	Ed. G. F. Malipiero (1931) / Ed. H. F. Redlich (1946, MS.)

Title (librettist)	Date, etc.	First Editions	Reprints	Performing Editions
La Finta Pazza Licori (G. Strozzi)	1627 Mantua	Music and Text lost		
Armida (T. Tasso)	1627 Mantua	Music and Text lost		
Intermedia (5) and Prologue* (Ascanio Pio)	1627 Parma	Music lost	Libretto: A. Solerti (1905)	
Mercurio e Marte (Cl. Achillini)	1628 Parma	Music lost	Libretto: A. Solerti (1905)	
Proserpina rapita (G. Strozzi)	1630 Venice	Music and Text lost		
La Delia e l'Ulisse (with F. Manelli?)	1630 Venice	Music and Text lost		
L'Adone (P. Vendramin)	1639 (Bologna?) Venice	Music lost, Libretto extant†		
Le nozze di Enea con Lavinia (Badoaro)	1641 Venice	Music and Text lost, Scenario extant†		
Il ritorno d'Ulisse in Patria (Badoaro)	1641 Venice	MS., State Library, Vienna, Nr. 18,763	DTOE, Vol. XXIX (ed. R. Haas, 1921) Coll. Ed. vol. XII (Malipiero)	1927 (d'Indy) (v. d. Borren) 1942 (L. Dallapiccola)
La vittoria d'Amore (Morandi)	1641 Piacenza	Music lost		
L'Incoronazione di Poppea (Busenello)	1642 Venice	(a) MS., Biblioteca Marciana, Venice (b) MS., Biblioteca di Conservatorio S. Pietro a Maiella, Naples	Libretto: A. Solerti (Riv. Mus. Ital. Facs. I, 1904) of (a): 1904 (H. Goldschmidt) Coll. Ed. vol. XIII (Malipiero) 1938 (G. Benvenuti) (Facs. Reprint) of (b): Coll. Ed.vol. XIII(Suppt.)	1904 (V. d'Indy) 1914 (v. d. Borren) 1927 (I. A. Westrup, MS.) 1937 (Malipiero, MS). 1937 (E. Křenek) 1938 (G. Benvenuti, MS.) 1937 (H. F. Redlich) (First performance May 1948, London, B.B.C.)

* Among which is 'Gli amori di Diana e di Endimione'. Cf. F. Walker, M. and L., Oct. 1948, p. 433.

† Cf. A. Loewenberg, 'Annals of Opera', 1943.

III. *Church-music*

Title	Date, etc.	First Editions	Reprints	Performing Editions
Sacrae Cantiunculae tribus vocibus, Liber I	1582	1582	Ed. Terrabugio (Orvieto, 1910). Coll. Ed. vol. XIV (1932) Ist. e Mon. della Mus. Ital. vol. VI (1939) (ed. Pannain)	
Madrigali Spirituali	1583	1583 Music (except the 'Basso') lost	Facsimile Reprint of the 'Basso' in Coll. Ed. vol. XVI (Suppt.) (1942) G.A. Vol. XIV	
Sanctissimi Virginis Missa senis vocibus . . . ac Vesperae pluribus decantandae . . .	1610	1610	Reprint of the 'Sonata supra S.M.' in Torchi (op. cit.)	'Sonata' (ed. Molinari, Rieti, Tommasini, etc.) 'Vesper and Magnificat I'. (ed. H. F. Redlich, 1934, publ. 1949; ed. G. F. Ghedini, 1950, U.S.) Magnificat II. (ed. K. Matthaei 1942)
Sacred monodies (published separately in contemporary collections)		1615–1627		
Selva Morale e Spirituale	1641	1640	Coll. Ed. vol. XVI (1942), 18 portions, individual portions from which were already printed by A. Adrio, op. cit., 1935.	
Messa a 4 Salmi	1649 (ed. All. Vincenti)	1651 (ed. All. Vincenti)	Coll. Ed. vol. XV 1/2 Missa a 4 therefrom (ed. Tirabassi and Ch. v. d. Borren, 1914) Coll. Ed. vol. XVI (1942),	

IV. *Fragments, sacred 'Kontrafakturen', and separate works*

Title	Date	First Editions	Reprints	Performing Editions
Lamento d'Arianna (Rinuccini)	1608	1623 (Bart. Magni) MSS. Copies in Florence, Ghent, Rome	E. Vogel (V. f. MW. III, 1887)	Ed. C. Orff (1929)
Madrigalized version thereof		1614 (Madr. B. VI)	Coll. Ed. vol. XI	Ed. H. F. Redlich (1945, MS.)
Sacred 'Kontrafaktur' of ('Pianto della Madonna')		1640 (Selva Morale)	Coll. Ed. vol. VI	
Lamento d'Erminia (Tasso)	1612 (?)		Coll. Ed. vol. XV/2 (1941)	
Fragment of 'La Maddalena' (Andreini)	1617	MS. by F. M. Fuci	Ed. F. Torrefranca ('Inedito', Rome, 1944)	
Lamento d'Apollo (A. Striggio jun.)	c. 1620	1617 (Gardano)	Coll. Ed. vol. XI	
Madrigal-cycle 'I cinque fratelli' (G. Strozzi)	1628	Music and Text lost		
Messa solenissima	1631	Music and Text lost		
Tre Ariette	1634	Music lost 1634 (A. Vincenti)		
Musica, tolta da I Madrigali di Cl. M. (Sacred 'Kontrafaktur' of Monteverdi's secular madrigals)		1607 (A. Coppini) 1611 (Melchior) 1608 (Coppini) 1623, 1641, 1649 (Profius) (from the VII M.B.) 1642 (Profius) (from the 'Selva')	Ed. D. de Paoli, op. cit. (1945)	

CALENDAR OF THE MOST IMPORTANT EVENTS IN MONTEVERDI'S LIFE

Date	Event
15 May 1567	Entry in baptismal register at Cremona.
1582	First publication as 'pupil of Ingegneri' (*Sacrae Cantiunculae*).
c. 1589	Journey to Milan.
c. 1590	Enters the service of the ducal court at Mantua as 'Violist'.
September 1594	Promotion to 'Cantore'.
c. 1595	Marries Claudia Cattaneo.
1595	Takes part in the Duke's campaign against the Turks in Hungary.
6 May 1596	Death of Jacques de Wert, Maestro di Cappella at Mantua. Monteverdi is passed over in favour of B. Pallavicino.
1599	Journey to Flanders in the Duke's retinue.
Beginning of 1600	Francesco, his elder son, born (Cremona).
6 May 1601	Retirement of B. Pallavicino.
c. 1602	Monteverdi becomes 'Maestro di Cappella' and is made a citizen of Mantua.
1603	The singer, Caterina Martinelli, comes to Mantua.
2 December 1604	Birth of his younger son, Massimiliano, at Cremona.
22 February 1607	First performance of the *Favola d'Orfeo* (Mantua).
10 Sept. 1607	His wife, Claudia, dies.
28 May 1608	First performance of *Arianna* (Mantua).
17 January 1609	According to a ducal decree of this date Monteverdi is to receive a pension for life.
August 1609	Publication of the music to *Orfeo* (Venice).
September 1610	Journey to Rome. Monteverdi dedicates the *Missa* and *Vespers* to Pope Paul V.
18 February 1612	Death of Duke Vincenzo I Gonzaga.
31 July 1612	Dismissal of Monteverdi by his successor, Francesco IV Gonzaga.
19 July 1613	Death of G. C. Martinengo, Maestro di Cappella of San Marco, Venice.
19 August 1613	Unanimous election and appointment of Monteverdi as his successor at San Marco.
April 1616	Yearly salary raised to 400 ducats.
1617	Beginning of his connexion with the court of Parma.
1620	Monteverdi visits A. Banchieri in Bologna.

Date	Event
25 May 1621	Ceremonial Requiem for the Archduke Cosimo II of Tuscany, composed and directed by Monteverdi.
1624	Tasso-Scene, *Combattimento*, first performance in the Mocenigo Palace, Venice.
24 Dec. 1627	Death of Vincenzo II, the last male descendant of the Gonzagas. End of Monteverdi's connexion with the Mantuan court.
1628	Schütz in Venice. Arrest of Massimiliano by the Inquisition in Mantua.
July 1630	Sack of Mantua, during which many of Monteverdi's manuscripts are destroyed. Plague in Venice.
28 November 1631	Plague officially declared ended. Monteverdi performs a ceremonial Mass in celebration thereof.
1632	Ordination as priest. He starts work on his projected theoretical treatise, *Melodia*.
September 1638	*Eighth Book of Madrigals* issued; Monteverdi's last secular publication.
1639	Period of late Venetian operas begins. *Arianna* is performed again in Venice.
May 1641	*Selva Morale* issued; Monteverdi's last sacred publication. New operas (including *Il Ritorno d'Ulisse*) for Venice.
Autumn 1642	First performance of the *Incoronazione di Poppea* at the Teatro Grimano, Venice. End of Monteverdi's creative activity.
May 1643	Last journey to Cremona and Mantua. Return to Venice in the autumn.
29 November 1643	Death in Venice.

BIBLIOGRAPHY

E. ARTEAGA: *Le rivoluzioni del teatro musicale Italiano*, 1783–5.

AMBROS-LEICHTENTRITT; *Geschichte der Musik*, Vol. IV. 3. Auflage. Leipzig, 1909.

H. ADRIO: *Die Anfänge des geistlichen Konzerts*, Berlin, 1935.

G. M. ARTUSI: *L'Artusi ovvero delle imperfettioni della moderna musica.* Venice, 1600–3.

G. BENVENUTI: *Facsimile dei MS IT Cl.* 4. *Nr.* 439 *della Bibl. Naz. di S. Marco in Venezia*, Milan, 1938. (Facsimile Ed. of the *Incoronazione*).

— *Il manoscritto Veneziano della Incoronazione di Poppea.* (Riv. Mus. Ital. Anno XLI, Fasc. 2), 1937.

— *Il Ritorno d'Ulisse in Patria non è di Monteverdi.* (Il Gazzetino, Venezia, 17 Maggio, 1942.)

CH. V. D. BORREN: Preface to the edition of the 'Messa a 4' from the *Selva* of 1641, ed. A. Tirabassi, Brussels, 1914.

MANFRED H. BUKOFZER: *Music in the Baroque Era—from Monteverdi to Bach* (London–New York, 1947).

G. CESARI: *La Musica in Cremona nella seconda metà del sec. XVI.* (*Ist. e. Monum. dell' arte musicale Italiana*, Vol. VI, 1939 (with G. Pannain).

A. CIMBRO: *I madrigali di Cl. Monteverdi* (Musica II. Sansoni, Florence, 1943).

P. COLLAER: *L'Orchestra di Cl. Monteverdi* (Musica II. Sansoni, Florence, 1943).

L. DALLAPICCOLA: *Per una rappresentazione di 'Il Ritorno d'Ulisse'* (Musica II. Sansoni, Florence, 1943).

E. DOHRN: *M. A. Ingegneri als Madrigalkomponist*, Hanover, 1936.

G. B. DONI: *Lyra Barberina* (ed. Gorius), Florence, 1763.

A. EINSTEIN: *The Italian Madrigal*, 3 vols., Princeton, U.S.A., 1949.

R. EITNER: *Quellenlexikon*, 1899–1904.

L. N. GALVANI: *I teatri musicali di Venezia nel secolo XVII*, Venice, 1878.

H. GOLDSCHMIDT: *Studien z. Gesch. der ital. Oper*, I–II, Leipzig, 1901–4.

— *Monteverdis Ritorno d'Ulisse*, SIMG, IV.

DONALD JAY GROUT: *A short History of Opera*, 2 vols. (London–New York, 1947).

R. HAAS: *Musik des Barocks*, Bückens Handbuch der Musikwissenschaft (Potsdam, 1928).

— Critical Commentary to DTOE Vol. XXIX (Ritorno d'Ulisse) and Suppt. IX thereto.

— *Aufführungspraxis der Musik* (Bückens Hdb. d. MW.). (Potsdam, 1931.)

A. HEUß: *Die Instrumentalstücke des Orfeo und die venez. Opernsinfonien.* (SIMG, 1903.)

V. D'INDY: Preface to his edition of the *Incoronazione*, Paris, 1908.

W. KREIDLER: *Heinrich Schütz und der stile concitato Cl. Monteverdis.* (Cassel, 1934.)

ERNST KŘENEK: Article on his edition of the *Incoronazione*, cf. Schweizer Musikzeitung, Nr. 20, 1936. Anbruch XVIII, Nr. 4–5, 1936.

H. KRETZSCHMAR: *Die venezianische Oper u. d. Werke Cavallis*, V. f. MW. VIII, 1892.

— *Monteverdis Incoronazione*, V. f. MW. X, 1894.

— *Geschichte der Oper*, Leipzig, 1919.

H. LEICHTENTRITT: *Cl. Monteverdi als Madrigalkomponist*, SIMG. XI. 1910.

— *Geschichte der Motette*, Leipzig, 1908.

E. E. LOWINSKY: *Secret Chromatic Art in the Netherlands Motet*, Columbia Univ. Press, U.S.A., 1946.

A. LOEWENBERG: *Annals of Opera, 1597–1940*, London, 1943.

B. Lupo: *Sacre monodie Monteverdiane* (Musica II. Sansoni, Florence, 1943).
Padre Giambattista Martini: *Esemplare o sia Saggio fondamentale di Contrappunto*, 1774–5, 2 vols.
G. F. Malipiero: *Cl. Monteverdi*, Milan, 1930.
— *Cl. Monteverdi in Cremona* (Rass. Mus. II/10, 1929.)
— *Cl. Monteverdi* (Musica II. Sansoni, Florence, 1943).
— Epilogue to Vol. XVI of the Coll. Ed., 1942.
H. J. Moser: *Heinrich Schütz*, Kassel, 1936.
K. F. Müller: *Die Technik der Ausdrucksdarstellung in Monteverdis monodischen Frühwerken*, Berlin, 1931.
J. M. Müller-Blattau: *Die Kompositionslehre Heinrich Schützens in der Fassung seines Schülers Chr. Bernhard*, Leipzig, 1926.
Domenico de' Paoli: *Cl. Monteverdi*, Milan, 1945.
G. Pannain: Introduction to Vol. VI of *Ist. e Monum. dell' Arte Musicale in Italia*, 1939, and critical commentary to the critical edition of Monteverdi's *Sacrae Cantiunculae*, 1582, and the *Canzonette a tre* of 1584.
H. Prunières: *Cl. Monteverdi*, Paris, 1924 (1926).
— *Monteverdi e la musica francese del suo tempo* (Rass. Mus. II/10, 1929).
— *Cavalli et l'opéra Venitien aux XVIIe siècle*, Paris, 1931.
A. Pirro: *H. Schütz*, Paris, 1913.
M. Praetorius: *Syntagma Musicum III*, 1619. (New edition by Ed. Bernoulli, 1916.)
G. Radiciotti: *L'Arte musicale in Tivoli*, 1921.
H. F. Redlich:
    (a) For the madrigals and in general:
        Das Problem des Stilwandels in Monteverdis Madrigalwerk (Dissertation, Frankfurt a. M., 1931) also published as a book under the title *Claudio Monteverdi, Vol. I. Das Madrigalwerk*, Berlin, 1932.
        Monteverdi-Gesamtausgabe (Anbruch, X/6, 1928).
        Article and bibliography *Claudio Monteverdi* in *Grove's Dictionary of Music and Musicians*, Supp. vol., 1940.
        Neue Monteverdiana (Anbruch, XIII/5, 1931).
        Cl. Monteverdi, by D. Paoli (Review), (in *Music and Letters*, April 1947).
    (b) For the operas:
        Zur Bearbeitung von Monteverdis Orfeo (Schweiz. Musikztg., Nr. 2/3), 1936.
        Monteverdis Incoronazione di Poppea (Schweiz. Musikztg., Nr. 23), 1937.
        Zu Monteverdis letzter Oper (Poppea) (Anbruch, XIX, 4/5, 1937).
        Notationsprobleme in Cl. Monteverdis Incoronazione (Acta Musicologica, Vol. V, Fasc. 3), 1938.
        Das Orchester Cl. Monteverdis (Katalog). (Musica Viva, Nr. 1, 1936, Ars viva, Bruxelles.)
        Monteverdi and Opera (*The Listener*, London, 14 May 1948).
        Monteverdi's last Opera (*Radio Times*, London, 14 May 1948).
    (c) For the church-music;
        Monteverdi's Religious Music (*Music and Letters*, London, October 1946.)
        Monteverdi's Vespers, 1610 (*The Listener*, London, 8 February 1947).
        Monteverdis Kirchenmusik (Anbruch XVII, 2/3 1935).
        Monteverdi als Kirchenmusiker (Neue Zürcher Ztg.), 19 February 1935, (Neue Zürcher Nachr.), 21 February 1935.
        Cl. Monteverdi—zum Problem der praktischen Ausgabe seiner Werke (Vespers, 1610). (Schweiz. Musikzeitung, Nr. 19/20, 1934.)
        Also under the title *Sulle edizione moderne delle opere di Claudio Monteverdi* in *Rassegna Musicale*, VIII/1, January/February 1935.
H. Riemann: *Eine 7sätzige Tanzsuite v. Monteverdi*, SIMG XIV.

O

C. Sachs: *Barockmusik* (Peters Jahrbuch, 1919).
A. Sandberger: Facsimile edition of *Orfeo*, Augsburg, 1927.
— *Ges.-Aufsätze zur Musikgeschichte*, Munich, 1921.
H. A. Sander: *Italienische Meßkompositionen des 17. Jahrh.*, Berlin, 1934.
A. Schering: *Aufführungspraxis alter Musik*, Leipzig, 1931.
Carlo Schmidl: *Dizionario Universale dei Musicisti* (and Suppl.), Milan, 1927 ff.
E. Schmitz: *Zur Geschichte d. ital. Continuo-Madrigals im 17. Jahrh.* (SIMG, XI, 1910.)
— *Geschichte der weltlichen Solokantate*, Leipzig, 1914.
L. Schneider: *Cl. Monteverdi*, Paris, 1921.
M. Schneider: *Die Anfänge des Basso Continuo u. s. Bezifferung*, Leipzig, 1918.
L. Schrade:-*Monteverdi—Creator of Modern Music*, New York, 1950.
W. Schuh: *Formprobleme bei Schütz*, Leipzig, 1928.
A. Solerti: *Gli albori del Melodramma*, Milan, 1905.
— *Le Origini del Melodramma*, Milan, 1903.
— *Musica, Ballo e Drammatica alla Corte Medicea*, Florence, 1905.
O. Sonneck: *Dafne the first Opera*, SIMG, Vol. XV, 1913–14.
— *Catalogue of Opera Librettos before 1800*, Library of Congress, 1913–14.
A. Tessier: *Les deux styles de Monteverdi* (Rev. Musicale, Paris, June 1922).
— *Monteverdi e la filosofia dell' arte.* (Rass. Mus. II/10, 1929).
F. Torrefranca: *Il Lamento di Erminia di Claudio Monteverdi.* (*Inedito*, quaderno musicale, Nr. 2, Rome, 1944.)
O. Ursprung: *Katholische Kirchenmusik* (Bückens Hdb. d. MW.). (Potsdam, 1931.)
E. Vogel: *Cl. Monteverdi* (V. f. MW. III, 1887).
— *Bibliothek der gedr. weltlichen Vokalmusik Italiens*, 2 vols. 1892.
E. Wellesz: On the *Incoronazione* in St. z. MW. I. 1913.
J. A. Westrup: *Monteverdis Lamento d'Arianna.* (The Music Review, I, Nr. 2, 1940.)
T. Wiel: *I codici musicali Contariniani*, Venice, 1888.
C. v. Winterfeld: *Gabrieli u. s. Zeitalter*, 3 vols., 1834.

GLOSSARY

AUFFUEHRUNGSPRAXIS (practice of performance). 'This term has been widely adopted by German and non-German writers to refer to the manner in which early music was performed and should be performed. In particular, it refers to the many problems connected with the attempts at restoring . . . the original sound of compositions from the early Middle Ages to Bach. . . .' (W. Apel, *Harvard Dict. of Music*, 1946, p. 61.) Cf. R. Haas, *Die musikalische Auffuehrungspraxis, Bueckens Hdb. der Musikwiss.*, 1929; A. Schering, *Auffuehrungspraxis alter Musik*, Berlin, 1931.

AKZESSORISCHES POINTENKOLORIT. A term coined by Curt Sachs (*Barockmusik, Peters Jahrbuch*, 1919). It refers to a practice of the Early Baroque Venetian Opera: i.e. the occasional employment of rare instruments such as flutes, trumpets, drums, in addition to the obligatory nucleus of strings (cf. Monteverdi's late operas of 1639–42) for the purpose of emphasizing special dramatic points such as the appearance of deities, martial pageants, etc.

CHROMA (Greek) = Chromaticism. 'The use of tones extraneous to the diatonic scale, e.g. in C major c– d– d sharp – e . . .' '. . . In the sixteenth century the word *cromatico* refers occasionally not to the use of semitones, but to the employment of the black notes (minima, semiminima, etc.). . . .' (W. Apel, *Harvard Dict. of Music*, 1946, p. 144.)

CORI SPEZZATI. 'The "separated" and alternating choruses of the Venetian polychoral style. . . .' (Cf. W. Apel, op. cit.)

DEVISEN ARIE (devise = device = inscription). 'Modern term (H. Riemann) for the da capo Aria with preliminary announcement of the initial subject. . . .' (W. Apel, *Harvard Dict. of Music*, 1946, p. 206, with Music example from Cesti's Opera *L'Argia*, 1669.)

GORGIA. '. . . Generic term for the late sixteenth-century method of improvised coloraturas such as were used in the performance of motets, masses, madrigals, etc. . . .' (Cf. W. Apel, op. cit.)

GRILANDA. Roman dialect expression for Ghirlanda, i.e. Garland. In this case translate: an anthology or miscellany of madrigals.

GROPPI. A kind of cadential trill, used more expecially at final clauses such as the following:

Cf. M. Praetorius, op. cit. p. 184.

o*

INTERMEDIUM. A precursor of opera, very popular at princely courts in Italy during the fifteenth and sixteenth centuries, comprising madrigals, dumb shows akin to the English masque, and occasional solo songs (anticipating the later operatic aria) with the accompaniment of instruments. A great number of instruments were employed particularly for the purpose of accompanying the splendid pageantry. The *Intermedia* (Intermezzi) were as a rule inserted between the acts of more serious dramatic entertainments. (Cf. op. cit., p. 97, for the orchestral table of the Intermedium *Psiche ed Amore* of 1565.)

KONTRAFAKTUR = CONTRAFACTUM. 'A vocal composition in which the original text is replaced by a new one, particularly a secular text by a sacred one, and vice versa. . . .' (W. Apel, *Harvard Dict. of Music*, 1946, p. 183.) Cf. also Monteverdi's *Lamento d'Arianna* and its 'Kontrafaktur' *Pianto della Madonna*.

MARINISM, derived from the name of G. B. Marini, the Renaissance poet. It indicates the exaggerated use of emotional, sensuous and even libidinous similes in the lyrical poetry of Marini and his lesser followers during the first quarter of the seventeenth century.

MUSEALER KLANGMATERIALISMUS. A term coined by the present writer in the Programme Book to his practical edition of Monteverdi's *Favola d'Orfeo* (Zürich, 1936). It denotes the tendency of some modern arrangers of old music to restore it according to the letter rather than to the spirit, by using obsolete and historical instruments (Cornetti, Viols, Portative, Chalumeau, etc.), but without simultaneously endeavouring to solve the problems either of 'Musica ficta', Basso Continuo or of the many special types of ornamentation. The belief that the employment of ancient instruments alone ensures a historically faithful reading of old compositions shows an exaggerated appraisal of the purely *material* side of old music. Unless the method of performance is supported by an equally faithful interpretation of the notation, the attempt at restoration is bound to remain ill-balanced and one-sided.

PARODIE MESSE (Parody Mass). 'The term refers to an important practice of sixteenth-century Mass composition, namely the use of musical material borrowed from pre-existent pieces (Motets, Chansons, Madrigals) for the composition of a Mass. Usually the term is understood not to include the mere borrowing of a Cantus Firmus—although, possibly, this widespread practice formed the point of departure encountered in Parody Mass. Occasionally, the process of borrowing went so far as the taking over *in toto* of the entire musical substance of a motet, the words of which were simply replaced by the text of the Mass item, a procedure which is equivalent to Contrafactum. . . .' (W. Apel, *Harvard Dict. of Music*, 1946, p. 554.)

PASSAGIO. '. . . In the sixteenth-century art of diminution . . . a generic term for improvised ornaments, usually other than plain scale passages or trill-like figurations. . . .' (Cf. W. Apel, op. cit.)

TEMPRO. 'Tempro la Cetra', a voce sola; the introductory Monody to Monteverdi's *Seventh Book of Madrigals*, 1619 (called 'Concerto'), based on a more or less unchanging basso ostinato theme in the Basso Continuo part, to which the elaborate variations of the vocal line form a significant contrast. That Monteverdi had a strong predilection for using this type of 'Ground' in his compositions is shown by other brilliant examples of the same kind, such as 'Ohimè dov'è il mio ben' (M.B. VII) and 'Amor' (Lamento della Ninfa) (M.B. VIII), which are based on the famous ground basses of 'Romanesca' and 'Malagueña' respectively. In all these compositions the essential thematic substance is to be found in the instrumental Basso Continuo part.

TESTO. '(It. text.) Narrator (in oratorios, passions, etc.) . . .' (Cf. W. Apel, op. cit.)

TORNEO. A combination of a tourney and an operatic presentation, one of the typical musico-dramatic spectacles of the later Renaissance. (Cf. J. Callot's engraving of *La Guerra d'Amore*, libretto by A. Salvadori, music by J. Peri, Grazi, Signorini and del Turco, produced at Florence Carnival, 1615; reproduction by R. Haas in *Musik des Barocks*, Berlin, 1929, Plate III).

TRICINIUM. A sixteenth century name for vocal compositions in three parts. (Cf. W. Apel, *Harvard Dict. of Music*.)

TRIONFO. A festive pageant of representational and pre-operatic character celebrating a major political event; especially popular during the Renaissance. (Cf. Jakob Burckhardt, *The Civilization of the Renaissance in Italy*, London, 1944, p. 255 et passim. Cf. also Hans Burgkmair's famous series of woodcuts, *Triumphzug*, in honour of the Emperor Maximilian I (*c.* 1519.)

VIVUOLA. Obsolescent Italian name for Viol. (Cf. the old Spanish form: VIHUELA.)

ZUFALLSORCHESTER. The term refers to the tendency during the transitional period between the Renaissance and the Baroque to rearrange compositions—originally of purely vocal character (Motets, Masses)—for Chorus and an accessory orchestra consisting in itself of groups (choros) of instruments which could be exchanged at will. (Cf. Monteverdi's frequently repeated indication for an a posteriori orchestral accompaniment in his liturgical compositions; for instance in *Et iterum a 3 voci, Basso et due Contralti, concertato con quattro Tromboni o viole da brazzo, qual si pono anco lasciare* . . ., *Selva Morale e Spirituale*, 1640, Coll. Ed., Vol. XV/i, p. 187. Cf. also M. Praetorius, *Syntagma Musicum*, III, 1619, Chapter VIII (reprint, Berlin, 1916, p. 134 et passim).)

LIST OF ABBREVIATIONS

1

M.B.	= Madrigal Book.
B.C.	= Basso Continuo.
V.	= Voice.
Coll. Ed.	= Collected Edition of Claudio Monteverdi's Works in 16 vols. (ed. G. F. Malipiero, Asolo, Treviso), 1926–42.
MS.	= Manuscript.
H. F. Redlich op. cit.	= H. F. Redlich, *Cl. Monteverdi, Vol. I. Das Madrigal*, Berlin, 1932.
SIMG	= Sammelbände der internationalen Musikgesellschaft.
V. f. MW	= Vierteljahrsschrift für Musikwissenschaft.
Z. f. M.	= Zeitschrift für Musikwissenschaft.
St. z. MW	= Studien zur Musikwissenschaft.
A. f. MW.	= Archiv für Musikwissenschaft
M & L	= Music and Letters, London.
Rev. Mus.	= Revue Musicale, Paris.
Rass. Mus.	= Rassegna Musicale, Turin.
Riv. Mus. Ital.	= Rivista Musicale Italiana, Milan.
DTOE	= Denkmäler der Tonkunst in Österreich.
Ist. e Monum.	= Istituzioni e Monumenti dell'arte Musicale Italiana, Ricordi, Milan, 1931 ff.
Schwz. Musikztg.	= Schweizer Musikzeitung, Hug & Co., Zürich.

INDEX OF NAMES

Where a reference is to an endnote it is printed in italic type in brackets, followed by the page on which the endnote appears.

INDEX OF MONTEVERDI'S WORKS

Compositions are headed under three main groups, in accordance with Part II.
Within their respective groups publications are listed in chronological order.

III. CHURCH MUSIC